Perpetuating Poverty

Perpetuating Poverty

The Political Economy of Canadian Foreign Aid

by Robert Carty, Virginia Smith

& LAWG

Published by: Between The Lines
                       427 Bloor St. W.
                       Toronto, Ontario, Canada

Typeset by: Dumont Press Graphix
                       97 Victoria St. N.
                       Kitchener, Ontario, Canada

Cover Design by: Richard Peachey

Printed and Bound in Canada by:
The Alger Press Limited

Between The Lines receives financial assistance
from the Ontario Arts Council.

Canadian Cataloguing in Publication Data

Carty, Robert.
     Perpetuating poverty

Includes index.

ISBN 0-919946-20-8 (bound)
ISBN 0-919946-21-6 (pbk)

1. Economic assistance, Canadian.
2. Canada — — Economic policy.

I. Smith, Virginia. II. Latin America Working Group.
III. Title.

HC60.C37   338.91'71   C82-094023-2

Table of Contents

Part V: Conclusions

Introduction

In the beginning, at the start of the post-war era, it was christened "foreign aid". A decade ago it was awarded a more dignified title — "official development assistance". Little else has changed during the intervening thirty years. Then, as now, aid has failed in its original mission, the development of a quick cure for Third World poverty. It has remained an under-achieving, post-adolescent ward of the governments of the industrialized capitalist North.

These governments agree that the problems of this embarrassingly mature dependant are chronic, and that it badly needs "reform". But effective reform programs have been perennially postponed. When the economies of donor countries periodically slump into recession, aid reform is criticized as too costly a welfare measure, and plans for its rehabilitation are shelved for an indefinite future. But when development assistance recipients plunge into crises that threaten to undermine the security of donors, traditional reform formulas are rehashed, relabelled, and marketed as ultramodern, guaranteed cures. But the advertisements about the new programs almost always prove false. Aid's deficiencies remain uncorrected because, in these emergencies, aid is applied as an inadequate, but politically expedient technique of crisis management. In the end, aid continues to limp along as an elderly problem child.

Canada and other donor countries are currently attempting to compensate for a period of neglect during the second half of the seventies by making aid the focus of renewed, earnest attention. In the early eighties, northern countries are stuck in a mire of economic stagnation, while the Third World is experiencing acute financial difficulties. The prospect of a global economic and monetary crisis is once again energizing western political leaders to refurbish development assistance programs as props to their now tottering post-war order.

One of the most highly publicized harbingers of the new wave of international development assistance was the how-to-do-it bestseller *Report of the Independent Commission on International Development Issues*, chaired by former German Chancellor Willy Brandt.[1] Issued in 1980 with the histrionic title *North-South: A Program for Survival*, the report presents a wealth of evidence that the current plight of the poor countries poses a serious threat to the international economic structures sheltering the North.

Members of the Brandt Commission and other aid experts are especially preoccupied with the problem of "recycling" — reintegrating the large pool of capital accumulated by the OPEC nations since 1973 into the global economic system. They hope to funnel it through channels that will both stimulate the sluggish economies of the North *and* rescue the deeply indebted countries of the Third World from the danger of default. The combined debts of underdeveloped countries shot up from $70 billion at the end of 1970 to an estimated $300 billion at the end of 1979, and defaults triggered by capital deficiencies could shake the West's economic house to its foundations.[2] Transfusions are vital to prevent the collapse of one or more of the debilitated southern countries. At the same time, the recycling project, which Brandt envisions increasing Third World purchasing power, is proposed as one of the few options open to the North in its drive to mitigate its own economic difficulties.

Hence, the Brandt Commission has resurrected the hoary notion of "mutual interests", and rejuvenated it for a return engagement in the corridors of power. "Mutual interests" mean simply that "a quickened pace of development in the South also serves people in the North", because, according to the Brandt study, the various sectors of the global economy are interdependent.

At the beginning of the 1980s the world community faces much greater dangers than at any time since the Second World War. It is clear that the world economy is now functioning so badly that it damages both the immediate and the long-run interests of all nations. The problems of poverty and hunger are becoming more serious. . . . The industrial capacity of the North is under-used, causing unemployment unprecedented in recent years, while the South is in urgent need of goods that the North could produce.[3]

More economic assistance — in traditional or new styles, labelled simply "foreign aid" or camouflaged with a new eighties slogan, and offered at concessional or more commercial interest rates — underlies many of the recommendations advanced by the Brandt Commission.[4] Although the report addresses non-aid issues as well, many of its findings return to the theme of developing and expanding mechanisms for transferring capital from the North, at the discretion of the North, and under the substantial control of the North, to the South. One such mechanism, development assistance, is to enjoy a rerun as a favoured method of reform. According to the World Bank, the globe's largest source of development finance, official development assistance must triple from $20 billion in 1980 to over $62 billion by 1990 to meet the capital needs of underdeveloped countries and assume some of the burden currently carried by private banks and foreign investors.[5]

Pierre Trudeau, always quick to spot a trend, leaped on the bandwagon already crowded by Edward Heath, Olof Palme, Eduardo Frei, Canada's Joe Morris, and other distinguished world "elders" who participated in the Brandt Commission's study and report. Six months after the Liberal Party's victory in the February 1980 elections, External Affairs Minister Mark MacGuigan announced that development assistance would be boosted to 0.5% of Canada's Gross National Product (GNP) by 1985, and to the internationally-accepted target of 0.7% of GNP by 1990. Ottawa's aid had previously declined from 0.56% of GNP in 1975 to 0.46% in 1979. Meanwhile, during his 1980-81 international excursions, Trudeau went out of his way to arrange stopovers in Third World countries where he could enhance his image as a pundit of North-South relationships and present himself as a champion of a "revolution in international morality"[6]

Like Canada, most other industrialized countries have recently promised increases in their aid to the Third World. Many also expressed support for a World Bank energy affiliate or similar mechanisms as a route out of the debt cul-de-sac. And the agendas of international summit meetings have increasingly turned to North-South relationships and questions of aid and recycling.

But the new enthusiasm for aid is not unanimous. The United States, the world's largest aid-giving nation, decreased the portion of its GNP allotted to development assistance throughout the 1970s and the hawkish administration of Ronald Reagan is implementing major cutbacks. Retrenchment in US aid volume, however, has been coupled with a return to the use of foreign aid as a Cold War weapon. Discussing the transition from the Carter to the Reagan administration, former Nixon administration official H.B. Malmgren explained that "aid for the sake of development alone may be replaced by aid used primarily as an instrument of US foreign policy."[7] The Reagan administration, in other words, is fashioning an aid instrument smaller than its old model, but equipped with a sharp political cutting edge.

The Brandt cheerleaders have so far generated little enthusiasm among southern nations for their old snake oil poverty cures and seemingly new prescriptions, which, like the old, were developed in northern laboratories. Despite the Brandt report, Tanzania's Finance Minister Amir Jamal criticized the industrial powers in late 1980 as bastions "of an outdated system, unwilling to change except grudgingly, slowly, and marginally."[8] The Third World's loosely representative organization, the Group of 77, has called the response of the North to the Third World's current difficulties "inadequate and halting".[9]

For example, at the 1980 UN Special Session, the United States, with the backing of West Germany and the United Kingdom, scuttled attempts to organize new global negotiations on better management of the world economy. As a result, the International Development Strategy, a set of development goals for the 1980s comparable to the development plans enacted at the start of the sixties and seventies, was agreed upon by the Group of 77 but not adopted lest the US claim "success" for the Special Session while glossing over the failure to agree on more significant North-South negotiations.

Representatives of the Third World speak from long experience of stingy donor *noblesse oblige*. For over 25 years, poor nations were the often reluctant objects of foreign aid experiments, undertaken to prevent revolutionary change both within recipient countries and in the North's relationship with the South. Then, in 1974, roles were suddenly reversed after OPEC shocked nations around the world by seizing, not begging, wealth from the advanced capitalist powers. Dramatic oil price hikes alerted poor countries to their potential power in the global political arena. Third World leaders served notice that foreign aid should be junked as the primary vehicle for North-South relationships and replaced by a truly new model. The South called for a New International Economic Order (NIEO) to transform international trade, investment, and monetary structures, which are the engines of Third World underdevelopment.

But movement towards the NIEO soon ran out of steam. The advanced capitalist economies, which keep a firm grip on the levers of global power, were easily able to thwart commodity producer associations similar to OPEC. The North also supported efforts to pry strong NIEO advocates loose from positions of leadership, and, during the past decade, Chile's Salvador Allende, Peru's Juan Alvarado Velasco, and Jamaica's Michael Manley were removed from office through varying levels of coercion and violence. (Of the three, only

Manley is still alive, and functioning as leader of a weak opposition within the Jamaican government.) The West's negotiators also managed to talk the NIEO agenda to death during apparently endless rounds of summits and UN conferences, while they reserved real decisions for where they monopolize power — institutions like the World Bank, the International Monetary Fund (IMF), and the General Agreement on Tariffs and Trade (GATT).

To the world's poor, the current revival of aid promises must sound like repetitious variations on the development hype of the past. Some must wonder if the new wave of aid giving signals the funeral of the NIEO itself. But promoters of the new wave in aid, like their predecessors, find that renewed development assistance efforts can conveniently meet their national, self-defined objectives while continuing to ignore the basic causes of Third World underdevelopment. They see the new aid as 1) providing short-term relief for Third World financial crises; 2) silencing some of the Third World demands for structural reforms by offering instead more aid and only minor adjustments to international institutions; 3) building a new network of political alliances to support the West in its renewed conflict with the East; and 4) helping northern economies export their way out of the economic slump. Third World leaders might well be skeptical of a "revolution in international morality" which so clearly serves *northern*, not mutual interests.

Periodic calls in Ottawa and other capitals for — alternatingly — expansion, retrenchment, or reform of aid make it difficult for Canadians to develop criteria for gauging a program that will soon absorb close to two billion dollars of the federal budget every year. *Perpetuating Poverty: The Political Economy of Canadian Foreign Aid* advances an analysis of the fluctuating trends in Canadian development assistance policies and programs during the three decades since their inception. Like any evaluation of foreign aid, this study starts from a particular perspective. Before examining our analysis, the reader might wish to situate this perspective among other common critical treatments of the theme.

Few and daring are the aid critics who maintain that they *don't* consider Third World development a good that should be promoted by all countries. But definitions of "development" and appropriate strategies for achieving this goal vary radically among students of North-South relationships. Three streams of thought can be perceived within the continuing debate about aid's shortcomings:

1) cynical, and often right-wing critics who maintain that most aid is wasted and should be cut back;

2) aid reformers who argue that aid should be increased in volume, improved in quality, and supplemented by new aid-giving mechanisms; and

3) frankly more radical critics who, in analyzing aid in the context of all North-South relationships, describe it as part of the problem, not the solution to poverty and underdevelopment.

The first group includes a vocal handful of right-wing journalists, politicians, civil servants and businessmen. Some advocates of this perspective attribute the failures of aid to aid bureaucrats, depicted as bunglers afflicted with addled brains and bleeding hearts. They delight in ferreting out mismanagement and mistakes within the Canadian International Development Agency (CIDA). *Toronto Sun* columnist Morton Shulman created front-page headlines in 1977 with the claim that millions of tax dollars had been wasted in "Foreign Giveaways". After a short trip to Haiti, Shulman announced that CIDA funds allotted to the western hemisphere's poorest country were being spent on pleasure yachts, useless studies, and nonsensical projects of no benefit to the Haitian people. His hastily concocted charges were easily refuted — and the serious real limitations of the CIDA Haitian program bypassed. Shulman claimed that his accusations were based on "front page" criticism of the CIDA program in a major Haitian daily newspaper. The newspaper was, in fact, a four-page technical newsletter which had published three times in the previous six months and which contained none of the quotes attributed to it.[10]

Other Canadian journalists have presented well-documented examples of CIDA errors overseas and have effectively worn down some public support of the agency. Such horror stories about incompetent aid administration easily lead to the conclusion that Canadian dollars should remain at home, where politicians presumably know how to utilize them, not wasted on ridiculous programs in remote jungle outposts. Some of these aid critics argue for aid cutbacks by stressing the unworthiness of recipient governments rather than the bungling of CIDA staff. *Maclean's* Barbara Amiel savaged Canadian assistance to Mozambique even before its leftist government treated her less than hospitably for neglecting to obtain papers required of all visitors.[11] *Toronto Sun* editor Peter Worthington's diagnosis of the problem of aid recipients verges on racism: "Some races or nationalities seem to have an inclination and talent for business, enterprise, hard work. Others do not."[12]

Proponents of this view portray many Third World leaders as either dangerous radicals or unbalanced megalomaniacs, who cannot be trusted to use aid money to build strong capitalist economies. They maintain that aid should be dispensed only to actual or potential political allies, governments devoted to the western spirit of free enterprise. Aid critics starting from this perspective also assert that Canada simply can't afford to spend money abroad when it is suffering a recession, a condition it has been trying to shake since the middle seventies. Canadian exporting companies, for example, hold that CIDA takes "an overly philanthropic giveaway approach to aid" and that aid should be extended only when it produces immediate benefits to the domestic economy — i.e., when it is tied to the purchase of Canadian goods and services.[13]

Generally, this first perspective on aid is often inspired by a view of the underdeveloped South as a strange and sometimes terrifying world rife with terrorism, subject to spectacular natural disasters, and stultified by too much sun. These conservatives, as the French philosopher Condorcet once remarked, try to "make nature herself an accomplice in the crime of political inequality". Subtle, and sometimes not so subtle, racist attitudes underlie this group's beliefs that the Third World's problems exist because of its populations' breeding habits and their lack of individual or racial ambition. They elect blindly to ignore the historical facts of colonialism and neo-colonialism and instead hold that western capitalist development is *the* model for southern progress. They show little sense of the multiple relationships, beyond the aid connection, that bind the nations of the South to the North.

Most of the aid debate in Canada is conducted within the camp of the second group, the aid reformers. Its members include liberal politicians and civil servants, many academics and professional aid experts, and members of some religious groups and non-governmental organizations. A number of Third World governments occasionally paddle along this stream of thought.

In Canada, this thought is reflected in most educational literature on international development and in the reports of several parliamentary committees.[14] But it also surfaces in the materials published by the aid agencies themselves. The World Bank, for instance, regularly announces a readjustment of its goals and aid organizations around the world promptly scramble to follow its example.

Aid reformers are a heterogeneous lot; some advocate more or less major surgery to development assistance programs, while others would be content with minor adjustments. Generally, the more intimate a reformer's ties with a donor government or agency, the more cautious he or she is in diagnosis and prescription. Reformers within the system — and there are many — are close enough to aid programs to know their shortcomings; but they are generally too close to conceive solutions other than tinkering with aid mechanisms or simply enlarging them (big is better). Their commitment to the goals of the advanced capitalist powers also prevents them from suggesting dramatic changes. And, frankly, this camp is where the "development mafia" earns and protects its daily bread, much of it, including development educational programs, funded by CIDA itself. Restraint is accordingly practised.

The reformers call on donor nations to give more aid, better aid, and in some cases, more than aid. Aid reformism is based on a vision of the South not as a dangerous "other" sphere, shrouded in the heart of darkness, but as a world of unfortunate people — the term "disadvantaged", coined originally to describe the domestic poor, is sometimes also applied to the Third World — who need more of what the industrialized nations have to offer with fewer strings attached. Its advocates are distressed that donor nations have erred in not committing enough capital, enough goods, enough services to the Third World. More inputs, and better quality inputs, will permit the poor to build prosperous societies, they maintain.

Thus, a common cry of all aid reformers is the extortion to donor countries to allot a greater proportion of their budgets to foreign aid. The United Nations constantly urges donors to meet the 0.7% of GNP target set over a decade ago. Nudged by the aid reformers, some governments loudly call for rapid advances towards this target, but subsequently ignore their own instructions. Ringing statements, like MacGuigan's pledge at the UN "to help my fellow Canadians become aware of the needs of our fellow citizens of the earth", are usually forgotten during hard dickering over the allocation of the national budget. Only Denmark, Norway, the Netherlands, Sweden, Iraq, Kuwait, Qatar, Saudi Arabia, and the United Arab Emirates have met or exceeded the 0.7% target.* The Liberal government's 1980 commitment to higher aid levels was not more than a repetition of a broken promise made five years earlier — itself a renewed commitment to similar promises, all broken, dating back to the early 1960s. Tinkering with this type of reformist targetry, the Parliamentary Task Force on North-South Relations, a creature of the Trudeau government, urged Ottawa to speed up MacGuigan's 1980 promise by attaining an aid level of 0.57% of GNP by 1985, a miniscule adjustment to a promise of questionable reliability.

---

* Development assistance from the centrally-planned economies is very small and explained by nations like the Soviet Union as the result of not having responsibility for colonialism in the Third World. Aid from the OPEC nations is downplayed by the western market-economy countries because OPEC countries are not members of the Development Assistance Committee (DAC) of the Organization for Economic Cooperation and Development (OECD). OPEC aid is thus outside the control and scrutiny of the western powers. DAC members criticize OPEC aid for being concentrated in a handful of Arab states, India and Pakistan. In comparison, however, DAC members such as Britain and France also highly concentrate their aid to former colonies or actual protectorates. Almost 43% of all US bilateral and military assistance is concentrated in just three countries of immense strategic interest to Washington — Egypt, Israel and Turkey.

Many aid reformers have long been calling on donor governments to improve the quality of their aid by untying it — i.e., not stipulating that a high percentage of bilateral development assistance be spent on goods and services supplied by the donor country. (Ottawa ties about 80% of its bilateral, or country-to-country, aid.) Advocates of untying argue that the requirement overly restricts recipients in the types of projects they can undertake. They also point out that tying decreases the value of Ottawa's aid, because Canadian goods are often more expensive than those available in other world markets. The Report of the Brandt Commission urges the strongest capitalist economies to untie their aid immediately, and those experiencing economic difficulties to accomplish the transition in stages.[15]

Since 1967, Ottawa has been minimally easing its tying restrictions, although its overall program remains substantially tied. The government's prominently public pledge to untie aid for procurement among underdeveloped countries — made in CIDA's *Strategy for International Development Cooperation 1975-1980* — was quietly but quickly withdrawn after Canadian businessmen expressed strong opposition to the move. Acutely conscious of slow economic growth at home in 1980, the Parliamentary Task Force further fudged the tying issue by taking an explicitly indecisive position, neither calling for untying nor for fixed tying regulations. Continued tying, some Task Force members argued, would be the only way Canada could justify increasing aid in troublesome economic times.

An idea which has recently been gaining greater currency among liberal-minded northern experts, and some recipient governments, is that of automatic aid transfers. Automaticity, which would involve collecting aid funds through mechanisms like an international income tax, and transferring them to the Third World without restrictions, would remove aid from national, political deliberations and allow southern governments to develop long-term development plans. The Brandt Commission's proposals for automatic transfers include a levy on international tourism, on military spending, or on international investment, but its report outlines no practical suggestions for tax calculation or collection. The notion, dreamily removed from the world of real political power, constitutes no more than an idealistic gesture of good will towards the Third World; northern governments might well view the creation of an international tax-man outside their control as comparable to the work of the unfortunate Dr. Frankenstein.

Other popular schemes promoted by the aid reformers include the creation of a World Bank energy affiliate or equivalent mechanism for recycling petrodollars, and a concentration of aid on the poorest of the world's poor countries, a policy supposedly in effect for the past decade. Many aid reformers call for a greater concentration of resources in multilateral agencies like the World Bank and regional development banks, an already-implemented shift that has produced questionable benefits for the underdeveloped world.

Finally, some, but by no means all, aid reformers flirt with the Third World's appeals for a New International Economic Order (NIEO). They view these as a set of non-aid issues more critical to the economic development of southern nations than mere development assistance. Debate just about the NIEO covers a wide spectrum of opinion. Reformers, however, too often stop short of a radical critique of the international systems developed to exploit the Third World. They either are not aware that a new order can't be created unless power relationships between and within nations are drastically readjusted, or they realize that revolutionary changes are required, but are unwilling to push for them. In the long run, aid reformers discard the core from the NIEO concept and focus on issues peripheral to it — for example, the creation of new financing facilities within existing international institutions. These schemes do nothing to disturb existing power structures, and preserve the traditional aid-giving perspective which divides the world into two categories of nations and peoples — givers and receivers.

This second group of aid critics occupies the middle ground in the Canadian aid debate. Reformers reject the ideology of right-wing critics as a rationalization for indifference or even hostility to the peoples of the Third World. They also dismiss more critical viewpoints as idealistic, simplistic, overly harsh, and in the end, too radical. Rooting themselves in a Canadian-style liberalism, they dominate much of the discussion.

Perpetuating Poverty: The Political Economy of Canadian Foreign Aid opts for the third perspective in the Canadian aid debate. It advances the discussion beyond the shifting middle ground of the aid reformers and tries to define, develop and support a critical assessment of development assistance within a systemic, analytical framework based on the affirmation that a new world order — both economic and political — must be constructed.

This is a nascent analysis currently being elaborated by *some* Third World political leaders, professional aid experts, church-related agencies and programs, and members of non-governmental organizations. Its advocates have stepped back from the often con-voluted discussion of aid techniques, and view development assist-ance as one element in the whole complex of North-South relation-ships.

Tolstoy has strikingly depicted the North's role in these relation-ships:

I sit on a man's back choking him and making him carry me and yet assure myself and others that I am sorry for him and wish to lighten his load by all possible means — except by getting off his back.

Underdevelopment, in other words, does not just "happen" — nor is it a problem solely generated within the Third World. External forces have substantially created it. In every situation of underdevelopment, there are *underdevelopers* — structures, powers and governments which ride the backs of the southern nations and choke off their development possibilities. The peoples of the Third World are not unfortunates suffering from a deficit of what the advanced capitalist countries can offer them, nor are they poor because the North has neglected them or left them out of the development process. The ties between the world's underdeveloped nations and the western powers have been far too intimate, both during the colonial period and the neo-colonial era when political subjugation has been replaced by economic domination. The Third World is trapped in the poverty cycle, not because western countries have failed to commit their capital overseas, but because they are continually draining massive amounts of capital from the South.

Capital is drained through investments by transnational corporations which remit profits on their overseas ventures back to home-based head offices or discreet tax havens. In the international marketplace, Third World countries still remain highly dependent on the sale of primary commodities like bauxite, copper, coffee and sugar at unstable and usually cheap prices while the northern countries sell their manufactured goods and technology dear. The international institutions controlled by the rich — the IMF, the World Bank and the GATT — keep the taps open through systems which the Third World, as yet, lacks the power to transform.

Within this analytical framework, development is not so much an economic process as a political one. What the Third World's poor most critically lack is not aid or northern inputs, or even reformist measures labelled a NIEO, but *power*. Foreign aid policies that ignore or justify the current power balance between and within nations are integral parts of the underdevelopment problem, not imperfect solutions. Lobbying for this or that aid reform in an attempt to create a more nearly perfect assistance program can divert attention from the central issues. It's like fussing over a flat tire on an automobile with a dead battery. The advocates of this third position in the aid debate are *not* against aid itself nor aid reforms. But aid, and its reform through measures such as automaticity or untying, is positive only if donor and recipient governments are committed to the promotion of an equitable distribution of wealth and power and not to the consolidation of a thin upper layer of global society. These are some of the perspectives the authors bring to this evaluation of Canadian aid programs and policies.

Perpetuating Poverty: The Political Economy of Canadian Foreign Aid is necessarily limited in its scope. It is not an examination of all Canada's relationships with the nations of the South, including trade and investment linkages, or of the many non-aid issues in the current North-South debate. Such a comprehensive view could be presented only in a much more ambitious study. This volume focuses on the evolution of aid as an instrument reinforcing under-development and dependence in the Third World without pretence that it is the main villain.

The locus of this study is in Canada. In assessing the impact of CIDA programs in Asia, Africa and Latin America, the starting view-point is the Canadian initiative, not the political and economic realities of the recipient nations. A chronicle of development assist-ance from a Third World perspective would likewise be an impor-tant undertaking, different and broader than the current project.

We extend our thanks to members and friends of the Latin American Working Group who offered analysis, criticism and encouragement during the preparation of this book. Financial sup-port by the Anglican Church of Canada, the United Church of Can-ada, the Canadian Catholic Organization for Development and Peace, OXFAM of Canada, and the Ontario Arts Council permitted us to research in the field and complete the manuscript. We are grateful to the many unnamed associates in Latin America, the Caribbean, Africa and Asia who shared with us their perspectives both on aid and the development of a new world order. Many have cooperated in our effort, but we are finally responsible for the contents which follow.

Robert Carty
Virginia Smith
July, 1981

At First Glance: Public Perceptions of Canadian Aid

1

Your Morning Gripe

Canadian programs to aid the overseas poor are always good material for cantankerous or concerned letters to the editor. The development assistance debate bobs from journalists to parliamentarians and back, but ultimately ends up in the court of the media consumer, the taxpayer who pays the bill for Ottawa's foreign aid. The volleys comes from a number of different angles in this often complicated exercise of charge and rebuttal. A glance at the morning paper reveals a cross-section of Canadian public responses to the arguments.

The Waste and Mismanagement Complaint

A *Toronto Sun* editorial cartoon depicts garbage cans crammed with dollars sitting outside the office of the Canadian International Development Agency.[1] A week later, a reader lamenting the reckless dollar disposal writes that "There isn't any sense in asking the Trudeau government to stop throwing away millions of taxpayer dollars on things like CIDA."[2]

A Variation on the Waste Complaint

"Charity should begin at home," M.W. Clarke writes to the *Montreal Star*.[3] "I suggest that anyone who is struggling with the high cost of living, including ridiculously high rents, write to their members of parliament, the department of external affairs, or Prime Minister Trudeau himself, protesting such a move." (Aid to the new government of Zimbabwe)

The Poor are Always With Us, and Not Only That, They're Undeserving Argument

"It is time to stand back and look at our tax money flowing into a country [Bangladesh or India] which produces babies at an overflow rate," Russ Powell writes to the *Toronto Star*. "I would rather see that $60 million of foreign aid go to a much more disciplined stock of people — namely CANADIANS."[4]

We've Got To Help

Christian Bay communicates to the *Star* his anger at "the gall, the abysmal inhumanity" of the argument "that it would be impractical to share with the victims of western man's greed."[5]

Let's Get To the Bottom of This

Penny Sanger criticizes the *Ottawa Citizen* for "mistaking office gossip for news" in its coverage of CIDA. "Some of us out here would like to know if our money is being spent wisely, not who's knifing whom."[6]

The letters to the editor debate was especially heated in the mid- and late seventies when many media representatives and politicians concentrated their fire on real or imagined errors in the administration of CIDA projects. Public ire was fueled by bizarre reports of ham slicers sent to Senegal, where religious rules prohibit the consumption of swine flesh,[7] Canadian dairy cattle dead on arrival in India,[8] and grain rotting in Ethiopian warehouses.[9] These media "horror stories" have often been distortions of fact, easily refuted by Agency officials, but still they linger longer in the collective consciousness than subsequent proofs of innocence.

The media must bear much of the blame for public misconceptions of Canadian aid, but some investigative journalists have probed beyond the superficial "horror stories" of Ottawa's errors overseas. These reporters have carefully drawn some aid profiles which suggest more fundamental flaws in Canada's development assistance program.

Aid Profiles

A) Rural Development in Lesotho

CIDA and its critics can agree on the basic facts about this landlocked African country. Lesotho has barely managed to keep itself afloat economically through subsistence agriculture and the earnings of workers who migrate to find employment in the Republic of South Africa. It has been designated a low income country by the World Bank, with a per capita GNP of $280 in 1978, an adult illiteracy rate of 45% and an average life expectancy of 50 years. As one of the world's most underdeveloped countries, it is a prime candidate for foreign economic assistance.

CIDA goes to Lesotho: When the Agency began assistance to the country in the mid-seventies, one of its primary goals was "support for agriculture and rural development".[10] One of its major initial projects was a $6 million integrated rural development scheme in the mountainous Thaba Tseka area which, according to CIDA, consisted of "implementing improved livestock management techniques and providing such social benefits as electricity, housing, a sewage system, clean water supplies and improved health facilities." By 1979, Agency officials were still confident that the Thaba Tseka effort "promises to exemplify the basic human needs orientation" officially adopted by CIDA in 1975.[11]

The Toronto Star visits Thaba Tseka: The Agency's continuing optimism about its work in Lesotho is testimony either to its tenacity or its capacity to harbour illusions. The myth about the Thaba Tseka project's social benefits was effectively exploded by *Toronto Star* reporter Jackie Smith during a 1979 visit to Lesotho.

Smith found that about three-quarters of the $6 million had been spent not on rural development, but on construction, including about 50 drab suburban-style homes she called "a chunk of Don Mills in Africa".[12] The homes, built mainly of materials imported from South Africa (when local stone might have been used instead), went up at a cost of about $25,000 each. Most were tenanted by Lesotho bureaucrats and Canadian advisors — the latter living rent free while earning $15,000 to $40,000 a year plus generous overseas allowances.

Unneeded garages and servants' quarters in 17 of these homes had to be converted to bachelor apartments at a cost of about $2,500 a unit. Canadian planners forgot that winters are cold in mountainous Lesotho as well as Ottawa, and so fireplaces had to be installed in large rooms that were originally meant to be heated electrically.

Instead of relying on a local generator, CIDA contributed $300,000 to a new $1 million transmission line which will be economical only when the town is 10 or 12 times the size it was at the end of the seventies. The cost of the unnecessary line doubled as work proceeded a year behind schedule, and the Lesotho government is responsible for its maintenance costs, estimated at $50,000 a year.

CIDA's most ambitious experiment, supposedly one of the major components of the integrated rural development program, was a pint-sized $35,000 seed potato project. Meanwhile the transplanted townsite mushroomed, creating "an even greater gap between the haves and have-nots", according to Smith.

B) Ghana: Wells and Water for the Thirsty

Ghana just barely makes it onto the list of what the World Bank describes as middle income developing countries, with a per capita GNP of $390 in 1978, an illiteracy rate of 70% and a life expectancy of 48 years. Ghana's economy has been extremely dependent on fluctuations in the world market price for a single crop, cocoa, which accounts for about 75% of its foreign earnings.

Poverty is especially acute in arid northern Ghana, on the edge of the relentlessly advancing Sahara desert. Drought and famine plague the area, and only about 50% of children survive until the age of five even in the best of years.

CIDA *takes a new tack in Ghana:*   Ghana has long been a recipient of large amounts of Canadian aid. In the mid-seventies, the Agency reported that its development assistance priorities in the country had been changing, "with the result that fewer types of assistance are now being provided." Agricultural assistance and "efforts to improve the quality of life in rural areas" rose to the top of CIDA's agenda.[13]

The Agency described a massive well installation project in northern Ghana as an outstanding example of its new initiatives. It reported in self-congratulatory tones that about 900 wells had been dug by the end of the 1975-76 fiscal year, "supplying the area with safe drinking water for the first time. In addition to improving health standards, the Canadian project will have an impact on agricultural production."[14] In 1977, the pumps were "in constant use as people eagerly take advantage of the chance to drink clean safe water for the first time in their lives," according to a CIDA publication.[15] The venture sounds an ideal form of assistance. What could be more basic to a decent human life than supplies of clean, fresh water?

The Fifth Estate *visits northern Ghana:*   A crew from the CBC's *Fifth Estate* visited the well digging site in 1978, and found that the Agency had indeed rapidly completed the first phase of its work. A Canadian firm, W.L. Wardrop and Associates, had been hired to drill enough wells so that everyone in the area would be within a mile and a half of clean water.

The basic holes in the ground were dug with an ease and haste that often amazed local villagers, but Canadian officials had a harder job finding a pump that could make the underground water supplies accessible. A Beatty pump manufactured by General Steelwares in Fergus, Ontario, which had been designed to meet the needs of Canadian farmers and cottagers, was purchased for duty in tropical Africa. The Beatty pumps balked at the unaccustomed task and wore out in months or, in some cases, within weeks.

CIDA kept on repairing its chronically malfunctioning pumps and started shopping around for a sturdier model. Four hundred wells had to be capped while the Agency did its comparison shopping. After examining 50 pumps from 10 countries, it concluded that a pump made in India was the best buy; it was manufactured through a Swedish aid project, and specifically designed for service in southern climates. Second in line was a pump produced by Winnipeg's Monarch Industries. The Agency decided to procure 400 Monarch pumps, and an additional hundred manufactured in the United States but assembled by Robin Meyers Ltd. of Brantford, Ontario. As is generally the case when CIDA goes shopping, Canadian aid officials decided to procure a commodity, not because it was best for Ghana, but because it was Canadian.

By 1981, the 400 capped wells were still not functioning, and the Agency was working to make them operational during the year. The project's other 2,100 wells have been experiencing "a percentage of breakdowns", says Gordon Walker of CIDA's Commonwealth Africa Division, and some pumps will have to be replaced with those "that have a better repair record". General Steelwares, which has developed a different model, as well as Monarch and Robin Meyers, are involved in the continuing push to build a better pump.

The protracted effort to draw water from the desert was only one aspect of the Agency's mandate in northern Ghana. When the wells were drilled, many local villagers didn't fully understand what was happening. Often they were not aware that the wells were being dug for their benefit, and were not familiar with maintenance procedures for the new machinery. Some didn't realize that clean water is better for health than contaminated water.

A nurse working in the area under the auspices of the Canadian University Service Overseas (CUSO) told the *Fifth Estate* crew that she didn't "know if they see a connection between clean water and health, or dirty water and disease. I don't think so. Certainly from the old tales they tell us, they said that the older people refused to drink the clean water, and when the market women sold the water in the market, they had to mix clay in it so that it had colour and it had taste."

CIDA personnel wouldn't necessarily twig to the problem immediately, because, unlike CUSO volunteers, they lived in an all-Canadian community. The government of Ghana built their ranch houses at a cost of about $100,000 and offered the accommodation to its benefactors rent free. The Canadian co-manager of the project, offering a bit of wisdom gleaned from his African experience, explained that "when you go overseas, you don't really change your style. You shouldn't try to change your style of life. The things you enjoy to do in Canada, you'd enjoy doing here."

When the Agency realized that the how and the why of the wells were a puzzle to many villagers, it trained and equipped a maintenance man in every village. Additional Canadians had to be hired to conduct further educational programs. Walker said in mid-1981 that CIDA personnel would remain in the area for at least three or four more years to do health education and training in pump repairs. A water-use education program for the whole region was then in the preparation stages. Agency employees were also involved in well-site improvements and construction of access roads to the wells.

C) Consolidating Indonesia's "New Order"

This strategically located Southeast Asian nation was the largest recipient of World Bank loans in 1979, and third largest in 1980. Indonesia is rich in natural resources like oil and nickel, but remains a low income country, with a per capita GNP of $360, an illiteracy rate of 38%, and a life expectancy of 47.

Massive amounts of aid flowing to Indonesia, which Richard Nixon called "the greatest prize in the Southeast Asian area",[16] began shortly after the right-wing General Suharto initiated what he called a "New Order" in the country. Estimates of the death toll immediately after Suharto's bloody 1965 coup range from 500,000 to one million.[17]

Many who survived the army rampage were held indefinitely as political prisoners, and Amnesty International estimated that at least 55,000 were detained as late as the middle seventies. In 1976, the Suharto government announced a plan to release post-coup prisoners who had still not been tried and for whom no trial had been planned. Over 30,000 prisoners were released between 1975 and 1979, according to Indonesia's state security organization.

But Amnesty International has expressed concern about restrictions which make it impossible for these ex-convicts to lead normal lives: a ban on their employment in government services and "vital industries", a mark on their identity cards indicating their former prisoner status, requirements that they report to military authorities regularly and ask for permission if they wish to travel.[18]

Fruitful collaboration: Contacts between Ottawa and Jakarta began to multiply after 1970, when the Trudeau government expressed its satisfaction that "in the last five years, the Indonesian government has provided evidence of its capacity to use increasing amounts of development aid."[19] Trudeau travelled to Indonesia in 1971, and Suharto was received in Ottawa four years later. CIDA's president visited Indonesia in 1976 to review the Agency's program there. Ottawa's bilateral aid to the Suharto regime peaked in 1975-76 at $36.7 million, then tapered off to $11.75 million in 1979-80.

Canadian assistance to Indonesia has included food aid and lines of credit offered to correct the nation's balance of payments difficulties, which were aggravated in the middle seventies because of debt incurred by Pertamina, the state oil corporation. In the mid-seventies, four 15-megawatt gas turbines were provided for the islands of Sumatra and Sulawesi. A $25 million loan was extended to support a civil aviation program.

"Cut off the rich":   This headline topped a 1974 *Ottawa Citizen* editorial critique of Canada's aid program. After the dramatic oil price hikes of the early seventies, some Canadian journalists started questioning CIDA aid to what the *Citizen* called "financially independent nations" — oil producers like Indonesia, Iran, Algeria and Nigeria.[20]

Late in 1974, when CIDA was rushing to use up its annual budget allotment, it secured quick government approval for a $12.5 million loan to Indonesia for 11 DeHavilland Twin Otters. The Indonesia deal facilitated the federal government's efforts to rescue the failing aircraft company, which it acquired from Hawker-Siddeley earlier that year. The Otters were to be used for regular freight and passenger services to cities not then served by Merpati Nusantara Airlines (MNA), a regional carrier. Reporters Robert McKeown and Christopher Cobb wrote at the time that "MP's opposed to further loans to oil producing countries will find this one particularly difficult to understand", because "MNA is a privately owned airline, not a government one, and is already the recipient of seven Twin Otters by a previous CIDA agreement."[21]

At the time of the speedily approved loan, MNA was subsidized by the Indonesian government, but was expected to become self-supporting within five years. The journalists expressed surprise that "on the face of it, Canada would seem to be contributing to the success of a private company with a no-interest loan to be repaid in 50 years." CIDA's chief attempted to correct the apparent inequities involved in "aiding the rich" on his 1976 Indonesia trip, when he took the approach that technical assistance should be the focus of future aid efforts, while support should still be extended for critical capital projects.[22]

War on Waste

Tales of Agency misadventures overseas — be they muckraking or investigative in approach — have prompted many Canadians to question the institution that sets up scenarios for chaos and failure. Many critics take up the "waste and mismanagement" complaint against CIDA, and argue that these twin scourges are at the root of deficiencies in Canada's development assistance program. This view is based on the facile assumption that the Agency's problems can be corrected simply through a thorough house cleaning.

In the mid-seventies, the media supplied a great deal of evidence to support this assumption during what CIDA has described as a "three year barrage of attacks by newspaper, radio, and TV commentators."[23] This attack on CIDA began in 1974, when the Agency's budget was rising 20% a year, and culminated in early 1977, shortly after the Auditor General issued a report highly critical of CIDA's administrative procedures. Reckless spending and poor management resulting in high staff turnover were two of the most frequently aired complaints against the aid bureaucracy in the middle seventies.

"Your career [in CIDA] depends on how you spend," a former Agency official told the press in 1975.[24] "It's not how well you spend your money, but . . . can you spend the budget allocated to you? That's what counts." A second official confirmed this assessment and maintained that "The whole criterion here is spend. Anyone who says that it isn't, doesn't know the facts."

The pressure to spend resulted in the approval of many projects of doubtful value, according to some who had been involved in the process. "Projects that go before the review committee get a rating of 'pass', 'fail', or send back for rewrite," according to one ex-official. "I've never seen one that failed." A university administrator who had submitted many projects to CIDA expressed surprise that none had been rejected.[25]

Another common charge in the "waste and mismanagement" debate was that Agency management had ordered an orgy of spending to get rid of $117 million budgeted for the 1974-75 fiscal year, so that it could ask for an even bigger allocation the following year. CIDA president Paul Gerin-Lajoie admitted that funds had unexpectedly become available because of a cutback in aid to India, but insisted that "it is totally incorrect and unfounded to say that we are rushing to spend this money inefficiently or ineffectively." He subsequently admitted that CIDA had "scrambled" to spend the money, and that the Progressive Conservative External Affairs critic had been correct when he observed that the Agency had been disbursing dollars "like mad" to use up the surplus.[26]

Foreign aid critics were also concerned that low morale at the

Agency was causing staff members to "quit in droves". The *Toronto Star* and the *Ottawa Citizen* both reported that 300 had left CIDA within a two-year period, "one of the highest turnovers of any department or agency in Ottawa."[27] Gerin-Lajoie refused to release the contents of a \$9,300 outside study on staff turnover and management improvement, explaining that it was based on interviews with former staff members, and that "those who leave a government department often feel sour about their former employer."[28] He asked for a further study on the subject.

The development of the mismanagement theme culminated in 1976 when the Auditor General, who regularly checks the financial errors of the whole government, singled out CIDA for special attention and produced a report including 92 recommendations for tighter reins on the Agency. He criticized the "very unsatisfactory state of financial control" which had prompted his decision to conduct "a very special major audit".

His critique catalogued "significant disbursements" made from accounts, set up for specific purposes, to finance projects other than those specified; food arriving at destinations in a condition "below standard, sometimes to the extent of complete deterioration", because of a "lack of operational co-ordination"; unlimited financial commitments to foreign governments; excessive project expenditures resulting from the failure of participating governments to meet their financial commitments; contributions made to governments without a written agreement about conditions; delegation of more than \$2 million in sub-contracting authority to architects and engineers working overseas with no provision for Agency review of their spending decisions; overcommitment of funds to various projects of up to 300% the allotted amount; and authorization of purchases after they had already been made.[29]

Publication of the report multiplied increasingly frequent rumours that the flamboyant, globe-trotting foreign aid chief would be dismissed and, in March 1977, career diplomat Michel Dupuy replaced Gerin-Lajoie as Agency president. In his first appearance before the Commons External Affairs Committee, Dupuy assured its members that CIDA had already dealt with 80% of the Auditor General's recommendations, that financial safeguard systems had been tightened, and that commitment controls had been overhauled.[30]

While acknowledging the Agency's past administrative errors, Dupuy attributed some of the faults of the Canadian aid program to the shortcomings of recipient Third World governments. He reminded legislators that CIDA deals with the world's poorest countries, which may not be able to meet their financial commitments because of their fragile administrative and political structures. The new president's remarks were, to some extent, a realistic assessment of the difficulties involved in working overseas. But they were also an attempt to pin the blame for the Agency's mistakes on absent fall guys, the world's less developed countries.

After Dupuy took control, the "barrage" of criticism slowed to an occasional potshot, indicating that most commentators were satisfied that financial discipline and spending cuts were creating an efficient CIDA doing more effective work overseas. They had accepted the reasoning that financial discipline means capable management which, in turn, means effective development aid.

Aid Profiles: A Reprise

But CIDA's experiences in Lesotho, Ghana and Indonesia show that the most serious problems with Canadian development assistance programs are not administrative foul-ups within a government agency, but systemic, structural, and political problems with Ottawa's basic concepts of aid dispensation. Certainly the three cases belie the implication that CIDA's institutional incompetence, or, as Dupuy suggested, the inexperience or incapacity of recipients, has been the major impediment to effective assistance. Two of the three profiles outlined above were reported *after* the Agency had supposedly rid itself of waste and inefficient management. The Ghana and Lesotho projects were initiated during the previous era, but their deficiencies had not been corrected by the late seventies.

Don Mills in Lesotho

The Thaba Tseka development is a product of a Canadian government decision, formally announced in 1975, to concentrate its development assistance on agriculture and rural development among the poorest of the world's poor people. This in many ways laudable policy had not been discarded by Ottawa as late as 1981.

The Agency readily acknowledged in the mid-seventies that it had little expertise in the field of tropical agriculture, but, in the past six years, it has done little to correct this deficiency. As late as 1979-80, CIDA had 180 advisors in the field of education posted to Africa, but only 156 specialists in renewable resources, which generally covers forestry and fisheries as well as agriculture.

Since its ostensible change in orientation, the Agency has, as a rule, continued doing what it has always done, and renamed it "rural development". What CIDA has always done is provide the Third World with products Canada can supply, and sponsored overseas the same sort of projects that involve Canadians at home. Adherence to the traditional approach usually generates profits for Canadian companies and spares Ottawa the challenge of revamping its aid systems. Canadians, well practised at protecting themselves from long winters, know how to build a good house, so Thaba Tseka has enjoyed a boom in construction rather than agriculture.

CIDA managers in Lesotho had greater than usual opportunities to evolve a development plan suited to local conditions. They were free to spend over two-thirds of the Agency's contribution to the project anywhere in the world. The scope of most comparable projects is more limited by a rule that about 80% of goods and services must be acquired in Canada. Despite their freedom, they adhered to the old style of Canadian aid dispensation. Of what avail is CIDA's pledge to aid the rural poor of the Third World if it lacks expertise in the field of tropical agriculture? Should the export of North American lifestyles be called "development assistance" or "cultural imperialism"?

Ghana Water Project

The basic flaw in what might have been a simple project, well suited to the needs of the people in arid northern Ghana, was Canadian commercial self-interest. Like most of CIDA's projects, this one was intended to boost the economy at home as well as benefit overseas recipients, and so was linked to the procurement of Canadian goods and services. CIDA's Peter Harkness maintains that the Indian product would have been inappropriate because there wasn't a guaranteed supply either of pumps or spare parts.

But the selection of Canadian-made pumps as replacements for the problem-prone original model was predictable because of the government's standard buy-Canadian requirement. An option for the Indian product would have fostered trade between two undeveloped nations, a development goal promoted by a number of northern donors, as well as by some Third World governments. CIDA's choice raises a basic question: when Canadian politicians express their concern about "development", are they talking about their own backyard or about the poverty of distant countries?

The Ghana case is typical of another major weakness in much Canadian aid programming — the overseas deployment of advisors and technicians who may have little knowledge of areas where they work. In 1980, only 52 of the Agency's total 1,077 employees were officers working in the field, where they attempted to manage Canada's entire overseas development budget, as well as the work of 735 advisors posted overseas on short term contracts.

Comprehension of Third World cultures and traditions is especially difficult when foreign technicians protect themselves from the rigours of life in poverty-stricken countries by ensconcing themselves in North American-style suburban homes.

Superficial contact with local cultures may result in costly mistakes, e.g., a failure to understand that wells are not necessarily a blessing if their users don't know how to maintain them or, in some instances, don't appreciate the differences between pure and contaminated water. Harkness says that if the Ghana project could be done again from scratch, it would make sense to start with sociological studies of the area. But are sociological studies an adequate substitute for the long, hard labour involved in really knowing your territory?

Indonesian Twin Otters

The loan extended to a private company, itself a dubious use of money allocated to aid the world's poor, raises a number of more serious questions about Canadian development assistance to Indonesia — matters which have generally not been addressed by the media. The problems include the use of aid to 1) promote Canadian trade and investment; 2) to consolidate the power of a repressive government; and 3) to bolster western political interests.

1) Like the pumps selected for the Ghana water project, the Twin Otters were dispatched to Indonesia because Canada could supply them. But the Twin Otters were not even components of a program designed to meet the needs of the poor in the recipient nation. MP Douglas Roche commented after a 1976 visit to Indonesia and Bangladesh that "much of Canada's bilateral aid there goes into big projects that are elitist in concept and seldom directly touch people's lives."[31]

CIDA billed its Twin Otters as vehicles to "provide pioneer air service similar to the bush services that contributed to northern Canada's development."[32] The analogy suggests that the air service will facilitate corporate resource extraction projects. The Twin Otter loan was only one aspect of CIDA's involvement in a drive to boost Canadian business interests in Indonesia. Canada's INCO Ltd. has launched a major nickel project on the island of Sulawesi, where Agency-supplied gas turbines were installed. CIDA has naturally been concerned about Pertamina's debt problems, because several Canadian oil companies have been involved in Indonesia, and Asamera of Calgary concluded one of the first production sharing agreements with the state oil corporation.[33] Trudeau's trip and CIDA's aid primed the pumps for increased trade, and Canadian exports to Indonesia tripled from 1973 to 1974.[34]

2) Aid to Indonesia is not inappropriate because it is a "rich" nation. Its per capita income — like its per capita GNP — is low, under $200. International aid cannot improve the lot of Indonesia's poor because its government is not committed to an equitable distribution of national wealth.

Through repression, Suharto has effectively silenced objections to his "New Order", which has dictated close collaboration with transnational corporations in the extractive sector. His regime has not developed a systematic plan for industrial development, and, by the middle seventies, Indonesia remained one of the world's least

industrialized countries.[35] Projects that might "directly touch people's lives" are clearly not a priority for Jakarta.

3) Canadian aid to Indonesia is politically expedient as well as financially rewarding. In 1976, the year CIDA's president visited
Indonesia, External Affairs Minister Allen MacEachen toured
Southeast Asia in what the *Toronto Star* billed as an attempt to
"Combat Communism" in the region. MacEachen promised firm
economic and political support for the Association of Southeast
Asian Nations (ASEAN), which includes Indonesia, Malaysia, Thailand, the Philippines and Singapore. He termed ASEAN "the last
bulwark against communism in this part of the world."[36] The use of
development assistance more as a political tool than an engine of
development in the recipient country has been a recurring feature of
Canadian aid programs.

The Indonesian case touches the most complex and disturbing
issues to emerge from the three profiles. How can CIDA's aid programs meet the needs of Indonesia's people if one of Ottawa's primary objectives there is the promotion of Canadian business? How
can programs for the poor be developed as long as Canada and other
western nations collaborate with a repressive regime because it is
perceived as a bastion of anti-communism in a politically turbulent
part of the world?

A close examination of three typical aid profiles suggests that the
problems central to CIDA's poor performance have escaped the
attention of Ottawa's financial watchdogs. Roche has pointed out
that, as late as 1977, the Auditor General did not do Agency evaluations in the field. Even if he had undertaken the task, he would have
scrutinized financial control systems rather than project content.
Prime ministerial and other political visits to Agency projects have
generally been staged only to generate puff pieces in Canadian and
local media. Muckraking journalists have seldom looked below the
flawed surface of Ottawa's projects.

The question "what's at the bottom of all this?" is finally tossed
back to the Canadian public, which foots the bill for a program that
is edging up to a cost of $2 billion a year. Throughout the seventies,
Canadians have expressed support for efforts to promote prosperity
in the impoverished Third World. Even in 1975, during the period
when CIDA's goofs and gaffes were regularly exposed to media consumers across the country, a Gallup poll determined that 53% of
Canadians felt that Ottawa's development assistance should be
increased.[37]

In 1981, four years after the mop-up operation at the Agency,
69% of over 1,000 Canadians in five regions interviewed by phone
thought that foreign aid should be increased or at least remain at the
same level. Fifty-nine percent thought that aid should be extended

for humanitarian reasons and only 4% felt that its goal should be economic benefits for Canada.[38]

But this poll also revealed a widespread lack of awareness about CIDA policies and the specifics of its programming. The Agency is not well known, especially outside Quebec, and 30% of respondents guessed that Canadian development assistance amounted to under $10 million a year, while only 6% correctly pegged it at over $1 billion.

Most Canadians are probably not aware that, during the past 30 years, foreign aid has become the most important instrument of Canadian foreign policy applied to the Third World. Citizens of far-flung countries know us better than we know them, if only because of the houses, hydro dams, transmission lines, airplanes and airports suddenly inserted into the local landscape. If Canadians don't know CIDA, the peoples of 89 Third World nations do, for better or for worse.

The recent poll shows a need for dissemination of interpretive materials about Ottawa's development assistance policies. It may also indicate that many Canadians have the interest and energy to push for effective programs of support for the world's poor. No one group or individual can, of course, come up with "the answer", the perfect program, because of the complexity of the problems confronting Third World nations. But well-informed labour unions, church organizations and community groups are no doubt capable of generating questions and proposals more creative than the by now tired themes played, and occasionally varied, by politicians, civil servants, and many of the journalists making the rounds of the international beat.

But Canadians need to explore "the bottom of all this" before they can act effectively. A full understanding of Ottawa's development assistance can be developed only through a scrutiny of CIDA's history, structures, programs, stated and implicit goals, and its role in international aid systems. The following chapters address themselves to these topics.

The Aid Program:

Uneven Growth &

2 Mixed Objectives

S ince 1951, Canadian taxpayers have paid over $11 billion to sup-
port international development assistance programs — over
$1,800 for every Canadian family. Today, the Canadian Interna-
tional Development Agency (CIDA) funds several thousand projects
in 89 countries, supports over 60 inter-governmental institutions
concerned with development, contributes to several hundred non-
governmental organizations, and covers the bills for shipping tons
of supplies and scores of experts to foreign shores. Annual foreign
aid disbursements of over $1.2 billion rank Canada — the world's
seventh most important industrial power — as the seventh largest
aid giver in the West.

Development assistance, now the chief instrument of Canadian
foreign policy towards the Third World, was originally conceived as
a series of emergency measures to repair the ravages of World War II
and to buttress free enterprise economies for the battles of the Cold
War. Lester Pearson, Canada's chief delegate to the 1950 Colombo
Plan conference, probably had little inkling that he was helping to
launch a solidly entrenched government bureaucracy which, by the
late seventies, would spend three times as much as its sponsor, the
Department of External Affairs.

Sketching CIDA's History: A Growing Bureaucracy

Because Canada had industrialized rapidly during the War, and had suffered no domestic destruction, it emerged from the conflict ready to assume new international responsibilities. Ottawa contributed $2,038 million toward the reconstruction of Europe and in 1949 offered more modest sums to the United Nations' technical assistance program.

In 1950, Canada became embroiled in a more complicated process when it started dispensing substantial sums, not for repairs to developed economies, but for development of countries where industrial prosperity was, at best, a distant prospect.

At the Colombo meeting in Ceylon (now Sri Lanka), representatives of the United Kingdom, Ceylon, New Zealand, Canada, India, Pakistan and Australia launched the Colombo Plan for Cooperative Economic Development in Southeast Asia, with the hopeful slogan, "Planning Prosperity Together". The Colombo Plan Bureau made a great show of its democratic structure, which it called "a collective concept of national effort".[1] But a Canadian official confided to aid historian Keith Spicer that "the consultative value of the Colombo Plan meetings was 'not worth a damn' ".[2] The Plan, which still operates today, was conceived as a six year crash program to build capitalist economies in Asia, a continent rocked by major post-war political upheavals.

The Colombo Plan was Canada's only bilateral assistance program for nearly a decade after its inception. But in 1958, the government initiated a full program for the Commonwealth Caribbean, and also began extending aid to Commonwealth Africa. Great Britain was dismantling its empire in these areas, as it had earlier in Asia, and it was reluctant to leave its old territories undefended against the influence of the socialist bloc. It was hoped that Canada could offer fraternal support and guidance.

These new programs, like their predecessor, were viewed as reactions to special circumstances, and were handled through ad hoc, patchwork administrative structures. For some time during the fifties, the Colombo Plan Group, or Interdepartmental Group on Capital Assistance, was the most powerful interdepartmental committee formulating foreign aid policy. But responsibility for aid was split among three ministries, which promoted distinctive, and sometimes conflicting, goals.

External Affairs sponsored the aid vote and chaired interdepartmental meetings on capital assistance, but administrative responsibility for the program was vested in the Department of Trade and Commerce. Yet a third ministry, the Department of Finance, exercised budgetary control, while most engineering and

purchasing jobs were delegated to two separate Crown Corporations. Within the three ministries, work was scattered over an
alphabet soup array of committees. Such divided authority naturally
created difficulties in developing long term goals for overseas aid.

During this period of confusion about responsibility and objectives, expenditures on development assistance rose slowly but
steadily. Between 1950 and 1955, Ottawa allocated $109.54 million
for bilateral assistance grants. The figure for the latter five years of
the decade was $219.48 million. The bulk of these resources were
concentrated in India and Pakistan, considered pivotal points in the
escalating Cold War. (See Table 2-I.)

By the late fifties, Ottawa bureaucrats, like foreign policymakers
around the world, realized that what they had perceived as an
emergency was in fact a chronic crisis situation. The task of recon-
structing Europe had been completed, and the threats presented by
Third World poverty and dependency were becoming ever more
explicit.

Table 2-I

Canadian External Assistance, 1951-1970
(allocation of appropriations by programs)

Fiscal year ending March 31	1951-60	($ millions rounded)									
		1961	1962	1963	1964	1965	1966	1967	1968	1969	1970
Bilateral Programs	359.8	61.1	52.9	41.7	45.7	122.1	129.7	199.3	204.7	232.1	269.9
Multilateral Programs	60.8	20.8	16.4	27.8	19.6	26.0	29.8	48.6	48.5	52.2	60.7
Total Allocations	420.6	81.9	69.3	69.5	65.3	148.1	159.5	247.9	253.2	288.6*	338.7*

* includes allocations to the newly-established Non-Governmental Organizations
Program.

Note: The budgetary planning process of the External Aid Office and its
successor, CIDA, entails several stages which may cause confusion in reporting
annual aid statistics. **Appropriations** are voted by Parliament for categories
such as grant aid, loans, food aid, and advances to multilateral institutions. The
approval of **allocations** to particular countries is done by Cabinet. Following
project or program requests made by developing countries to CIDA,
commitments of specific funds are taken. **Disbursements** are the last stage in
the budgetary process. The above table reflects allocations of appropriations
and is not the same as actual disbursements. Allocations for a given country or
project may actually be disbursed over several years. Throughout the 1960s,
disbursements fell short of appropriations with the result that by 1969-70 the
cumulative undisbursed balance of appropriations reached about $400 million.
Although CIDA attempted to close the gap in the early 1970s, there continued to
be undisbursed balances with the result that in 1976-77 the government stopped
the practice of carrying over unspent appropriations, these being allowed to
lapse at the end of the fiscal year.

Sources: CIDA, **Annual Review**, 1969 and 1970-71; CIDA, **CIDA Commitments
and Disbursements**, (February 1971); CIDA, **Contact**, no. 59, June 1977.

By late 1961, the United Nations launched what it called the First International Development Cooperation Decade. The General Assembly set two main goals for the sixties: an annual increase of 5% in total production by the developing countries, and an annual net transfer of financial or other support from the rich countries equivalent to 1% of their Gross National Products.

In Ottawa, the Colombo Plan Group readied itself for the new era of aid dispensation by proposing the establishment of a new agency and the centralization of all aid administration within the office of the Department of External Affairs. The old confusion among ministries ended in the fall of 1960 with the establishment of the External Aid Office (EAO), accountable to the Minister of External Affairs.

The new chief aid administrator, Herbert Moran, reported directly to the minister, and was a more powerful figure than his old counterpart. But Trade and Commerce maintained its influence through the External Aid Board, an interdepartmental committee set up for aid policy coordination. The launching of the EAO meant that the cabinet "recognized aid as a momentous activity of long range Canadian diplomacy", according to Spicer.[3]

In the sixties, the EAO initiated a bilateral aid program for Francophone Africa, designed to thwart Quebec's ambitions for bilateral international relationships, and, in 1964, began extending a limited amount of aid to Latin America. The development assistance budget expanded dramatically, and, in the middle sixties, Ottawa launched a program of bilateral development loans, extended on easy terms. All bilateral assistance had previously been extended as grants. During the first half of the decade, bilateral grants and loans totalled $558.39 million, more than double the amount expended between 1955 and 1960. (Grants from 1960-61 to 1964-65: $286.09 million; loans from 1960-61 to 64-65: $272.30 million.)

By the late sixties, a number of forces pushed western capitalist powers to expand their foreign aid programs even more rapidly. In 1969, the Commission on International Development, chaired by Lester Pearson, issued a report which critically reviewed past efforts and urged developed nations to improve the quality and quantity of their assistance.

The UN began developing new targets for the second development decade, and, using a new concept, Official Development Assistance, urged the rich northern countries to aim for aid budgets equivalent to .7% of their GNP.

Ottawa moved with the prevailing winds by overhauling its assistance program once again in 1968, when the External Aid Office was restructured as the bigger and better CIDA, headed by Maurice Strong, who assumed control of the External Aid Office in 1966.

Strong dispelled any remaining illusions that quick cures could be devised for underdevelopment when he acknowledged that "international development is a long term process."[4]

Strong, a former Power Corporation executive, was well matched with Canada's dashing new Prime Minister, Pierre Elliot Trudeau: both hoped to create a more active and creative Canadian presence in the international arena. Trudeau began preparing the unobtrusive middle power for its new role by undertaking a major review of Canada's foreign policy, which was published in 1970. He often treated the new development agency like a favourite son, and, for a time, CIDA expanded far more rapidly than other agencies.

CIDA's departments and divisions quickly multiplied. It rounded out its global commitments by inaugurating a bilateral assistance plan for Latin America in 1970. A planning and economics branch was organized within the Agency to do systematic evaluations of individual projects and country programs. Various operating divisions responsible for the capital assistance program, dispatching Canadians abroad, and training foreign students in Canada, were consolidated within a single operations branch. Canada's first permanent aid field workers were posted overseas.

In the late sixties, Ottawa also decided to modify what it termed the "responsive character" of the Canadian aid program. "Instead of relying entirely on passive response to requests from nations overseas," task forces were sent abroad to "make on-the-spot assessments of overseas needs in strategic economic areas."[5]

As it sprouted new divisions, the Agency mushroomed into a hefty bureaucracy. By the middle seventies, it employed 980 permanent staff, as well as 1,988 advisors and educators hired on contract to serve overseas.

A complex system was devised to control the sprawling bureaucracy. Commercial interests are represented through an interdepartmental committee, the Canadian International Development Board, which includes representatives of CIDA; External Affairs; Finance; Industry, Trade and Commerce; the Bank of Canada; the Treasury Board; and the International Development Research Centre. The Board meets three or four times a year to review the Agency's work and discuss new policies.

A lower level committee, the Interdepartmental Committee on Development Assistance (ICDA), including delegates from all departments represented on the Board, meets more frequently and informally. In 1974, still a third committee, the Interdepartmental Committee on Economic Relations with Developing Countries (ICERDC), was created to monitor Canada's relationships with developing countries. The ICERDC, which gathers deputy minister level representatives from 12 departments, ministries and agencies, is currently the principal focus for foreign assistance policy discussions.

The proliferating committees and divisions dispensed a budget which was shooting up in dramatic leaps. In 1970, the government announced its intention of boosting aid expenditures to the UN's revised aid target, .7% of Gross National Product. The aid budget grew by nearly 20% a year during the early seventies. By 1976-77, it had climbed to $973.3 million, nearly triple the 1969-70 total of $339 million. Canada was approaching the UN target by the middle seventies, when its allocations totalled .54% of GNP. (See Table 2-II.)

Table 2-II

Official Development Assistance — Disbursements by Program, 1971-1980

($ millions rounded)

(Fiscal year ending March 31)	1971	1972	1973	1974	1975	1976	1977	1978	1979	1980
Bilateral Aid (including food aid)	268.8	283.2	329.2	367.7	498.4	525.7	466.5	541.4	559.3	598.8
Multilateral Aid (including food aid)	74.4	97.4	153.8	185.1	200.0	318.5	428.7	425.5	490.4	500.5
Non-Governmental Organizations	8.5	11.9	16.1	20.7	26.0	31.8	41.8	49.1	70.8	78.1
IDRC	2.5	2.5	8.0	14.0	19.0	27.0	29.5	29.5	35.8	35.6
Other Programs	— —	.1	.1	.2	16.5	.4	6.5	4.9	9.6	27.9
Total Disbursements	354.3	395.1	507.3	587.8	760.0	903.5	973.1	1050.5	1165.9	1241.1

Notes: This table reflects actual disbursements of Official Development Assistance (ODA) as opposed to appropriations or commitments by CIDA. Since 1969, the OECD's Development Assistance Committee has defined aid as having the promotion of economic development as its objective and as being concessional in its terms. All CIDA disbursements qualify as ODA and these disbursements represent over 96% of Canadian ODA. Non-CIDA ODA includes, for example, contributions by provincial governments to NGOs.

In this table, constructed from CIDA annual reports which have shuffled categories several times in the past decade, bilateral aid includes international emergency relief up until 1976; afterwards it is placed in the "other" category. Omitted from the 1978 figures is CIDA's debt cancellation of $232 million which represents no new ODA disbursement. Statistics for the NGO Program include allocations to the International NGO Program since fy 1974-75 and the statistics for this category since 1977 encompass donations to some agencies previously considered under multilateral. "Other Programs" includes scholarship programs and support of the Business and Industry division as well as post-1976 emergency relief; it also accounts for a special item in 1975, the forgiveness of obligations made by the Export Development Corporation to Pakistan and later repatriated by Bangladesh.

Sources: CIDA, **Annual Report**, (1971 to 1979-80).

Even as divisions, budgets, and, apparently, expectations, burgeoned, a more sombre mood began to infect CIDA and other development agencies around the world. As early as 1969, when the Agency was flexing its newly developed muscles, it acknowledged that "the gap between the rich and the poor continues to widen."[6]

An increasing number of statesmen realized with dismay that their aid dollars weren't building strong, prosperous, free enterprise economies in the Third World. At the same time, many less developed countries, dissatisfied with the charity dispensed to them by their richer neighbours, cooperated in formulating demands for redistribution of the world's wealth. They called not for more aid dollars, but for nothing less than a New International Economic Order.

World Bank President Robert McNamara kicked off still another supposedly new era of development assistance at the 1973 meeting of Bank governors, when he admitted that the post-World War II aid programs had failed the world's poor. McNamara pledged that, in the future, Bank resources would be concentrated on meeting the most basic needs of people in the world's least developed countries.

CIDA took up the tune played by McNamara's band, and, in 1973, Strong's successor, Paul Gerin-Lajoie, ordered an "intensive and extensive review of Canadian international development programs, policies, and procedures. . . ."[7]

Gerin-Lajoie, who was not a high powered businessman, but a former Vice-Premier of Quebec and the province's first Minister of Education, told the House of Commons Standing Committee on External Affairs that "the sixties witnessed a concentration on economic development and growth rates, with too little account taken of the social development of the people affected."

The product of the review, CIDA's *Strategy for International Development Cooperation 1975-80* was published in 1975, the year Canada allotted a higher percentage of its GNP to foreign aid than it has before or since. The *Strategy* pledged to redirect Ottawa's aid program to assist "the poorest countries of the world" and reaffirmed "its determination to achieve the official United Nations target of .7% of GNP."[8]

But the *Strategy*, a glossy red book proudly presented to a meeting of the UN General Assembly, was irrelevant as soon as it was published. In the middle seventies, the developed capitalist economies were hit by the worst recession they had endured since the thirties. As Canada's economic situation deteriorated, so did Ottawa's good intentions, and development assistance budgets were frozen in the late seventies. During the second half of the decade, aid disbursements increased less than $100 million a year, except in 1978-79 when the increment was slightly higher. Development assistance as a percentage of GNP dropped from .5% in 1976-77 to .45% in 1979-80. During a period of rapid inflation, these small increases meant actual cutbacks in aid recipients' purchasing power. In 1979, Canada's disbursements fell in US dollar terms for the first time in ten years.

Gerin-Lajoie had been a presentable exponent of the new aid

style promoted in the *Strategy*, but hard-headed elements within business and government considered him woolly-minded and careless about finances. He was ill-suited to a regime of penny pinching, and was replaced by a career bureaucrat, Michel Dupuy, in March, 1977. The Agency later explained that CIDA had become "a significant target for criticism", and that Dupuy was brought in to tighten up budgets and administration.[9]

Table 2-III

Official Development Assistance Expenditures as a Percentage of Gross National Product

Calendar Year	Canada	Total DAC Countries
Average 1966-1968	.30	.40
1970	.42	.34
1971	.42	.35
1972	.47	.33
1973	.43	.30
1974	.48	.33
1975	.54	.35
1976	.46	.33
1977	.50	.31
1978	.52	.35
1979	.46	.34

Note: The Development Assistance Committee (DAC) of the Organization for Economic Cooperation and Development reports aid expenditures by calendar year in contrast to CIDA's use of the government's fiscal year ending March 31.

Sources: OECD, **Development Cooperation: Efforts and Policies of the Members of the Development Assistance Committee** (Paris: OECD, various years); CIDA, **Annual Reports** (various years); — — —, "Recent Trends in Aid", **OECD Observer**, no. 105, July, 1980.

By the close of the seventies, few of the *Strategy*'s promises had been realized, and Trudeau, who had hoped to play an increasingly prominent role in North-South negotiations, had suffered a humiliating electoral defeat. Pundits predicted that development assistance would continue its slow slide to the bottom of the government's agenda, as Ottawa became increasingly preoccupied with domestic economic problems.

Then, a decade after the Pearson report, the Independent Commission on International Development Issues, chaired by Willy Brandt, reminded the industrialized world that attention to the problems of the Third World was not only a moral imperative, but a matter of "sound self-interest".[10] After Trudeau's re-election in 1980, the Department of External Affairs pledged, in September of the same year, to boost aid expenditures to .55% of GNP by 1985, and aim for the .7% UN target by 1990. Dupuy was replaced by Marcel Masse, a former World Bank employee with extensive travel experience in Third World countries.

A parliamentary task force on North-South relations, including representatives of Canada's three major political parties, urged the government to meet this goal by quickly increasing aid budgets. Task Force recommendations included the by-then old pieties that Ottawa's aid resources should be concentrated on meeting the basic needs of people in the world's poorest countries, and that the terms of its dispensation should be liberalized.

The Trudeau government's commitments to the Third World at the start of the eighties were simply a re-run of promises made and broken during the seventies. They protected CIDA, at least temporarily, from further cutbacks, but did not augur major changes or advances in the field of development assistance.

Multiple Channels

As Canadian aid planning became more sophisticated, channels and styles of distribution multiplied. CIDA both disburses aid directly, and supports a large number of domestic and international aid dispensing institutions.*

Bilateral Aid

About three-quarters of all aid ever disbursed by Ottawa has been bilateral, i.e., extended directly from government to government. At the start of the eighties, about half of CIDA's budget is allocated for bilateral aid to 89 countries. But over half of this total is funneled to ten recipients: Pakistan, Bangladesh, India, Egypt, Tanzania, Upper Volta, Ghana, Ivory Coast, Zambia and Malawi. Recipient nations are divided into two categories — *program countries* where Canada has a long-term commitment to development assistance, and a smaller number of *project countries* where aid is distributed on a project by project basis.

In most years, about 20% of the bilateral budget is devoted to food aid. Less than 10% is spent on technical assistance, which covers the costs of sending Canadian advisors overseas or of training programs for Third World students. A small amount of bilateral funding ($16 million in 1977-78) goes to Mission Administered Funds (MAF), disbursed through Canadian embassies in Third World countries.

---

* In 1969, the Development Assistance Committee of the Organization for Economic Cooperation and Development, a club of rich donor nations, refined the original loose definition of aid and developed strict criteria for what it terms Official Development Assistance (ODA). ODA excludes military assistance and commercial transfers such as foreign investments, private bank loans, and export credits. Under the terms of the old definition, Canada had technically been the world's largest aid recipient.

External Affairs describes the MAF program as "singularly effective in achieving both political benefits and developmental impact." Canadian ambassadors use the MAF to respond quickly to requests for assistance, up to a maximum of $25,000 per project. MAF funds are generally distributed to grassroots organizations like agricultural cooperatives, village development committees, or hospitals. The Fund permits the ambassador to support pet projects, and to build his personal prestige in the host country. This generous discretionary allowance supplied by CIDA also makes it less likely that the ambassador will be critical of Agency projects within his jurisdiction.

The remaining seventy percent of bilateral aid is extended in grants and loans for various kinds of economic assistance. By the middle seventies, the proportion of grants to loans was 63% to 37%. Over 90% of the loans are provided according to the 0/10/50 formula — 0% interest, 10 years of grace for repayment of the principal, and 50 years to maturity. Other loans are offered according to a concessional 3/7/30 formula.

CIDA requires that 80% of all bilateral aid be spent on the purchase of goods and services in Canada, and two-thirds of the value of this merchandise must actually be added in Canada.

Multilateral Aid

An increasing proportion of Canadian development assistance is channeled through multilateral institutions, organizations which pool the resources of donor governments and include both the industrialized and less developed nations as members. In the 1975 *Strategy*, CIDA pledged to devote up to 35% of its budget to these institutions, but by the early eighties, the percentage had risen to about 40%.

There are several types of multilateral aid: a) grants to international organizations, especially to United Nations agencies like the UN Development Program (UNDP) and the World Food Program (WFP). The most powerful developed countries treat the UN agencies, where each nation, rich or poor, is allocated one vote, as the poor relatives within the family of multilateral institutions; b) loans to special funds of the major international development banks such as the International Development Association, a World Bank affiliate. The IDA and other similar special funds offer soft loans to the world's poorest countries; c) capital subscriptions to development banks and financial institutions including the World Bank, the Inter-American Development Bank, and other regional development banks. These are considered Canadian assets or shareholdings. A specified amount of the subscription is actually paid into the Bank, but a high percentage is callable. Power within these banks and development institutions is generally determined by the amount of the members' contributions.

Canada supports 65 different multilateral institutions, but the bulk of its contributions go to international financial institutions (over 70% of the non-food multilateral budget) plus food aid programs like the WFP. The major development banks sometimes cofinance large projects which have been partially funded through CIDA's bilateral program. Ottawa's multilateral aid is not tied to procurement in Canada, but most multilateral aid is generally spent on goods and services available only in the industrialized countries of the North.

Special Programs

CIDA has created programs to involve Canadian non-governmental organizations (NGOs), the Canadian business community, and Canadian universities in its work overseas. Its NGO Division was established in 1968 with a budget of $5 million. The division matches funds raised by non-profit Canadian agencies operating in the Third World, e.g., OXFAM, church and missionary societies, the Red Cross, and the YWCA.

A substantial portion of NGO money (over $16.5 million in 1979-80) goes to three para-statal agencies which send Canadians to work overseas: the Canadian University Service Overseas (CUSO), which funds educators and technicians; the Canadian Executive Service Overseas, which pays retired Canadian businessmen to train Third World entrepreneurs; and Canada World Youth, which finances teenagers to work and travel in developing countries. In 1974, Ottawa broadened the program's parameters to include non-Canadian voluntary organizations, and CIDA has subsequently funded agencies like the International Council for Adult Education and the World University Service Overseas. In 1979-80, CIDA allocated over $61 million to 195 Canadian NGO's and over $7 million to international NGOs.

CIDA has often lamented the fact that "Canada has trailed other developed nations in investing abroad."[11] In 1970, the Agency offered a stimulus to Canadian business overseas by establishing its Business and Industry Division, which offered grants up of to $5,000 on a matching basis for starter studies, i.e., trips to prospective business sites, and up to $50,000 for more in-depth feasibility studies. The amount of CIDA resources allotted to the Division more than tripled between 1976 and 1977, from $200,000 to $750,000. This relatively small amount of seed money spawned investments totalling $8 million during 1976-77 alone, according to Agency administrators. In 1978, the Business and Industry Division was reshaped as the Industrial Cooperation Program, which has expanded eligibility and increased funding for pre-feasibility and feasibility studies.

Besides attracting business support for the aid program, Industrial Cooperation projects provide CIDA with a means of continuing relationships with middle-income, rapidly industrializing countries where traditional aid mechanisms are being phased out.

CIDA's Special Programs Division also allocated more than $35 million per year to the International Development Research Centre (IDRC), a para-statal corporation which maintains strong ties with the Agency. The IDRC involved Canadian and Third World intellectuals in research programs designed to close the technology gap between the industrialized and underdeveloped countries.

Juggling Objectives

The styles and structures for distribution of Canadian aid have changed frequently during the past three decades, but the objectives of the program show a basic unity and consistency over the years. In many cases, the real purposes of a given program have been papered over by a rhetoric designed for public scrutiny, leading to confusion among both Canadians and recipients about Ottawa's foreign aid goals.

CIDA's current official formulation of its primary objective is a repetition of many past similar statements:

The objective of the Canadian development assistance program is to support the efforts of developing countries in fostering their economic growth and the evolution of their social systems in a way that will produce a wise distribution of the benefits of development among the populations of these countries, enhance the quality of life and improve the capacity in all sectors of their populations to participate in national development efforts.[12]

This is the *humanitarian* rationalization for CIDA's programming. The expression of this objective has grown increasingly sophisticated over the years, and the Agency administrators no longer speak of "aid" or "charity" to the poor, but about rigorously defined "official development assistance" which will permit what they call "developing", not "underdeveloped", countries to assume their rightful position as equals in the global village.

The humanitarian explanation for aid is the one that prompts many Canadians to support the disbursement of their tax dollars overseas. It is the motive most often expressed in public statements to international agencies like the United Nations.

Reflection about aid's humanitarian objectives tends to move Canadian politicians to eloquence. External Affairs Minister Mitchell Sharp, who could equally well advance opposing arguments, made a convincing case for exclusively philanthropic objectives:

There is one good and sufficient reason for international aid and that is that there are less fortunate people in the world who need our help.... The inspiration for what we do must be essentially humanitarian and unselfish. . . . If it is not, if the purpose of our aid is to help ourselves, rather than to help others, we shall probably receive in return what we deserve and a good deal less than what we expect. Many of the troubles with which international aid is beset today may be laid to the fact that we of the free world are losing this humanitarian inspiration. We have got ourselves into an international rat race, using aid in an effort to win friends, influence customers and outbid the communists.[13]

A review of the content of Agency programs rather than its press releases shows that the humanitarian aim is in fact close to the bottom of Canada's aid agenda. National self-interest rather than philanthropy has always been the basis for Ottawa's development assistance programs. In some contexts, Canadian statesmen have been quite frank in their assertions that aid can, and indeed must, first of all serve Canadian purposes. "The government believes that development objectives can complement and reinforce other Canadian objectives in the developing countries," the Liberal government emphasized in its 1970 Foreign Policy Review.[14]

The national development objectives of recipient countries must compete for attention. Often this contradiction is ignored, and Canadian policymakers, like the members of the Brandt Commission, assume that "sound self-interest" is complementary and compatible with the objectives of less developed nations. "There is always a relationship between what can be done in Canada for people who need help and what can be done in Pakistan for people who need help," Lester Pearson assured his colleagues as early as 1961.[15] This primary assumption includes another premise: that the people of the Third World can make good use of the commodities Canada has to offer.

In reality, no invisible hand has arranged for such a happy coincidence of objectives. Aid based on Canadian interests has not fostered, and in many cases has discouraged "a wise distribution of benefits" among the populations of Third World countries.

Because Canada has evolved from a political colony of Britain to an economic colony of the United States, its national objectives are often indistinguishable from those of its patrons. "We are no more independent in our aid policy than we are in our defense or foreign policy", according to Professor Stephen Triantis, a major contributor to CIDA's original policy development.[16]

National self-interest has dictated a set of *political* and *commercial* rather than *humanitarian* objectives. *Political objectives* prompted Canada's original involvement with foreign aid, and remain a dominant factor in the development of CIDA programs. They include distinctively Canadian goals, as well as those common to all advanced capitalist powers.

• Aid was originally forged as a weapon in the Cold War, and is still considered a force in what is often termed the "war for men's minds". Pearson positively and succinctly stated this goal during discussion in the House of Commons after the Colombo Plan Conference. "If Southeast Asia and South Asia are not to be conquered by Communism, we of the free democratic world must demonstrate that it is we and not the Russians who stand for national liberation and social progress."[17] This goal became less important as the Cold War abated, but even as late as 1976, Canada's Minister of External Affairs Allen MacEachen considered aid to the Association of Southeast Asian Nations, a grouping of non-communist countries in the region, a vital support for "the last bulwark against communism in this part of the world."[18]

Canada has often played surrogate for the US and Britain in the Cold War, and this role has dictated the geographical spread of its aid programs. The Colombo Plan was conceived because Asia was, at the time, the hottest spot in the spreading East-West struggle. Representatives to the Colombo Plan Conference, a gathering of Commonwealth nations, acted as plausible advance men for the United States and Japan, who joined the program shortly after its inception.

This pattern has been repeated on numerous occasions. Ottawa was attempting to fill Britain's shoes when it initiated the Commonwealth African and Caribbean programs, and helping the US to contain the Cuban Revolution when it started dispensing aid to Latin America through the Inter-American Development Bank.

Canada has represented western interests in nations financially punished by Washington because of doubtful loyalties. In 1969, after India had started securing military and economic support from the USSR, the Nixon administration reacted by drastically cutting its aid program to a government perceived as fickle. Canada tried to fill the gap by increasing the level of its support. There were several rationalizations for this move. "One popular one was that the Americans had misunderstood their own true interests and that Nixon and Kissinger had overidden the knowledgeable advice of the State Department."[19]

• During the era of detente, Ottawa, like other advanced capitalist powers, realized that the North-South split was as threatening to global political and economic stability as the primal East-West conflict. The formulation of demands for a New International Economic Order, and especially the OPEC offensive, put the industrialized northern powers on notice that there were powerful new players in the international political arena.

Trudeau has spoken publicly about the danger of North-South tensions as early as 1968.

... in the long run, the overwhelming threat to Canada will not come from foreign investments or foreign ideologies, or even — with good fortune — foreign nuclear weapons. It will come instead from the two-thirds of the people of the world who are steadily falling farther and farther behind in their search for a decent standard of living.[20]

By the early eighties, aid had assumed a new significance, not as an actual solution for the problems of underdevelopment, but as a demonstration of serious concern for the plight of the poorest of the world's poor. Canada simply could not remain a respectable member of the club of rich nations if it did not run a development assistance program. Foreign aid is no longer voluntary largesse, but an obligation expected of every developed country by both rich and poor nations around the world.

• Canada has its own limited domestic agenda to promote through development assistance. Ottawa's foreign policymakers tend to equate the size of the aid program with the amount of weight Canada can swing on issues in which the nation has a direct stake, e.g., Law of the Sea and Multilateral Trade Negotiations. The Foreign Policy Review issued during the early Trudeau years acknowledged that:

We could not expect to find the same sympathy for Canadian interests or support for Canadian policies amongst the other nations with which we are associated in the world community if we were unwilling to bear our share of our collective responsibilities. Development assistance is one of the ways we can meet these responsibilities.[21]

On a few occasions, Canada has also launched or continued aid programs that were clearly dictated by its own political priorities, not by the needs of the bigger powers. The Francophone Africa program, for example, was essential to minimize political frictions at home. Diefenbaker insisted on Ottawa's independence from Washington by maintaining ties with Cuba when the US was trying to enforce a complete embargo on Fidel Castro. An aid program was developed to complement trade contacts. Trudeau, who is generally much less ornery about Americans than Diefenbaker, also likes to prove that Canada is an authentic nation by ignoring Washington's instructions from time to time. In the late seventies, he continued financial support for the government of his friend, Michael Manley, despite US pressure to cut aid to Jamaica.

Commercial objectives cannot be separated from the *political* and the two generally work hand-in-glove. The drive to guarantee western political dominance in the Third World has always been fueled by the need to secure supplies of raw materials, new markets, and investment opportunities.

• Canadian aid has facilitated post-war· investment by American,

European and Japanese corporations. Some Canadian corporations, which may or may not be controlled in Canada, have also started up overseas operations. These initiatives have been supported by CIDA's programs for business, and protected by the good will generated through the aid program as a whole. But Canadian investments abroad, though increasing, have always been dwarfed by those of bigger powers.

Aid has always been used to grease the wheels of corporate growth by providing the energy, transportation and communications systems necessary for large-scale capital investment. Through its infrastructure projects, Ottawa supplies the power lines that may later be used by Volkswagen, General Motors, or even in a rare case, a Canadian company.

An increasing proportion of western development assistance was channeled through multilateral institutions during the seventies, partly because they have the resources to undertake massive development projects that most donor countries could not execute unilaterally. Ottawa's contributions to multilateral institutions do not guarantee immediate rewards, because Canada's procurement record within these agencies is uneven, but they promote the general welfare of the western economic system.

• Within the context of the drive to open up new corporate frontiers, Canada has unobtrusively used aid to promote its own trade interests. The trade possibilities presented by aid programs have been especially important to the Canadian government. The tying of a high proportion of Canadian bilateral aid ensures immediate business for Canadian companies.

CIDA spokesmen are sometimes quite direct in their public statements about the Agency's commercial objectives. They generally wait until they are addressing the appropriate constituency. In 1977, incoming CIDA president Michel Dupuy justified Canada's aid program at the prestigious Empire Club of Toronto with what he called the "charity begins at home" argument:

Yes it does. That is why sixty percent of our total aid budget is spent in Canada for goods and services provided in developing countries. The sum is close to $650 million annually. It is estimated that over 100,000 jobs can be related to our foreign aid program. The bilateral aid programs provide foreign markets for key Canadian industries and may sometimes represent a major source of contracts. [22]

In the longer term, Canada uses its aid as free samples, enticing potential customers to make commercial deals. Aid can in fact make Canadian aid recipients dependent on Canadian inputs — replacement parts, repairs, and services for aid-funded projects.

These commercial objectives are central to Canadian aid programs partly because they are backed by a strong lobby — the Canadian business community. Canadians who support the humanitarian objectives are generally unorganized or gathered in groups that simply don't have the clout of the Canadian Export Association (CEA), the Canadian Manufacturers Association (CMA), and the Canadian Association-Latin America and the Caribbean (CALA). These associations regularly meet with top CIDA officials or pressure the government indirectly through their government representative, the Department of Industry, Trade and Commerce (ITC).

The business lobby is alert to any sign that CIDA may be neglecting sound self-interest. In 1975, Ottawa announced that Canadian aid would be untied immediately for bidding by Third World countries only. The Development Aid Committee of the Canadian Export Association expressed loud dismay at this minor concession to recipient nations and, in meetings with top CIDA officials, insisted that they be consulted before implementation of the decision. One ITC official showed his instinctive distrust of any Agency initiative when he privately remarked that "the people at CIDA either have their hearts on their sleeves or are so far left that they make Marx look like a fascist."

Government spokesmen soon became equivocal in their statements on the change, stressing how complex a process it would be. By the end of 1977, they had stopped mentioning it even as a possibility.

The self-incriminating words of ITC official James Whiteside are a clear illustration of how pro-commerce concerns bring their pressure to bear on CIDA. At a 1973 meeting of businessmen in Toronto, Whiteside was asked about the relationship between his ministry and the Agency. His reply reveals as much about the business community's real view of aid as it does about the shaping of policy objectives:

You have in CIDA — I hope there are no members of the press, I'd like to ask you to take this one off the record — you have in CIDA a lot of people of what we call do-gooders, bleeding hearts, you know, the kind of guy that wants to do good. I see nothing wrong with that, except that when I also see Canadian funds or a project coming up, and the Japanese are there with their soft money, the Brits are there, the Yanks are there, and old Canada isn't there, you get pretty upset. So what we at Trade and Commerce have been trying to do is to move CIDA into areas where they are more commercially oriented. We are saying to CIDA basically, "Look you take so much money and go out into the world and do good, but we would like some for export." And I think the people at CIDA are starting to see the need to create jobs in Canada and so on. You see aid money is often a device, a tool, to get into a market. It's a toehold. Now where you people can benefit is by coming to us at Trade and Commerce, especially in the Financing Branch because we are the official contact with CIDA, and say, "Look, I've got the project in Bongo Bongo and we would like to do such and such. . . ." We'll look at the project and say, "Now look, what have you got in there now? If it's just cold hard exports, CIDA will probably have a nightmare over that one." But what we can do is turn it around. We can appeal to their sentiment in the sense that we can say, "Look, if you put in there a technical assistance package to help these people identify what they want, or if you throw in a management contract so that we can actually help them run the thing 'til we get it off the ground," I think we could sell it to CIDA. And that is why we at Trade and Commerce would like to see what you are going to present to CIDA before you actually present it. We can get the hangups out of the way.[23]

Ottawa states one or more of its aid objectives on appropriate occasions. When confronted about the contradictions among the three, government spokesmen insist that there is no conflict, and that the achievement of political and commercial objectives does not prevent the realization of aid's humanitarian objectives.

But the effort to keep juggling priorities is one of several factors that prevents CIDA from working out a coherent program for Third World development. The business community exerts constant pressure on the Agency, forcing it to renege on its "development" promises that resources will be concentrated on meeting the basic needs of the most oppressed sectors of the world's poorest countries which require few Canadian inputs. Political objectives, on the other hand, keep aid administrators from focusing on middle income Third World nations — clients that commercial interests hope to wean from aid to hard export credits.

CIDA's success or failure in meeting its objectives can finally be gauged only by reviewing the development of its programs in recipient nations, not by reading Ottawa's policy statements and reports. A quick look at the spread of its aid projects during the past three decades shows that Canada's self-interested political and commercial goals invariably edge out the supposedly primary humanitarian objectives.

CIDA's Regional Programs:

3

Global Reach

At the heart of Canada's foreign aid program are CIDA's bilateral programs, divided for administrative reasons, for Asia, the Commonwealth Caribbean, Commonwealth Africa, Francophone Africa and Latin America.*

Asia Program

Three-fifths of all bilateral aid ever transferred by Canada has gone to the countries of South and Southeast Asia and the region is still the biggest program administered by CIDA.

Politics have always dominated Canada's aid program to Asia. From the outset the objective was to stop communism. In front of this overriding goal, the development of peoples and societies was incidental. Even before Lester Pearson informed the House of Commons of the anti-communist intent of the Colombo Plan, John Diefenbaker upstaged him by bluntly telling a CBC audience that "$50 million a year... would be cheap insurance for Canada... to halt communism in Asia."[1] Five years after the initiation of the Colombo Plan, Pearson would admit that Canada wouldn't have started giv-

---

* "Commonwealth" and "Francophone" programs in Africa and the Caribbean also administer aid for countries other than the former colonies of Britain and France.

ing aid if not for the perceived communist threat and he even went
so far as to thank the communists for drawing Canada's attention to
the plight of the Third World.[2]

Canada was quite unprepared to initiate an aid program in a
region where it had limited experience and familiarity. But with
Britain and the United States pressing Ottawa to shoulder its Cold
War responsibilities, Commonwealth Asia (which was all there was
of the non-white Commonwealth until Ghana's independence in
1957) provided an opportunity to begin in countries where English
was spoken and which had inherited British administrative and
planning systems of supposed reliability. And there was always the
promise of commercial returns from the venture; a Colombo Plan
administrator told Parliament in 1956 that as the needs of the people
of Asia increase "so will their ability to buy . . . creating a market for
ourselves in the area".[3]

While the longer-range growth of these markets was awaited,
aid supplied an immediate outlet for Canadian goods. Canada's first
shipment under the Colombo Plan — a $10 million donation of
surplus wheat — was followed by a supply line of more food, other
commodities (metals, fertilizers, pulp and paper), transportation
equipment, and materials to build hydro-dams and transmission
lines. The hydro-dam category, Canada's *forte*, absorbed fully 61%
of the non-commodity aid up until 1967.[4] As a result, aid-supported
exports monopolized Canada's trade with Asia during this period;
over half of Canada's exports to India during the 1950s, for example,
were financed by the aid program.[5]

The heavy use of Canadian inputs was part and parcel of the aim
to build a defence line against communism in Asia. The assumption
was that Asian hearts and minds could be swayed by the construction of conspicuous examples of western economic development.
So, Canadian aid planners preferred large, technically-advanced
and photogenic infrastructure projects to serve as both monuments
to Canadian generosity and symbols of progress. Some of the most
expensive and visible forms of Canada's assistance ever provided to
Asian countries were prepared at this time: the Warsak Hydro-
Electric and Irrigation project in Pakistan ($35 million disbursed
between 1952 and 1959), the Kundah Hydro-Electric Power Development in India ($44 million between 1955 and 1965), steam locomo-
tives to India ($21 million between 1952 and 1955), and the Canada-
India Atomic Research Reactor at Trombay ($11 million between
1958 and 1965).[6]

The Warsak Dam — a concrete structure almost 750 feet long and
220 feet high which can generate up to 240,000 kilowatts of electricity — demonstrates the showcase mentality of the donor. Built on
the border of Pakistan and Afghanistan, the project was undertaken
to strengthen one of the eastern fronts in the Cold War. By employ-

ing local workers in constructing the dam, Warsak's planners hoped to root the wandering Pathan tribesmen of the area in sedentary occupations and the wage economy. This would create a new stability in the region and thwart Soviet plans to unite the Pathans of both Afghanistan and Pakistan into an independent nation.[7] Over twenty years later, the failure of such showcase strategies was symbolized by the hastily-erected camp at Warsak for Afghan refugees from the Soviet invasion of their country.

The Cold War preoccupation of donor countries continued to dominate the development of aid programs as the nations of South Asia matured through the 1960s and 1970s. When the United States suspended aid to Ceylon (now Sri Lanka) in 1963 in reprisal for the nationalization of American petroleum companies, the possibility of Ceylon's isolation from the West frightened both Washington and Ottawa. Ever sensitive to its role on the world stage, Canada played the understanding good-guy foil to Washington's policeman bully; Ottawa increased its aid assistance to Ceylon and picked up on the project of constructing a runway extension and new terminal for the Katunayake international airport. The $6 million project appears in retrospect a small price for keeping doors open to the West.[8] In a later instance, the only apparent reason for $10.6 million in Canadian aid to South Vietnam, Cambodia (now Kampuchea) and Laos during the American escalation of the war between 1966 and 1969 was to show that the low-profile but decidedly pro-American Canadians were there.[9]

The clear inability of aid programs to decisively win western allies in Asia has, over the years, made CIDA less pretentious and more cautious about its aid programming. The severe embarrassment of India's explosion of a nuclear device in 1974 — employing technology and equipment from the original aid-financed Canada-India Atomic Research Reactor and a CANDU power station sold to the country in 1963 — and India's use of both Soviet and western aid has caused a cooling of Canada's traditional affinity for the country and a decline in its aid allocations from CIDA (1980 levels are less than half of 1976 disbursements). CIDA's programming is also complicated by more recent internal and border conflicts in Vietnam, Kampuchea and Afghanistan; aid to Vietnam and Afghanistan was suspended in the late 1970s and early 1980s respectively as a result.

Asia is clearly the favoured region among western development agencies and nowhere is Canada the most important donor. Asia is no longer the greatest recipient of CIDA bilateral disbursements. Since 1975, Asia received less than half of total bilateral expenditures, surpassed by the combined programs for Commonwealth and Francophone Africa. (See Table 3-IV.) The decline is partly because of political concerns about countries of the region but also a consequence of expanding programs in Africa and Latin America.

Still, the region receives a hefty 39% of the bilateral budget. Eleven countries (down from 17 at one point in the 1970s) count on regular CIDA allocations compared to the original three recipients — India, Pakistan and Ceylon — at the start of the Colombo Plan. But the aid is highly concentrated in the subcontinent where a half-billion of the world's poorest live; India, Pakistan and Bangladesh absorb three-quarters of all bilateral aid to the region. (See Table 3-V.)

Table 3-IV

Regional Breakdown of CIDA Bilateral Aid Disbursements (including bilateral food aid)

(in millions of dollars)

	1970/71	1974/75	1979/80
Asia	180	244	235
	(69%)	(50%)	(39%)
Africa:			
Francophone	30	99	148
	(11%)	(20%)	(25%)
Commonwealth	25	109	138
	(10%)	(22%)	(23%)
Latin America	9	21	35
	(3%)	(4%)	(6%)
Commonwealth Caribbean	19	20	31
	(7%)	(4%)	(5%)
Other			12
			(2%)

Sources: CIDA, **Strategy for International Development Cooperation 1975-80,** (Ottawa, 1975); CIDA, **Annual Report 1979/80.**

Canada also supports multilateral aid efforts in the area through the Asian Development Bank in which it holds $95 million worth of equity. Since joining the bank at its inception in 1966, Canada has contributed $268 million in the form of capital subscriptions, loans to special funds, and grants. The Bank annually dispenses almost half-a-million dollars in the region.

In the 1980s, CIDA plans to use the same old moulds for its aid giving to Asia. Although heavily criticized both in Canada and abroad, food will continue to occupy a large space in the aid package. Even CIDA admits that attempts to direct bilateral aid towards meeting "basic needs", especially in the rural sector, are having limited success. Recent annual reports suggest a return to traditional, large-scale infrastructure projects in the hydro-electric, transportation and resource development fields. Canadian business leaders have been lobbying for increased attention to the South East Asian Nations (ASEAN) — Indonesia, Malaysia, Philippines, Singapore, Thailand and Vietnam — which represent a fast-growing market of over 250 million people. Consequently, CIDA recently announced a major commitment to spend $122 million over the next five years in Indonesia, a country where Canada's INCO Ltd. is a

Table 3-V

Asia — Bilateral Aid Disbursements, 1971-1980
($ millions)

fiscal year ending	1971	1972	1973	1974	1975	1976	1977	1978	1979	1980	Total 1971-1980
Afghanistan	.73	2.27	1.01	.23	1.77	.40	.25	2.92	4.22	6.62*	20.42
Bangladesh	—	—	48.28	59.27	73.80	29.48	37.27	72.10	71.79	65.18	457.17
Burma	2.94	.37	3.04	1.72	1.39	.70	2.87	5.46	3.77	6.33	28.59
India	103.14	101.49	78.26	69.28	96.40	98.91	80.86	57.16	31.91	42.60	760.01
Indonesia	3.57	3.95	14.75	21.64	19.52	36.70	22.43	13.19	12.72	11.75	160.22
Kampuchea	.35	.03	.04	.09	.55	.03	.01	(.02)	—	—	1.08
Korea (Rep.)	2.59	.05	.02	.01	—	.01	.03	(.04)	—	(.04)	2.62
Laos	.23	.20	.16	.28	.20	.18	2.59	(.01)	—	—	3.83
Malaysia	2.36	3.59	2.84	2.31	1.61	1.48	1.59	2.97	2.36	1.75	22.86
Nepal	.29	.94	.78	1.06	.07	.21	.55	2.56	3.37	6.74	16.57
Pakistan	47.50	24.32	9.41	37.51	27.56	63.94	62.65	68.85	60.91	67.17	469.82
Philippines	.05	.05	.01	.02	.02	.07	1.29	2.84	.33	.37	5.05
Singapore	.34	.51	.47	.63	.34	.10	.05	—	—	—	2.44
Sri Lanka	5.18	6.41	7.53	5.65	10.84	8.37	18.75	16.93	30.04	15.94	125.64
Thailand	.98	.58	.32	.42	.41	.21	.35	.32	2.54	6.79	12.92
Turkey	8.00	.70	5.51	.33	4.85	—	—	—	—	—	19.39
Vietnam	1.56	2.39	1.91	2.76	2.07	1.49	(.05)	6.07	.24	—	18.44
Regional, Special and Other Programs	.77	.54	.30	.59	2.85	15.53	1.94	2.11	2.86	3.42	30.91
Total	180.58	148.39	174.64	203.80	244.25	257.81	233.43	253.41	227.05	234.62	2,157.98

* suspended after the Soviet invasion

( ) signifies net payment back to Canada

Sources: CIDA, **Annual Reports** (various years)

major investor in the mining sector and where Canadian businesses are anxiously investigating projects in the mining, transportation and power generation fields.

And here the history of Canadian aid to Asia comes full circle. CIDA is still intent on funding large projects of commercial benefit to Canada with the intention of building "a bulwark against communism in this part of the world", as former External Affairs Minister Allan MacEachen puts it. Because Asia is an area where the interests of four major world powers (the US, the USSR, China and Japan) intersect and sometimes clash in complex patterns, the region has lost none of its strategic significance for Canada's foreign policy-makers who still view the world through Cold War glasses.

Commonwealth Caribbean Program

The expansion of Canada's aid program beyond Asia in the late 1950s was undertaken to support Britain's decolonization program in the Caribbean and Africa.

The English-speaking Caribbean was of special and immediate concern to Ottawa. Here, more than anywhere else in the world, the Canadian government and Canadian corporations have earned the label "imperialist". Throughout the islands, Canadian banks dominate street corners and much of the region's financial activity. Canada's ALCAN corporation is a pillar of the Jamaican bauxite industry. Overall, Canadian direct investment in the Commonwealth Caribbean now exceeds $850 million.[10] Trade with the area, while not large, is deeply rooted in history, pre-dating Confederation, when schooners from Atlantic Canada traded fish, livestock and lumber for Caribbean rum, molasses, sugar and spices. Over 400,000 Canadian tourists annually flood Caribbean beaches, their chilled, white complexions seeking relief from northern winters. And the ebb and flow — mostly the former of late — of Canadian immigration policy stands as a continuing frustration for Caribbean emigrants with yearnings for Canadian destinations.

Canada's economic investment in the countries of the Caribbean is matched by political preoccupations about its security. That the preoccupation is justified was brought home in February 1970. Trinidadians rioted in downtown Port of Spain protesting, in part, the arrest and trial of a number of West Indian students involved in an occupation at Sir George Williams University in Montreal. Canadians were shocked to learn that the windows being smashed in Port of Spain were those of branches of Canadian banks. The federal government and Canadian businessmen were equally unnerved when later that same year the government of Forbes Burnham in Guyana announced the nationalization of ALCAN's bauxite subsidiary, the Demerara Bauxite Company (DEMBA).

At the same time, in mid-1970, the Canadian Senate's Standing Committee on Foreign Affairs released its report on the state of Canada-Caribbean relations. The report said little that was not already the basis of Canadian foreign and aid policy toward the region. Nevertheless, it initiated a reappraisal of that policy — the need for which was all the more emphasized by the inexplicable omission of the Caribbean as a major discussion point in the Trudeau government's *Foreign Policy for Canadians*. "Canada can expect continuing, and even growing criticism and hostility from some sectors of opinion in the Caribbean," the committee explained. To contain such criticism, the report suggested, Canada should not take the Caribbean for granted. Canada's special relationship with the area should be maintained and should demonstrate that Canada, "while interested in stability in the Caribbean, is not committed to the status quo and recognizes the case for progressive change".[11]

The implication for aid giving was that assistance would have to deal with some of the festering social sores of poverty and unemployment if Canadian interests were to be protected. A confidential Cabinet document issued in the mid-1970s succinctly summarized the policy basis for aid giving:

The region is a highly volatile one, beset with racial tensions, high unemployment, greater underemployment, and immense income distribution inequities. To the extent that the Canadian bilateral development assistance programme, in cooperation with the governments concerned, is directed toward the solution of these problems, then our aid programme may be seen as a useful support for peace and stability within the region and hence an effective support for all Canadian interests.[12]

The federal government first began discussing Canadian aid for the Commonwealth Caribbean in the autumn of 1956 when Lester Pearson convened a conference of Caribbean leaders in Ottawa. It was left to the government of John Diefenbaker to actually launch the program in 1958. Ottawa allocated $10 million over a five-year period for the newly established Federation of the West Indies; the funds went to construct a residence of the West Indies in Jamaica, upgrade water and port facilities, support elementary schools, fund port and water surveys, and provide two ships to improve communications among the islands. The Federation itself — designed to be a new Commonwealth state comprising Jamaica, Trinidad and Tobago, Barbados, Antigua, St. Kitts-Nevis, Montserrat, Grenada, Dominica, St. Lucia and St. Vincent — disintegrated after four years, but the Canadian aid program survived.

By the mid-1960s, a bilateral aid program had been scaled up to about $10 million a year. The major aid donors to the area — Canada, Britain and the United States — decided among themselves in 1966 to divide it into sectors for assistance purposes. Canada got water resources, air transport, education and agriculture, and most of its aid projects over the next decade were concentrated in these areas. The US and Canada seemed to agree on another kind of division of responsibilities at the same time; although the Caribbean is the immediate backyard of the United States, Canada, with its historic and Commonwealth relationship, seemed willing to take over the task of "looking after" the region for the interests of both Washington and Ottawa. Thus, the Caribbean became the only Third World area where Canada is regularly a top-ranking aid donor, in some countries outpacing even the US and Britain as a source of funds.

In line with its early aid to the Federation of the West Indies, CIDA continued to actively support the process of regional integration in the Caribbean. By supporting institutions which coordinate economic policies within the region, CIDA hopes to maximize the potential for trade with a strengthened common market (instead of with individual, small nations), to modernize government structures and administrations and to contain corrupt and demagogic rulers.

The most important effort in this area is CIDA's support of the Caribbean Development Bank (CDB). The idea for the bank first came up at the Canada-Commonwealth Caribbean Conference in Ottawa in 1966. When established in 1969, Canada joined Britain as one of the Bank's two non-regional members and has since become its largest donor. By 1979 the Bank was disbursing about $32 million annually in loans to projects in the region, making it one of the most important sources for development financing. Since joining the CDB, CIDA has contributed over $43 million in the form of loans and advances.

The bilateral aid program also contributes to integration and modernization in the region through grants to the University of the West Indies. In particular, CIDA — in conjunction with the University of Western Ontario — has helped develop the Department of Management Studies at both the Mona, Jamaica and the St. Augustine, Trinidad campuses. Although often rated a success story by both Canadian and Caribbean government officials, problems with the program include the cultural imposition of teaching methods and content based on North American experiences. The University of Western Ontario relies heavily on the "case method" of Harvard, although "cases" in the Caribbean are just not the same as ones from industrialized North America which are mostly employed. The program's general orientation toward strengthening the private sector is also viewed by some Caribbean academics as a service for Canadian commercial interests.[13]

By 1980, CIDA was disbursing about $31 million a year to the Commonwealth Caribbean region, making it the highest per capita recipient of Canadian bilateral aid, although with only 5% of the bilateral budget. The program supports over 143 projects in fifteen countries or protectorates, but over half the program's budget is concentrated in Jamaica, Belize and Guyana; since the mid-1970s there has been some growth in support for the poorer Leeward and Windward Islands in line with overall CIDA policy. (See Table 3-VI.) The Agency claims its Caribbean program focuses on the generation of productive employment. But it continues to finance the construction of airports for the tourist industry, education, public services and programs of balance of payments support under the guise of food or commodity aid, none of which get at the roots of the economic problems of the region. Instead, much of it might cynically be viewed as supplying infrastructure, both physical and social, to fulfill the needs of Canadians — as tourists to the area or as investors in its tourist and low-wage industries. Although not strictly part of the aid effort, Canada also supplies a small military training program for some countries in the Caribbean. Since 1970 the Military Training Assistance Program administered by the Department of External Affairs has helped train police and military forces from Jamaica and Trinidad and Tobago consistent with Canadian foreign policy interests in maintaining the "internal security and stability" of these nations.[14]

In the early 1980s, Canadian aid to the Caribbean is taking off from its current plateau. During an official visit to Jamaica in January 1981, External Affairs Minister Mark MacGuigan promised to double bilateral flows within three or four years and later committed CIDA to tripling annual disbursements from $31 million in 1979-80 to as much as $90 million by 1986-87. Motivating the minister were both broad political and more particular commercial considerations.

Boosting aid to the region is part of Ottawa's strategy for promoting Canadian exports generally and for re-asserting Canada's commercial status in the Caribbean in particular. Canada's share of the Commonwealth Caribbean market plummeted from 17% in 1950 to a mere 5% by 1978. A new Trade and Economic Agreement signed in 1979 between Canada and CARICOM — the Caribbean Common Market, whose members are Antigua, Barbados, Belize, Dominica, Grenada, Guyana, Jamaica, Montserrat, St. Kitts-Nevis, St. Lucia, St. Vincent and Trinidad and Tobago — is one framework under which Ottawa hopes to expand Canadian trade with the region. Foreign aid is the other tool MacGuigan seems eager to wield in order to recapture part of the Caribbean market for Canadian companies.

MacGuigan's announcement is also clearly part of Canada's response to the new strategic importance which the United States attaches to the Caribbean. American foreign affairs analysts

Table 3-VI
Commonwealth Caribbean – Bilateral Aid Disbursements, 1971-1980
($ millions)

fiscal year ending	1971	1972	1973	1974	1975	1976	1977	1978	1979	1980	Total 1971-1980
Antigua	1.38	.25	.50	.14	.15	.40	1.01	3.63	2.06	1.90	11.42
Barbados	1.05	.77	1.74	2.93	.77	2.14	1.49	4.62	4.61	2.16	22.28
Belize	.24	.49	.80	.41	1.39	1.46	1.06	2.63	6.19	3.77	18.44
Dominica	1.35	.44	.62	.61	.56	.41	.43	1.75	.34	1.95	8.46
Grenada	.49	.47	.54	.35	.24	1.18	1.82	.59	.29	.07	6.04
Guyana	4.18	2.36	1.54	2.85	4.05	2.33	2.21	1.80	4.83	5.95	32.10
Jamaica	2.52	3.91	4.74	3.24	3.11	3.43	3.57	13.61	9.34	7.76	55.23
Montserrat	.15	.46	.79	.51	.68	.61	.13	.25	.32	.28	4.18
St. Kitts	.40	.35	.41	.37	.21	.26	.13	.21	.18	1.50	4.02
St. Lucia	1.68	1.72	1.35	1.39	2.93	1.39	1.93	1.25	.39	.24	14.27
St. Vincent	.89	.72	.53	.17	.76	1.26	.89	.66	.26	.12	6.26
Trinidad & Tobago	1.72	.63	.65	.90	.57	1.80	.69	(.10)	.47	(.09)	7.24
Turks, Caicos & Caymans	—	—	—	—	—	—	—	.02	.03	.02	.07
Virgin Is.	—	—	—	—	—	—	—	—	.01	.02	.03
Regional Programs	.99	.28	.02	.12	.17	.70	2.66	2.19	1.66	1.76	10.55
Leeward & Windward Is.	—	.21	.08	.36	3.31	3.42	4.24	3.73	2.48	3.01	20.84
University of the West Indies	1.85	.57	1.19	.99	.73	1.11	.47	.49	.10	.46	7.96
Total	18.89	13.63	15.50	15.34	19.63	21.90	22.73	37.33	33.56	30.88	229.39

( ) signifies net repayment to Canada
Sources: CIDA, Annual Reports (various years)

sounded alarms in the late 1970s that the leftward orientation of old and new governments in the Caribbean basin — those of democratic socialist Michael Manley in Jamaica, leftist Maurice Bishop in Grenada, and the Sandinista leadership in Nicaragua — was making the Caribbean a "red sea". Washington pressed Ottawa to limit its aid to both Jamaica and Grenada, but in a small manifestation of independence CIDA maintained aid to both countries. However, the Agency's plan to rapidly inflate its aid program to the Commonwealth Caribbean, coinciding with US intentions to do the same, included significant promises to the new Jamaican government of anticommunist Edward Seaga who defeated Manley in the 1980 elections. MacGuigan assured the right-wing Seaga government of an immediate injection of $3 million in addition to aid already committed by CIDA for the 1980-81 fiscal year ($8 million). He also suggested an overall increase in allocations for future years, the possibility of a special balance of payments credit of $10 million, and a willingness to discuss a longer-term aid program consistent with an economic recovery program Jamaica was then discussing with the International Monetary Fund.

MacGuigan shares the US view that the continuing economic and political crisis of the Caribbean and Central American region could nurture political unrest, and he believes Canada can play a distinctive role. As he told the *Toronto Star* in early 1981, the security of the Caribbean "is important to us because Britain is largely withdrawing from the area and because so many of them find Canada more acceptable than the United States as a more-developed friend."[15] To advance this friendship, MacGuigan announced in mid-1981 that Canada will soon join the United States, Mexico and Venezuela in a coordinated effort to increase aid and trade with the countries of the Caribbean and Central America.

Commonwealth and Francophone Africa

The continent of Africa receives more Canadian aid than any other region. In the 1979-80 fiscal year, over $286 million was spent by the Commonwealth Africa and Francophone Africa programs — equivalent to 48% of the total bilateral budget — making them the fastest growing of CIDA's divisions. This growth has paced the transformation of Ottawa's attitude toward Africa. From casual disinterest twenty-five years ago Ottawa has been steadily drawn into African involvement in both the political arena — Canada is now an important member of both La Francophonie, the association of French-speaking countries, and the western "contact" group of five industrialized nations which are trying to resolve the independence of Namibia from South African control — and in the commercial sphere through expanding trade deals.

Political motives dominate the historical development of Canadian aid to Africa. The export potential of the region has long been assessed as minimal and only recently recognized as a possible bonanza, at least in selected nations. In contrast, political considerations of both a domestic and international character have provided sharp definitions for Canadian policies. "Our interests in Africa," explains Africanist Robert Matthews, "were, at least initially, derived in large part from our broader concern to maintain a strong and united alliance with the West (including Britain, France and Portugal) against the Soviet bloc."[16] As the colonial powers of Europe prepared to withdraw beginning in the late 1950s onward, fears arose in the West that anti-colonial sentiments in Africa could easily be stirred into anti-western sentiments which the Soviet Union, in the context of a power vacuum, could take advantage of. Both Europe and the United States turned to countries like Canada. With neither colonial possessions nor aspirations, such nations could support the decolonization process through economic assistance aimed at promoting a western model of liberal democracy and capitalism.

In casting its support for decolonization, Canada was inevitably drawn deeper and deeper into the tense debate about the future of Africa's white settler states (Rhodesia and South Africa) and Portugal's African colonies. Prior to decolonization these states had monopolized Canadian diplomatic and commercial attention and Canada was associated with Portuguese colonialism through the latter's membership in the NATO alliance. After decolonization, Canadian foreign policy showed a willingness to verbally criticize white minority rule and even to take some related boycott actions — some more symbolic than effective — but always remained passive and ambiguous on support for liberation movements which would, and will, eventually bring about majority rule.

As aid programming for Africa matured, the mixture of international political concerns was coloured by domestic political considerations: the striving to achieve a balance between Commonwealth and Francophone programs and the effort to counterbalance Canada's traditional commercial ties with the white settler states by expanding contacts with black Africa which would offer longer-term markets of greater significance.

Commonwealth Africa Program

Canada's delegates to the March 1957 independence celebrations in Ghana returned to Ottawa with a sense of the material expectations of the first new black African state. Under strong urgings from Britain, Canada's Conservative government initiated a small technical assistance program for Ghana in 1958. External Affairs Minister Sidney Smith warned the House of Commons that unless Canada stepped into the breach "these underdeveloped countries... may be prone to accept blandishments and offers from other parts of the world."[17] From its single focus on Ghana, the Canadian aid program moved to encompass all the Commonwealth countries in Africa by the 1960 creation of the Special Commonwealth Africa Assistance Plan. During the early years of the plan, the External Aid Office concentrated on the provision of technical assistance because it was assumed that new African governments couldn't use capital assistance properly.

The next innovation was the establishment of the first military training assistance program. Although no longer considered a form of aid giving, military assistance to Asian, African and Caribbean countries has been described by External Affairs as "complementary to the much larger Canadian foreign aid program."[18] The Department sees the benefits of Canada providing military assistance to parts of the world where western powers and policies were usually suspect as a means of pre-empting or neutralizing aid from communist countries; additionally such programs could gather a little intelligence for the West and promote sales of Canadian military equipment. The Cabinet gave approval to the program in 1961 and, with the support of London and Washington, began providing military training to the armed forces of Ghana (beginning in 1961) and Tanzania (1964). By the end of the decade, Canada had spent over $23 million training the military forces of seven African and Asian countries.[19]

The program still survives in modest form today, directed by the Department of External Affairs with a budget not to exceed $500,000 annually. For public consumption Ottawa's interest in maintaining the stability of Third World governments is explained in palatable, neutral terms: "Canada's small but highly-trained professional forces are well-suited to provide the impartial assistance required by a number of developing countries."[20] Beneficiaries of the program to date include Barbados, Guyana, Jamaica and Trinidad and Tobago in the Caribbean; South Korea, Malaysia and Singapore in Asia; and Cameroon, Ethiopia, Ghana, Gabon, Kenya, Nigeria, Swaziland, Tanzania, Uganda and Zambia in Africa.[21]

Allocations to Commonwealth Africa increased from $3.5 million annually in the early 1960s to over $18 million by 1968. Then the program's budget soared, increasing seven-fold by 1980. Fueling the expansion was the need to keep the Anglophone program more or less in balance with the even faster growing Francophone Africa program. CIDA also recognized the need to counteract Canada's South Africa connection so as not to alienate the greater potential for commerce with emerging black Africa. The winners of increased aid funds were Botswana, Ghana, Kenya, Lesotho, Malawi, Nigeria, Tanzania, Zambia and several nations of Francophone Africa. A $10

Table 3-VII

Commonwealth Africa – Bilateral Aid Disbursements, 1971-1980
($ millions)

	1971	1972	1973	1974	1975	1976	1977	1978	1979	1980	Total 1971-1980
Botswana	.03	4.18	15.00	8.98	7.20	1.84	1.61	2.89	2.40	3.56	47.69
Djibouti	—	—	—	—	—	—	—	—	—	.03	.03
Egypt	—	—	—	—	—	—	9.87	6.39	.31	27.78	44.35
Ethiopia	.08	.10	.51	1.51	6.47	.90	.54	.48	.82	2.09	13.50
Ghana	7.01	10.00	9.21	9.66	13.17	17.63	12.34	14.35	17.76	17.97	129.10
Kenya	2.07	2.53	2.24	6.19	5.20	6.48	9.34	9.49	6.64	12.78	62.96
Lesotho	—	.07	.07	.19	.62	2.70	3.11	6.35	3.65	7.02	23.78
Malawi	.04	.36	1.09	.27	9.11	14.91	3.57	18.65	15.80	15.96	79.76
Malta	—	—	—	—	—	.44	.02	.11	.01	.40	.98
Mauritius	.04	.04	.08	.14	.12	.09	.22	.15	.22	.24	1.34
Mozambique	—	—	—	—	—	—	2.81	2.03	2.60	.06	7.50
Namibia	.01	.01	.02	.04	.02	.01	.02	.02	.01	.02	.18
Nigeria	6.63	11.95	12.61	11.98	10.20	13.95	8.14	2.86	1.69	.56	80.57
Seychelles	—	—	—	—	—	—	.04	.09	.10	.05	.28
Sierra Leone	.01	—	—	.30	.29	.06	.03	.04	.23	.37	1.33
Somalia	—	—	—	—	.99	.39	4.06	.01	—	.02	5.47
Sudan	—	—	—	—	.01	.01	.05	.49	.82	2.40	3.77
Swaziland	.05	.03	.04	.30	.65	.54	1.48	1.80	1.99	1.69	8.57
Tanzania	3.13	6.02	6.22	17.67	38.34	24.38	14.75	24.99	32.98	27.64	196.12
Uganda	1.84	1.54	1.66	1.15	.36	.75	.57	.56	.29	.27	8.99
Zambia	.78	1.51	2.10	2.35	4.39	6.59	11.85	6.93	18.06	15.98	70.54
Zimbabwe*	.04	.04	.08	.09	.01	—	—	.05	.04	.04	.39
Regional: East Africa	3.14	11.27	1.87	2.50	11.39	15.73	6.66	1.44	.43	.18	54.61
Other	.24	.01	.07	.51	.24	.29	.59	.67	.30	.52	3.44
University of BLS	—	.27	1.08	.39	.70	.63	.81	.48	.76	.72	5.84
Total	25.14	49.93	53.95	64.22	109.47	108.32	92.48	101.32	107.91	138.35	851.09

* Includes training Black Zimbabwean students in countries other than their homeland up to 1979.

Sources: CIDA, "Canada's Development Assistance to Commonwealth Africa", (Briefing Paper no. 3, December 1976); CIDA, Annual Reports (various years)

million per year aid program for the promising market of Zimbabwe, formerly Rhodesia, has recently been committed.[22] (See Table 3-VII.)

Through the 1970s CIDA supported 22 countries under its Commonwealth Africa program with five countries — Tanzania, Ghana, Nigeria, Malawi and Zambia — accounting for two-thirds of the total. By 1980, the program claimed $138 million or 23% of the bilateral aid budget.

Francophone Africa Program

French-speaking Africa received only grudging attention from the Diefenbaker Government in the early sixties. A Francophone program initiated in 1961 after Patrice Lumumba's visit to Canada, doled out only $300,000 annually between 1961 and the defeat of the Conservatives in 1963, mostly for food aid and technical assistance.

Quebec commentators quickly recognized the discrepancy between the Anglophone and Francophone programs. In 1960, Le Devoir journalist André Laurendeau grumbled that "le Commonwealth n'est pas toute l'humanité . . . il existe des pays sous-développés où la langue de communication est le français. . . . Il y a là une question d'égalité et de justice."[23] Another spokesman, Paul Gerin-Lajoie, then a member of the Quebec cabinet, called in the early 1960s for Quebec's right to undertake international activities in fields under its jurisdiction such as education — a position later accepted by Ottawa as was Gerin-Lajoie when he became president of CIDA in 1970. But at that time, such comments caused great consternation in the capital. Prime Minister Lester Pearson began to increase the budget for Francophone Africa aid after 1964 in parallel with, although not equal to, increases in the budget for Commonwealth Africa. From this point on, aid to Francophone Africa closely tracked the rising demands of Quebec within the Canadian confederation.

The turning point for parity between Anglophone and Francophone programs was 1968. In that year, shortly after the 1967 visit of French President Charles De Gaulle (and his explosive "Vive le Québec libre" speech), Quebec moved to establish, with De Gaulle's assistance, direct ties and perhaps future aid programs with Francophone African states. Quebec won a near-coup by receiving an exclusive invitation to the Gabon meeting of Francophone education ministers. Pearson dispatched Pierre Trudeau to Africa as his personal emissary in an attempt to obtain an invitation for Ottawa to the meeting but none was forthcoming.[24] Ottawa then suspended diplomatic relations with Gabon (restored a year-and-a-half later) to warn other African states that Canada would not recognize them if they chose to treat Quebec as a sovereign nation. Ottawa's use of

the stick was cushioned by offering the carrot of increased development aid: the Chevrier Mission to Africa in 1968 hastily identified
and began funding aid projects with a value of up to $40 million.[25]
Subsequently, Ottawa succeeded in being invited to other conferences of the same nature. One country, Niger, learned quickly how
to play the game; in return for some modest, if timely, help in 1970
in getting Canada accepted as a full member of the Francophone
states' Agence de Coopération Culturelle et Technique (while
Quebec was given lower status as a "participating government"),
CIDA became engaged in a large development program in Niger.[26]

In its intensifying struggle with Quebec over relations with Francophone Africa, CIDA rapidly expanded its aid program with five
countries — Tunisia, Cameroon, Niger, Ivory Coast and Senegal —
taking almost half of the total. By 1980 the division was allocating
over $148 million a year or about 25% of the bilateral budget. (See
Table 3-VIII.)

Aid remained an important tool in the federal government's bat-
tle with Quebec, especially after the election of the Parti Quebecois.
In his drive for political sovereignty, Premier René Levesque wrote
19 African leaders in 1978 asking for full participation in *La Francophonie*. But Ottawa was still able to use the diplomatic stick and the
aid carrot to keep Francophone African states sensitive to the federal
position. The 1980 meeting of Francophone heads of state was cancelled when France refused to attend because Quebec was denied
separate representation. Shortly afterwards, early in 1981, Prime
Minister Trudeau visited Senegal and discussed rescheduling the
meeting with local leaders. To sweeten the discussion Trudeau
promised a major expansion of Canadian aid to assist the country's
exploration for oil and to build a major dam project.[27]

External Affairs still prefers to explain Canada-Francophone
Africa relations as Ottawa's way of "seeking to extend its linguistic
duality into the international sphere."[28] What that means is pre-
empting Quebec's attempts to use African contacts as a way to
legitimize Quebec sovereignty while conveying to Quebecers an
impression that their federal government indeed has a foreign policy distinct from Washington and pertinent to their interests.

Canadian aid to the African continent as a whole includes multilateral support for the African Development Fund (AFDF). Since join-
ing the Fund at its inception in 1972, Canada has become one of its
major donors, providing almost $110 million in loans and advances
by 1980 with the prospect of becoming a non-regional member of the
Fund's sponsor, the African Development Bank (AFDB). Ten African
countries (out of 12 throughout the Third World) were also affected
by Canada's decision in 1977 to forgive loan repayments to CIDA
from the world's poorest states.

Table 3-VIII

Francophone Africa — Bilateral Aid Disbursements, 1971-1980
($ millions)

fiscal year ending	1971	1972	1973	1974	1975	1976	1977	1978	1979	1980	Total 1971-1980
Algeria	4.01	4.24	4.96	5.06	9.21	10.70	6.52	3.21	.80	.88	49.59
Benin	.67	2.62	2.16	1.30	4.50	6.35	4.16	3.44	2.73	5.03	32.96
Burundi	.09	.19	.23	.20	.14	.10	.09	.04	—	.03	1.11
Cameroon	3.26	4.51	4.58	3.91	4.58	11.05	6.98	12.15	16.25	15.29	82.56
Cape Verde	—	—	—	—	—	—	—	.99	.03	.02	1.04
Central African Republic	.09	.19	.20	.16	.06	.06	.08	.12	.09	.02	1.07
Chad	.25	.26	.24	.96	3.42	.02	1.25	3.21	.35	.20	10.16
Comoros	—	—	—	—	—	—	—	.05	—	.01	.06
Congo	.03	.05	.11	.48	4.03	6.46	2.91	2.60	2.70	1.62	20.99
Gabon	.16	.27	.35	.52	.77	1.21	1.08	.95	.59	.29	6.19
Gambia	.02	—	—	—	—	—	.04	3.22	.10	.03	3.41
Guinea	.03	.03	.01	.02	.51	.07	.74	.11	.16	.05	1.73
Guinea-Bissau	—	—	—	—	—	—	—	.02	.05	.03	.10
Ivory Coast	1.39	2.89	6.54	4.23	4.24	4.83	7.04	6.60	15.13	16.99	69.88
Madagascar	.47	.57	.63	.43	.48	1.27	.65	2.01	2.99	3.65	13.15
Mali	.10	.72	.70	1.79	6.57	3.95	2.87	4.65	5.08	12.79	39.22
Mauritania	.05	.10	.50	1.42	3.13	.70	2.61	6.07	1.25	.72	16.55
Morocco	4.77	4.45	4.31	5.55	4.86	3.45	3.25	5.59	4.01	2.58	42.82
Niger	2.47	7.19	8.59	8.40	16.84	17.38	9.69	3.71	4.07	4.08	82.42
Rwanda	1.29	1.46	1.66	1.55	3.68	4.07	7.35	8.54	6.56	5.84	42.00
Senegal	3.18	5.38	4.85	5.62	5.69	5.31	7.10	9.60	9.57	8.76	65.06
Togo	.86	2.70	2.37	1.01	1.44	1.96	1.60	1.77	5.01	9.17	27.89
Tunisia	5.49	5.93	13.59	13.06	11.72	16.42	14.44	6.92	23.21	10.87	121.65
Upper Volta	.08	.50	.95	1.51	4.02	.83	1.89	1.65	3.64	18.09	33.16
Zaire	.95	.59	1.08	3.54	6.33	4.28	2.71	3.87	8.73	8.18	40.26
Regional Programs	—	—	—	5.93	2.28	.72	3.05	2.67	.08	.72	15.92
Francophone Institutions	.01	.29	.47	—	—	3.22	—	—	2.13	2.28	7.93
Sahel Region	—	—	—	—	—	.50	—	8.95	15.43	19.50	44.38
Council of the Entente	—	—	—	—	.04	.08	.06	—	.02	—	.20
Total	29.72	45.13	59.08	66.65	98.54	104.99	88.16	102.71	130.76	147.72	873.46

Sources: CIDA, **Annual Reports** (various years)

While political objectives determined the selection of aid-receiving countries in Africa, commercial objectives within the aid program defined the content of aid shipments and its impact on recipient economies. In most African countries, the dramatic increase in Canadian exports during the 1970s was due almost entirely to aid allocations.

All of CIDA's talk about aiding the poorest sectors of African societies was compromised by the commercial tying of aid. Most aid went to develop infrastructure for industry — power generation and transmission, railways and roads, harbour projects and airports, telecommunications networks — all sectors where the "trickle-down" theory is blocked up at the top. According to one study of Canada's aid program in southern Africa, an average of 70% of all bilateral aid went to these infrastructure works up to 1978.[29] With only a handful of African states making a genuine effort to distribute national income and power, such aid almost inevitably concentrates benefits for existing elites.

The commercial mandate of aid is likely to be reinforced in the 1980s. Canadian exports to Africa quadrupled between 1970 and 1980 with particularly strong gains in North Africa which surpassed South Africa as the largest buyer of Canadian goods. Identified as a growing world market, Africa was deemed worthy of the first visits by Canadian prime ministers to the continent in 1979 (by Joe Clark) and 1981 (Pierre Trudeau); their visits, like the increasingly frequent missions by senior government officials, were aimed at cementing Canada's political relationships and at promoting Canadian exports. The federal government's commercial strategy toward Africa entails the use of EDC financing for the energy-rich countries of North Africa, as well as Nigeria, in place of CIDA aid. Elsewhere, CIDA is working to break into markets that are difficult to penetrate because of traditional longitudinal trade links between African countries and their former European colonizers. Egypt's status as the number one African recipient of Canadian aid in 1980 foreshadows a growing market development mandate for CIDA. "Egypt is of special interest," explained CIDA's annual report, "in that the relatively high level of development in certain sectors of that country's economy can cause significant commercial benefits to accrue to Canada."[30]

The limits and the two-facedness of Canada's foreign policy in Africa is best seen in CIDA's stingy aid to liberation movements in southern Africa. From 1973 to 1978, the Agency dispensed only $5.1 million to these movements, mostly for the education of southern Africans outside of their home countries and for humanitarian aid channelled through NGOs. The gesture made a small reparation for the damage caused by Canada's past association with South Africa and Portugal. But the aid fell well short of meaningful support for groups fighting for liberation from white minority rule. Federal officials justified their timidity by trotting out arguments about non-violence in both South Africa and Namibia.

External Affairs Minister Don Jamieson tried in 1977 to both have and eat his cake — to be seen verbally castigating South Africa without jeopardizing Canada's significant trade and investments there. He announced Canada would scale down its trade promotion efforts in Pretoria and eliminate the availability of the EDC's "government account" for the support of trade. But that account hadn't been used by South Africa in 15 years. The main EDC account remained open for business, and Canadian companies operating in South Africa expressed little worry that Jamieson's policy would cost them business. Canada's position, as the 1970 *Foreign Policy for Canadians* explained, was to limit its "support of the principle of freedom" because of the interests of many "businessmen who see better-than-normal opportunities for trade and investment in the growing economy of the Republic of South Africa."[31] Despite statements in favour of reform, Ottawa's fence-sitting posture translates as support for the status quo.

Latin America Program

Latin America was last in line to receive Canadian aid. During the 1950s, Ottawa felt it didn't have to worry about the southern half of the hemisphere. Significant Canadian investments were located in the region, as was most Canada-Third World trade, but also omnipresent was Uncle Sam. Canadian commercial interests felt safe under the protective umbrella of the State Department and any policing jobs — the overthrow of progressive governments for example — were left to Washington. Canada seemed content limiting itself to regions where it had a linguistic affinity.

The Cuban Revolution of 1959 changed this established order. Washington began to press Ottawa to join the Organization of American States (OAS) and to pick up its share of the responsibility for the economic development President Kennedy thought could forestall other revolutions. The US couldn't understand Canada's initial reluctance to blaze new frontiers to the South. In June 1963, Senator Wayne Morse complained that "Canada... is not willing to participate at all in... economic aid to Latin America.... We must say to these countries, 'We have to cut back until you come in and do your share.' "[32]

Canada decided to start doing its share when, in 1964, the External Aid Office began lending $10 million a year to the Inter-American Development Bank (IDB), a regional multilateral institution. Over the next eight years, Canada contributed $74 million to a special Canadian Fund in the IDB. Eighty percent of the contribution was tied to the purchase of Canadian goods and services, and over half of the total amount was allocated to constructing hydro-electric projects with most of these funds staying in Canada to benefit Canadian suppliers of related technology and equipment.[33]

But, using the same reasoning it applied to OAS membership, the Canadian government decided to refrain from membership in the Bank to avoid direct involvement in institutions dominated by US foreign policy objectives. Nonetheless, the fledgling Canadian aid program evidenced political concerns in line, if not in league, with US strategies. Between 1961 and 1964, the Canadian Export Credits Insurance Corporation — the forerunner of the Export Development Corporation — whose loans were considered integral to aid giving at the time, provided almost $20 million in export credits to Jorge Allessandri's government in Chile at the same time as massive US aid was being mobilized to prevent the election of socialist Salvador Allende in that country's 1964 elections. The electoral victor, Eduardo Frei, subsequently received $8.6 million from the Canadian Fund of the IDB during the first four years of his government. In another incident, Ottawa made an exceptional grant of $298,000 in food aid to the Dominican Republic in 1966 as part of the mop-up in the wake of the 1965 military invasion of that country.[34] Such gestures were welcomed by Washington as indications that Canada was shouldering some responsibility for the politically volatile region.

Canada's still passive attitude toward Latin America began to change in 1968 with the creation of CIDA. By that year the massive Alliance for Progress effort of the US government had been almost totally discredited as a front for gradual militarization of the area, an instrument of foreign political intervention, and a mechanism for increasing Latin American dependence on the US economy and its multinational corporations. The entry of an apparently disinterested aid giver such as Canada appeared appropriate in Latin America as it had during decolonization in Africa.

Also in 1968, a ministerial mission to the region reported that the Spanish-, Portuguese-, and French-speaking republics to the south represented a growing market where Canada was losing opportunities. In May, Prime Minister Trudeau announced his decision to review Canada's foreign policy, and that Latin America would be an important element of the review.

We have to take greater account of the ties which bind us to other nations in this hemisphere — in the Caribbean, Latin America — and of their economic needs. We have to explore new avenues of increasing our political and economic relations with Latin America where more than four hundred million people will live by the turn of the century and where we have substantial interests.[35]

As part of the foreign policy review, a CIDA task force prepared a report on development assistance options for Latin America.[36] This document recommended the establishment of a bilateral aid program consisting solely of technical assistance. Capital assistance to large infrastructure projects, the task force argued, would probably "contribute to the maintenance of the existing situation with limited effects on economic development." For this reason the IDB was judged an unsuitable channel for effective development aid and the report recommended against membership while supporting the political compromise of maintaining financial support for the institution.

The purpose of starting a technical assistance program, according to CIDA, was to assist the process of "transformation" of economic and social structures so that the poorer groups among Latin American populations could participate in the wealth of the existing modern sector. This was pretty heady, even radical sounding, material emerging from CIDA's new bureaucracy. Foreseeing possible business opposition to a direction in aid giving that offered minimal commercial returns, CIDA also suggested the creation of programs to aid the private sector in expanding its activities in Latin America and endorsed greater use of the EDC's export credits for the region.

The federal government accepted all these proposals and incorporated them, using appropriately vague and diplomatic language, in the 1970 *Foreign Policy for Canadians*. The Latin American bilateral aid program was launched in the 1970-71 fiscal year with an $8.5 million allotment, or 3.4% of the total bilateral budget. The countries originally targeted for the aid — Peru, Colombia, Brazil and Central America as a region — were selected simply by eliminating countries which seemed too rich and others which seemed too poor to appropriately use Canadian technical assistance. At the same time, CIDA's Business and Industry Division started up with a keen eye towards Latin America, the NGO division expanded funding to the region, and EDC's business with Latin America broadened.

The Canadian business community, however, was less than enthusiastic about the approach. They whined that a region particularly suited to commercial returns was substantially excluded from the market development opportunities provided by aid programs elsewhere. Business lobbies such as the Canadian Export Association (CEA) and the Canadian Association for Latin America (CALA) mounted a drive to secure commercial benefits from the newest CIDA program. Under the corporate cajoling CIDA's policy on the IDB was reversed and full membership in the Bank taken out in May 1972. The Agency would later justify the about-face by claiming that membership was "helping Canadian suppliers to become more familiar with Latin American markets and increasing the interest of Latin American buyers in Canadian goods and services."[37] In 1975, the establishment of an aid program in Cuba was, anomalously, also due to commercial concerns. By keeping diplomatic relations with Cuba despite the US boycott, CIDA admitted, "Canada has profited from Cuba's ostracism."[38] Ottawa decided to promote foreign aid to Cuba, coupled with EDC export financing, in order to protect Canada's trade position from the competition expected should the US re-establish normal relations with the island. The combined effort more than tripled Canadian exports to Cuba between 1973 and 1976 making it Canada's fourth largest export market in Latin America.

Later, in 1977, CIDA announced a shift in emphasis in its Latin America program to give "a better balance of technical assistance and capital aid."[39] The shift meant a retreat from CIDA's original objectives of transforming economic and social structures to traditional aid programs which facilitate the more ample use of Canadian goods and services. The nature of the technical assistance offered also fosters underlying commercial objectives. CIDA is currently bankrolling technical assessments of the mining sector in Brazil, Colombia and Peru; of the forestry sector in Bolivia, Brazil, Colombia, Honduras and Peru; of the telecommunications field in Brazil and Peru; and of the electric power sector in Bolivia, Brazil, the Dominican Republic and Haiti.[40] Such technical assistance conveniently coincides with the pattern of Canadian export sales and direct investments in the region.

Political and "development" considerations determined the selection of countries if not the content of the aid package for Latin America. After 1976, several of the poorest nations, Haiti and Bolivia, were included as "program" countries in line with CIDA's evolving policy. Brazil was quietly dropped from the program list because its repressive military regime impeded any attempt at transforming social structures and was a source of political embarrassment for CIDA at home.[41] Similarly, Chile's program was cut after the 1973 military coup d'état because, as a confidential cabinet document explained, "the attention which the churches and various Canadian groups have focussed on the Chilean Government's use of repression against its opponents has led to an unfavourable reaction among the Canadian public — a reaction which will not permit any significant increase in Canadian aid to this country."[42]

In 1977, Ottawa stopped giving aid to Cuba. CIDA and the Department of External Affairs had simply decided to replace the aid program, which in any event had run its course without Cuba's request for renewal, with solely commercial credits from the EDC. But the opposition's criticism of Cuba's military involvement in Africa prodded federal ministers to make political mileage with the suggestion that Canada was disciplining Castro. In 1981, while visiting the Caribbean, External Affairs Minister Mark MacGuigan formally, and in convenient retrospect, explained that the program ended because "we felt that if Cuba can finance foreign adventurism, then it can also finance development on its own."[43]

Today, Canadian aid to Latin America supports 106 projects in twelve countries. Allocations of $35 million in bilateral aid during the 1979-80 fiscal year represented 6% of total bilateral spending, a drop from disbursements in previous years which elevated Latin America's share to 9% of global bilateral expenditures in 1978-79. The aid is concentrated in the rural development and resource development sectors, with four countries — Haiti, Colombia, Honduras and Peru — monopolizing two-thirds of the regional total. Recent changes include the suspension of aid to El Salvador in late 1980 because of Ottawa's "concern about the situation" of widespread government repression and, more to the point, CIDA's inability to continue operating the program because of internal strife. Also in 1980, CIDA began cautious planning of a foreign aid program for the revolutionary government of Nicaragua, and in June, 1981, a $4.5 million grant of food aid was consigned to Managua.[44]

CIDA is deeply committed to financing the work of the Inter-American Development Bank. Since becoming a full member in 1972, Canada has provided over $439 million in the form of capital subscriptions, loans and grants to the Bank — more than to any other regional development bank. This is CIDA's way of gaining a more substantial presence in a region where its bilateral aid program is relatively small.

Latin America will probably not significantly increase its share of total bilateral spending. Although great portions of its population are very poor, its economies are generally regarded as "middle class" by policy-makers who find it hard to justify large allocations under the Agency's current criteria. But the region will likely continue receiving its share of a growing CIDA budget, primarily for commercial reasons. Canada's export trade with Latin America quadrupled during the 1970s and is now worth more than $3 billion annually. Canadian chartered banks are deeply involved in financing the capital needs of the regimes of the region and the book value of Canadian direct investments in Latin America, at over $1.6 billion in 1977, ranks it second only to the United States as a location of Canadian overseas investment.

Because of Latin America's awkward status as a region of high commercial priority but low developmental priority, CIDA is examining new forms of aid-giving for the future. Under consideration are programs for balance of payments support, joint ventures (e.g. Canada's Petro-Canada linking with private oil companies and state oil agencies of oil-exporting nations) for developing energy supplies, parallel financing endeavours with the Export Development Corporation, and the expanded use of the Agency's own Industrial Cooperation Program. Both current and planned programs, however, clearly take into account the government and business view that Latin America, more than any other Third World region, offers the best short-term prospects for expanding exports and investments.

Table 3-IX

Latin America — Bilateral Aid Disbursements, 1971-1980
($ millions)

fiscal year ending	1971	1972	1973	1974	1975	1976	1977	1978	1979	1980	Total 1971-1980
Bolivia	—	—	—	.56	.99	.21	.05	.09	1.77	1.01	4.68
Brazil	1.28	2.42	3.10	1.13	1.44	2.70	2.78	2.06	2.01	2.39	21.31
Chile	2.36	.75	2.11	2.15	.30	.08	(.14)	(.17)	(.33)	(.25)	6.86
Colombia	4.05	4.36	5.28	3.71	1.74	2.11	4.05	5.77	8.83	7.11	47.01
Costa Rica	—	—	—	.05	.15	.14	.04	.20	.16	.17	.91
Cuba	—	—	.05	.43	.43	3.68	4.26	4.52	1.06	—	14.43
Dominican Republic	—	—	—	.16	3.71	1.81	1.62	.09	.03	.34	7.76
Ecuador	.11	1.33	.57	1.07	3.33	3.35	.88	.53	.45	.30	11.92
El Salvador	—	—	.07	.11	1.42	2.07	.72	.35	.63	1.37*	6.74
Guatemala	—	—	.13	.05	.02	3.32	1.48	1.88	4.61	2.94	14.43
Haiti	—	—	—	.15	1.34	2.90	4.33	6.68	10.97	7.59	33.96
Honduras	—	—	.53	.31	2.19	1.44	.43	1.79	9.88	4.62	21.19
Nicaragua	—	—	.01	1.41	1.02	.13	.57	.40	—	.20	3.74
Peru	—	—	—	.66	1.61	2.51	2.90	8.67	4.30	4.02	24.67
Other	.77	1.56	—	—	—	—	—	—	—	—	2.33
Regional:											
Central America	—	—	.15	.27	.13	.11	.15	.07	—	—	.88
Latin America	—	—	.33	.55	.80	.42	1.32	1.64	2.91	3.52	11.49
Total	8.57	10.42	12.33	12.77	20.62	26.98	25.44	34.57	47.28	35.33	234.31

* suspended in late 1980 due to internal strife

( ) signifies net repayment to Canada

Sources: CIDA, "Canada's development assistance to Latin America", Briefing Paper no. 5, April 1979; CIDA, **Annual Reports** (various years)

Underdevelopment
4   Assistance

"Development is our business."
— CIDA Annual Review 1969.

When the subject of the Bakery is raised, CIDA officials groan. Unlike some horror stories about aid that the Agency readily refutes, the Bakery stands out as a festering example of one aid project that went terribly wrong in ways that throw into relief the basic defects of Canadian aid policies and programs.[1]

In 1969, Tanzania's National Milling Corporation (NMC), a government-owned enterprise, decided to centralize bread-baking in Dar es Salaam. The idea of building a large-scale, modern, automated bakery was dubious from the start. Previously, the city's bread was baked in a number of small, labour-intensive bakeries. They were locally-financed, relied on Tanzanian-made equipment, used local coal or charcoal as fuel and could substitute for raw materials — maize was experimented with during previous wheat shortages. They had always been run efficiently. But NMC's management longed for the prestige of a big bread factory. The automated bakery idea was explained by NMC's General Manager, J.K. Chande, one of Dar es Salaam's leading businessmen, as a logical use of modern methods, if only for their own sake, toward a corporate goal of expanding NMC's activities from milling into baking. Chande planned for the bakery to be financed by foreign aid and to begin production by 1971.

The Tanzanian government first approached the Netherlands government for aid, but the project was turned down and Tanzania turned to Canada. CIDA was sympathetic but ploddingly slow. Before signing a loan agreement, the Agency insisted that a Canadian consultant, Angus Butler Engineering Company of Alberta, be retained to conduct a feasibility study and to later supervise technical matters relating to engineering, design, construction and the purchase of machinery and equipment. In 1971, Canada agreed to lend $1 million for the project on the further condition that Canadian equipment be used. But the subsequent tender submitted by the only Canadian manufacturer of large-scale bakery equipment (and hence the only possible bidder), Canadian Baker Perkins Ltd. of Brampton, Ontario, exceeded the $1 million amount. To cover the equipment costs plus Angus Butler's fee of $170,000, CIDA agreed in mid-1972 to increase its loan to $1.35 million. An additional $350,000 was later kicked in to hire a Canadian manager and a maintenance supervisor, and to train Tanzanians in Canada as bakery technicians. With CIDA's total contribution of $1.7 million, plus an equal amount spent locally by NMC, the ill-fated bakery only began baking bread in early 1976, five years late and at triple the original budget.

The whole project — from conception and design to construction and start-up — shows how development assistance can in fact be *underdevelopment assistance*. The Canadian consultants designed a building suited for the climatic conditions of Alberta instead of those of Tanzania. Its low ceiling, enclosed-wall architecture requires a complicated system of fans and vents to remove excess heat created by the ovens. In contrast, other bakeries in Dar es Salaam have simple, concrete foundations and high ceilings for air circulation — and they cost a fraction of the CIDA-sponsored building. On top of that, the design itself was over-priced, according to the Tanzania Investment Bank. The high price tag for the design work was the result, the bank says, of a lack of local cost control due to dependency on a distant foreign consultant: "the situation was one where the consultants [Angus Butler] were in another continent with more easy access to information from the manufacturer/supplier [Canadian Baker Perkins] than from the client."

The tying restrictions on Canada's aid also locked Tanzania into purchasing uncompetitive bakery machinery. A UN-financed project in Dar es Salaam, Indcentre, which carries out industrial feasibility studies, discovered that Tanzania could have bought equivalent capacity bakery equipment from West Germany or Japan for half the Canadian price.

Besides the cost and design problems, the project also proved directly counterproductive in development terms. Tanzania is unlikely to become self-sufficient in wheat production in the medium term, a fact that CIDA is trying to remedy through another project — one equally dependent on Canadian technology and equipment — the Basotu wheat growing scheme where "Canadian

wheat farming practices as employed on the prairies may be introduced." In the meantime, the government will have to use scarce
foreign exchange to import wheat to make a plastic-wrapped Wonder Bread, a luxury item for much of the population. When the
bakery breaks down — and Baker Perkins officials suggest that such
breakdowns are more common in Tanzania than in North America
because of lack of familiarity with the foreign technology — all bread
supplies are cut off and replacement parts have to be imported from
Canada. The bread factory also has to import expensive oil instead
of relying on local fuels. In a country where unemployment is high
and surplus labour a ready resource, the bakery employs fewer people than the six existing bakeries it replaced. Each job cost an investment of $46,000 to create, compared to $2,000 had existing Dar es
Salaam technology been used.

There were also clear alternatives to the mechanized bakery
scheme, alternatives more in line with Tanzania's commitment to
"self-reliant development" and to President Julius Nyerere's beliefs
in labour-intensive rather than capital-intensive industrialization.
According to a 1972 study by Indcentre, ten small bakery units could
have been designed for Tanzanian conditions at a cost of one-third
of the capital invested in the CIDA project. Ten smaller units would
have avoided dependence on foreign technology and spare parts.
And they would have hired people instead of buying machines,
employing 320 people instead of the 60 hired for the automated
bakery.

CIDA is not solely to blame for the fiasco. Tanzania might have
avoided most of the problems had it opted for the alternative plans.
But by the time government officials became aware of the many
faults in the venture, it was deemed both politically and financially
more problematic to cancel than to get on with it. Generally, Tanzania is one of the few nations in the Third World with a coherent
set of national development policies and a genuine commitment to,
although often-faulty execution of, self-reliant development concepts. In the case of the bakery, however, Tanzania has learned the
difficulty of putting theory into practice, especially when outside
agencies are influential.

The bakery also strikes out against all Canadian aid-giving objectives. Strike one is the obvious failure to connect with development
goals; in many ways, the project has done more harm than good.
Strike two is the out-of-bounds political impact; far from reinforcing
Canada's friendly ties with Tanzania, the bakery has caused some
Tanzanian officials to cynically regard the project as an insidious
way for Ottawa to sell Canadian wheat (according to CIDA, one-third
of Tanzania's wheat imports in 1974-75 came from Canada).

The third strike is the call on the questionable commercial benefits of the project for Canada. Given the uncompetitiveness of the

Canadian supplier relative to other countries, Canadian Baker Perkins would probably never have sold such equipment to Tanzania if it had not been for the support of the aid program. A company official explains that the sale would not likely have been made from the Canadian plant of the international firm — and in fact the company would not even have known of the sale opportunity — had it not been contacted by CIDA. In other words, it was a one-time, taxpayer-subsidized export deal. For Canadian Baker Perkins, the single Tanzanian sale was the equivalent of over one-quarter of the company's 1972 total sales. But as much as it contributed a significant portion of the firm's sales — and profit remittances to its foreign parent, Baker Perkins Holdings Limited of England — the deal failed to stimulate longer-term export opportunities or exporting ability. CIDA was unable to assemble other bakery equipment aid projects and three years after the Tanzanian sale, Canadian Baker Perkins closed its Canadian manufacturing operations, sold its inventory, machinery and equipment, and terminated all manufacturing employees. Without more CIDA-supported sales, a company official claimed, the manufacturing operations could not be profitably continued in the small Canadian domestic market.

Today, the company is but a shell of its former self. Maintaining a small sales and service office in Brampton, it continues to supply replacement parts and equipment to the Tanzanian bakery — a drain of $25-40,000 annually on Tanzania's foreign exchange reserves. But since the Canadian sales office of Baker Perkins does no manufacturing itself, parts are ordered from other Canadian suppliers and when necessary imported from the company's US affiliate or other foreign suppliers. In the end, the bakery project achieved only the temporary propping up of a foreign-owned company which, without CIDA subsidy, was not economically viable. Development occurred neither in Tanzania nor Canada.

The bakery scheme, like the case examples presented earlier, raises issues more fundamental than the flaws in an individual project. Although CIDA officials contend that lessons have been learned from the bakery experience — the past is past, they say — the Agency provides little evidence that its thousands of projects are not, to a greater or lesser degree, similarly flawed. But Canadians are unable to judge for themselves. CIDA's reports on program countries are classified, and individual project evaluations — an area where CIDA admits its own inadequacy — are likewise kept secret. Canadians may have a long time to wait before CIDA accounts for its spending of taxpayer dollars with a comprehensive evaluation of its worldwide programs. In the meantime, examples like the bakery fiasco provide an insight into the concepts and policies which, more than simple mismanagement, are at the root of the problems that afflict Canadian aid.

Development Deceptions

When then CIDA vice-president Pierre Sicard addressed the Canadian Export Association in 1977, he groped for a simile to explain that the Agency's work cannot be measured by the simple profit and loss criteria familiar to his business audience. "One learned authority has come to the conclusion that development is like a giraffe," he told Canada's private sector exporters. "It's hard to describe but you recognize it when you see it!"[2]

CIDA should not be chastised for trying to explain its work in colourful and popular images instead of bureaucratic dialects or acronym-filled developmentese. But after 25 years of aid-giving experience, Canadians might expect a senior administrator of a billion dollar program to be somewhat more lucid on the raison d'etre of his work.

Misconceptions of what development is all about begin the list of aid's shortcomings. There are as many definitions as there are economic theories, but most aid experts have trumpeted one of a handful of theories to explain the particular role of foreign aid during the past thirty years. The significance of these theories needs to be kept in proper perspective. Although each attempts a logical rationale for development assistance, the real reasons for aid giving are often the political, strategic, and commercial goals of the donor. Nonetheless, development aid theories play an important part in defining and orienting aid and they share some of the responsibility for aid failures. To the degree that they miss the boat in defining what development is all about, such theories doom the best-administered and altruistically-motivated aid programs to the deep six. The confusion and eclecticism of these theories also explains why aid experts have difficulty in describing the development giraffe — in most places they've made it an endangered species.

Several US-born concepts of development blazed the trail of aid thinking and most of today's theories stumble in these footprints. During the early aid-giving years, development concepts were as underdeveloped as the countries being aided. Colombo Plan designers relied not so much on a theory as on a model — the Marshall Plan for the reconstruction of war-torn western Europe. As in the Marshall Plan, aid experts expected that the insertion of missing inputs — capital and technical assistance — would result in rapid development in the Third World and the eventual phasing out of aid. But the analogy was misleading. The objective of the West in the Marshall Plan was the quick restoration of western Europe's industrial and trade capacity. But unlike the Third World, post-war Europe possessed the social, economic and institutional infrastructure to be able to absorb large amounts of aid, and much of its industry was still intact. Aid to the Third World has never come close to the levels reached during the Marshall Plan. At its height Canada allotted over two percent of its GNP (four times today's level), and the US almost three percent, towards the rebuilding of western Europe.

A more elaborate notion about development aid replaced Marshallian concepts in the early 1960s. Walt Rostow, an economist and advisor to US Presidents Kennedy and Johnson, formulated the "stages of growth" prescription for the stable modernization of the Third World.[3] The world's poor, Rostow insisted, should imitate western, capitalist styles of development with aid playing a dual role of catalyzing rapid economic growth and cushioning the social and political shocks of the forced march to modern industrialization. His influential and ideologically loaded book, *The Stages of Economic Growth: A Non-Communist Manifesto*, claimed that aid could help underdeveloped countries achieve a "take-off" point — analogous to an airplane which can get off the ground only after it has attained a certain critical speed — by emphasizing the accumulation of savings for growth-producing investments. This theory openly advocated the acceleration of growth at the expense of income distribution and the concentration of aid efforts in those countries closest to the take-off point.

Canada's External Aid Office eagerly embraced Rostow's ideas on aid giving and occasionally referred to the stages of growth concept until the mid-1970s. Canadian aid was concentrated "on high priority projects in countries which are following general economic and financial policies conducive to growth and which are effectively mobilizing their own internal resources," the EAO explained in its 1966-67 Annual Review. But although the Agency claimed to be concentrating on countries "which are in the best position to benefit from Canadian aid", in practice Rostow's admonitions were never followed. The Department of External Affairs preferred the shotgun approach of scattering aid over dozens of countries and programs to accomplish its multi-pronged political objectives.[4]

Since Rostow, tangles of other theories have sprouted up to explain the role of aid in the development process. Stemming from Rostow is the idea that development assistance provides the external capital to make up for the inability of poor countries to accumulate enough domestically to stimulate a desired rate of GNP growth. The logic of these *capital* or *savings* theories, popularized by World Bank officials during the 1960s and still employed today, is based on accepted western doctrines about economics.[5] Growth results from investments. Investments in turn are dependent on the availability of an unemployed stock of capital or savings. As most capital in poor countries is immediately spent, by both governments and individuals, to keep the people alive, little can be saved, with the result that the rate of investment is low. Development aid, therefore, supplies savings capital from external sources to supplement domestic savings. Inflows of capital are also encouraged from other sources such as foreign investment and commercial loans. Donor countries can also supply commodities, equipment, and infrastructure in place of cash since this theoretically allows the recipient to free domestic resources for growth-producing investments. Either way, foreign aid supposedly breaks the vicious circle of underdevelopment wherein low levels of savings means low levels of investments which result in low levels of growth and inability to generate more savings.

A related theory stresses *population control* as a primary focus for development efforts and foreign aid. While capital theories say that there is too little capital in relation to population, the population theorists say there's too many people in relation to the available resources, including capital for investment. This neo-Malthusianism began to creep back into vogue in the 1950s after half-a-century of slumber. In the seventies it found a demagogic exponent in Garrett Hardin, an American biologist who transferred his discipline into the political teachings of social Darwinism (i.e., survival of the fittest is not just a law of evolution but a basis for economic and social policy).[6] Hardin believes that there are no poor countries, only overpopulated ones. Overpopulation hampers economic growth because the "surplus" population, largely unemployed, consumes resources — food, education, health care, etc. — which otherwise could be used for investment. Therefore, aid is wasted unless it goes toward, or is conditional upon, the implementation of mandatory population control programs.

Although the population-based theories about development and aid have only been partially swallowed by international aid agencies, aid funds for population programs increased from about $3 million in 1960 to over $300 million by 1975. Not to be left out, CIDA has kept in step by increasing its disbursements for population control from $1.5 million in 1970 to $12.5 million in 1980.[7] This, however, is still far short of the desire by some conservative commentators that Canada should "concentrate all of its foreign aid on birth control measures of every conceivable type and variety."[8]

Also related to the savings concept is the notion that besides capital, what poor countries lack is western knowledge and culture. Lack of education and training means that poor countries don't have the know-how (managerial, entrepreneurial, technical) and the socio-economic institutions to do things the way they're done (with presumed success) in the West. Third World cultures, religions and social ethics are pejoratively labelled superstitious, archaic and primitive, and considered decisive in counteracting development-creating forces. As a 1976 editorial in *Fortune* magazine declared: "the poor nations aren't poor because they have been exploited by the rich ones, but because of various combinations of meager natural endowment, adverse climate, cultural impediments, and inappropriate policies."[9] This knowledge-deficiency analysis of underdevelopment travels well with simplistic racial and climatic explanations of Third World poverty.

A problem which permeates all of the above theories is that they deal with only one aspect of people and societies. While some grant great importance to Third World culture and religion, if only in denigrating them, most theories simply ignore culture and non-economic aspects of the human condition. They tend to see the universe as peopled by "economic persons", all equal in their aspirations, all subject to the same immutable laws of economic behaviour, all fulfilling their pre-ordained functions as, alternately, producers and consumers. Population theorists go one step further by mixing the two myopias, denigrating Third World cultures, and at the same time considering people only as consumers of scarce resources — ignoring the fact that people are at the same time the producers of capital and value. Economistic theories thus reduce planning to something done with a slide-rule or calculator. All of these abstractions remarkably overlook, or relegate to secondary importance, notions of culture, nationality, and above all, social class.

Population-based theories, like creatures with weak eyes, can't stand too much exposure to daylight. They are important because they have so deeply imbedded themselves as myths in North American public opinion, even though they have recently lost some credence in certain international aid organizations. Agencies like the World Bank and CIDA now recognize that birth rates are noticeably on the decline in many Third World countries due not to birth control planning but to improvements, for some social classes in some societies, of socio-economic conditions.[10] Contrary to what Malthus originally held, population increases slow down as people become more prosperous. In many Third World societies, large families are not the result of irrational behaviour, but rather of the fact that they need many children — for example, to help in agriculture and to look after them in old age. In other words, population increase does not create misery, but rather misery causes population increase. Thus, as Domingos Donida, a former professor at the University of Ottawa who went on to become a CIDA planner, explains:

Giving priority to the population problem over and above economic and social [development] means we are bound to fail. Underdevelopment is the end result of a whole international system which is based on colonial dependency and which is perpetuated by trade relations biased in favour of the industrialized countries.[11]

But population theorists have a convenient myopia which measures only today's imbalance between population and the amount of capital available in a nation for development. By its own system of logic, such a problem could be solved by simply adding more capital. As World Bank economists Mahbub ul Haq has pointed out, "even a slight redistribution of the world's income can help ease the pressure on the world's resources far more than any possible reduction in the population growth of the Third World."[12] This is because while the Third World may contain 70% of the world's people and account for 80% of the world's population growth, it consumes only one-tenth of the world's resources. Population control appears to the underdeveloped countries as a plot hatched in the First World to both deprive it of a just share of the world's resources and continue the northern grab for southern raw materials.

The proponents of population theories reject these arguments because they deal with the systems of capital accumulation and distribution rather than with breeding habits. Generally political conservatives, they hold capital systems sacred. Their insistence on population control as the answer amounts to adjusting the population to the amount of capital which one class — the owners of capital — determines is available for investment. The use of population planning in this way — as the decisive tool instead of one, secondary element for planning popular well-being — can only be accomplished by coercion.[13]

Prominent in post-war thinking has been a deterministic view according to which development in different lands follows a set course as time goes by. If General Marshall's plan worked for western Europe, it was assumed to be the solution for the Third World. Rostow believed that all societies could be placed on one of five rungs of a linear development ladder ascending towards industrialization and development. Such views assume that fundamental similarities exist between different cultures and countries at different periods of time. It expects a given Third World nation to repeat in several decades what western countries did in their industrialization stages between 100 and 150 years ago under completely different conditions. Such reasoning is like a "Connecticut Yankee in King Arthur's Court" vision of development, entertaining as storytelling but more hallucination than history. Even 100 years ago, the northern nations were already higher up the theoretical ladder than most of the Third World today. For instance, measured in 1965 dollars, the United States had a per capita GNP of $474 in 1843, an amount greater than the 1965 GNP per capita of all but a handful of underdeveloped countries.[14] The problem is that the northern nations, having climbed up the ladder in stages themselves, took the ladder away by imposing international economic and political systems that perpetuate underdevelopment.

Rostow's followers claim Taiwan and South Korea as outstanding examples of the stages of growth theory. But the theory was little more than a glossy rationalization for US strategic goals. It justified the dumping of massive amounts of aid into these countries to make them patron states of Washington. In the case of South Korea, between 1958 and 1974, the United States funnelled a whopping $8.8 billion in economic and military assistance to Seoul — an amount more than twice what Canada had allocated by 1974 to over eighty countries.[15] These capital injections contributed to an increase in GNP averaging 7.4% yearly between 1960 and 1977, but, together with the presence of 39,000 US troops, such aid thoroughly compromised the nation's independence and made it a virtual military and economic colony.

Korea's model of rapid industrialization is founded not on Rostow's abstract prescriptions but on the cold exploitation of cheap labour. According to the Seoul government itself, wages for men in the export-oriented manufacturing industries are only one-third of the amount required to support an average family's cost of living. The labour force works the longest hours per week in the world with the highest accident rate. The military dictatorship of President Park Chung Hee (1961-1979) and his successors, has made this super-exploitation of labour possible through repressive measures including media censorship, denial of freedoms of speech and assembly, rigid government control of trade unions, workplace purges, political arrests, torture and disappearances.

By 1980, however, with inflation rising, economic growth plunging, and the foreign debt ballooning, South Korea lost its success status and turned to the International Monetary Fund for bailing out. As a model, South Korea's experience is neither widely duplicable nor desired by other Third World countries. Its "take-off" never achieved self-sustaining flight.[16]

In South Korea as elsewhere, aid experts reveal their penchant for quantifying the concept of development. But the most important measure they have employed during the past thirty years — Gross National Product — is like judging a wine by measuring its quantity. GNP is a statistical yardstick, often broken down in per capita terms, gauging measurable output of all goods and services in an economy.* Designed for use in industrial societies, it makes little sense in underdeveloped, largely rural, often subsistence economies of the Third World. On the one hand, current GNP statistics only measure gainful employment and underestimate unpaid and subsistence work. On the other hand, the rate of GNP increase in itself says nothing about the social welfare for most of the population, as demonstrated by examples from two Caribbean islands. National

---

* Another indicator used to measure development is Gross Domestic Product (GDP) per capita. GDP differs from GNP by including profit remittances by foreign companies and interest payments on foreign loans in calculating the total output of goods and services — amounts which can be significant for some Third World countries.

income per capita increased in Trinidad an average of 5% yearly from 1953 to 1968. But at the same time, unemployment grew steadily to include more than 10% of the labour force. In contrast, on the island of Cuba, GNP per capita decreased, on average, by 0.6% yearly between 1960 and 1970 according to the World Bank. But because of the socialist government's economic planning and social programming, open unemployment fell from roughly 25% to practically zero, illiteracy dropped from roughly 25% to under 4%, and malaria and polio were practically eliminated.[17]

While GNP measures the monetary value of goods and services produced, it doesn't distinguish between desirable and undesirable production, nor does it measure the social costs of such production. For example, social costs of increasing GNP include depletion of non-renewable minerals, consumption of forest resources, and erosion of land by intensive agriculture lacking protective actions. Human costs of accelerated industrial production include more work injuries, accidents and deaths. Production of luxury goods for a sliver of the population, and corruption in government and business, are examples of undesirable economic activities. Yet statistics like the GNP mix these in with socially useful economic production and view as positive even the most socially costly, parasitical, and criminal of economic activity.

Making economic growth the touchstone of development avoids a crucial question: who benefits from the increased output? For most of the past 30 years, development aid planners answered with the "trickle-down" theory. This is the naive view that any type of economic growth is good and slowly filters down to benefit the common people. But again, the experience of showcase countries contradicts the theory.

In Brazil, for example, GNP grew at over 10% yearly between 1967 and 1973 largely spurred by multinational investments. But the economic miracle did not improve living standards for most. Instead, the rich got richer and the poor got poorer; the top 1% of Brazil's income earners saw their share of national income increase from 12% in 1960 to almost 18% in 1970 while, for the same period, the bottom 80% saw their share decline from 45% to 36%. Not only did the poor's share of a growing pie shrink, many experienced a real decline in incomes and by 1970 it was estimated that 74% of the population had real earnings of less than the government's minimum subsistence level. The effects of the economic model are most strikingly shown in infant mortality figures. Between 1962 and 1975, the period of rapid growth, it increased by 45%.[18]

Ottawa has long been aware of these problems. In a confidential brief to the federal Cabinet in the mid-1970s, CIDA admitted that:

The development model outlined in [Brazil's] is that of creating wealth first and leaving the distribution problem for later.... However, a recent estimate, attributed to the Brazilian Finance Minister, is that only about 5% of the population have benefitted from 5 years of unprecedented economic growth; 45% actually saw their standard of living go down; and the remaining 50% are relatively no worse and no better off than they were before the economic boom started.[19]

To its credit, the same report went on to recommend a downgrading of Brazil as an aid recipient. The reasons given, however, were more political than economic or humanitarian. With a frankness reserved for the secret society of policy makers and Cabinet Ministers, the brief writer admitted that in order to keep political stability, maintain subsistence wages, and attract foreign investment, the regime had to be very authoritarian:

Brazil is frankly a fascist state. The term is used to describe the complexion of the regime rather than its ideology or institutional structure. Dissent is stifled and allegations of the torture of prisoners under interrogation are too widespread and too well documented by organizations, such as Amnesty International, to be dismissed . . . any decision on the part of the Canadian government to strengthen and diversify relations, developmental or otherwise, with Brazil will almost certainly come up against prevailing public attitudes in Canada on the question of the alleged torture of prisoners.[20]

Trickle-down and take-off models fail in part because they tend to foment a dual economy.[21] A modern sector monopolizes foreign inputs and the benefits of economic growth — only it takes off — while the traditional sector, large parts of which are outside the money economy, benefits little from development plans and projects. In both sectors, there are privileged minorities and impoverished or disenfranchised majorities. The policies of national governments perpetuate such divisions by pro-modernization schemes coupled with calculated indifference to the poor. Extending aid to nations where dual economies are severely structured, unless directed to the poor, will inevitably benefit the rich first if not exclusively. A study prepared for the US Agency for International Development (AID) concluded that in countries with severely dualistic economies (for example, Peru and Zambia), GNP growth generally cut the share of income going to the lowest-paid 60% of the people. In countries where the modern sector is primarily foreign-owned and financed, higher GNP growth tended to result in lower income shares even for middle-class households.[22]

Such findings raise serious doubts about CIDA's construction of hydro-electric infrastructure the world over. In dualistic economies the result is the electrification of cities — to the benefit of local and foreign investors — while the rural poor are predictably left in the dark pondering the meaning of the hum from overhead, made-in-Canada transmission lines. A case in point is the Alto Anchicaya hydro-electric project in Colombia. Built with funds from the Canadian contribution to the Inter-American Development Bank in the sixties, this hydro dam on Colombia's Pacific slope employs Canadian General Electric turbines and equipment to produce electricity and transmit it through the very poor and unelectrified Anchicaya valley to the booming city of Cali where, among its beneficiaries, can be found a subsidiary of Alcan Aluminium.

Capital or savings approaches, because they usually apply to investments in the modern sector, only reinforce the dual-economy blockage to the trickle down of aid inputs. But in addition, external capital inputs such as development assistance often replace, not supplement, the stock of domestic savings available for investments in the Third World. For example, if foreign aid helps finance a Third World hydro-electric project it theoretically helps the recipient government by absorbing the costs of a priority project that would ordinarily be met out of general government tax revenues. The government revenue "freed up" by the aid supposedly expands the total amount of capital available, in public or private hands, for investments. But if foreign aid merely allows the recipient government to lower or forego taxation of the wealthy, then the aggregate amount of savings at its disposal is not supplemented at all. And when the rich are allowed to squander their untaxed wealth on luxury imports, a potential source of domestic savings is lost. Such practices provoked World Bank economist Hollis Chenery to conclude in the mid-sixties that aid to Latin America had been a "substitute for savings, not an addition to investment."[23]

Another classic example of the same savings-drain problem is CIDA's funding of infrastructure projects aimed at boosting tourist industries. In the Caribbean region, at least seven nations have received CIDA support for building or expanding airports specifically designed to increase tourism. But a government-initiated study into these transportation projects by P.F. Wickenden, a transportation specialist from the Department of Industry, Trade and Commerce, concludes that CIDA promoted these projects without having a concrete regional development plan. The study went on to underline that investments in Caribbean tourism can actually worsen the underdevelopment situation. Wickenden gives an example using a fictional island:

Let's say this island decides to improve its airport. It wants to be able to handle full-size jet traffic. It needs about $40 million and gets it through grants but mostly loans, which is the trend. The island has real tourist potential and after the airport is finished the numbers increase. But money spent by tourists can have up to 90 per cent leakage. Most of the tourist dollar goes to foreign-owned hotels, food importers, liquor importers and is drained right back out of the country. At 10 cents on every dollar spent, that country has to get incredible numbers of tourists to pay off the debt it incurred building the airport. Unless it can get $40 million, the island is in worse net shape than it was before.[24]

In concentrating on tourism, both CIDA and recipient governments in the Caribbean have sought an illusory easy way out of underdevelopment instead of tackling greater priorities such as agriculture.

The credibility crisis in mainstream theories about development and foreign aid are obviously profound and pervasive. The periodic unveiling of new development approaches — such as "basic needs" aid to the rural poor, a type of savings theory that has become a new phase in development thinking (see chapter 6) is evidence of the groping by aid agencies of the North for new formulae to replace failed ones. For its part, CIDA now confesses the contradictions in its earlier concepts:

Aid and development cooperation were undermined by false assumptions about the speed at which a developing society could be transformed or the ability of western science and technology to eliminate poverty... many donors have pursued policies related more to their immediate self-interests than those of recipients, and have maintained an over-simplified view of the requirements of genuine development. Many recipients have squandered resources, refused to adopt rational trade and taxation policies, avoided land reform, or delayed changes in administrative systems. A major misconception of donors was the assumption that the relatively modest volume of resource transfers represented by aid flows could alone and in isolation eradicate poverty and guarantee development.[25]

But CIDA's caveats continue to be contradicted by the Agency's practice. Flawed theories of the past are still applied even as they are confessed. These atavisms — one dictionary definition of which is "the recurrence in a descendant of a particular abnormality or disease manifested by a remote ancestor" — can be diagnosed in two general categories.

Firstly, the practice of western aid giving is still based on an "input deficiency" analysis of underdevelopment: that what the Third World most needs, or even significantly needs, is the capital, technology, know-how and products of the northern, capitalist world. This is an aid-blinkered outlook on reality. Because what the industrialized West has to offer and needs to sell to the Third World are its own products and services, then the lack of these inputs defines the problem of underdevelopment for aid officials. In fact, foreign aid accounts for only 7% of the total capital available to Third World countries; over 80% of the total comes from domestic savings and the rest from commercial loans and foreign investment.[26]

But a more frontal challenge to the input-deficiency concept is the historical experience of China. Though some observers find much to criticize in China, no one can dispute that China has managed to meet the basic needs of its 930 million people. And it achieved this during a quarter-century of planned isolation from externally-induced mechanisms of development such as private investment, foreign aid and extensive international commerce. Rejecting top-down models of development, China emphasized food production, labour-intensive and appropriate technology, and local community participation in the economic and political process. It is not a perfect model, nor one readily transferable to other countries. But China's experience mocks capitalist theories of development and the underlying assumptions of aid giving.

The Chinese experience also shows up western, externally-induced mechanisms of development as instruments of underdevelopment. The input-deficiency concept of the problem conveniently sidesteps the causes of underdevelopment that originate in the capitalist West. It ignores the role played by colonialism, neo-colonialism, and the current international trade, monetary and investment structures. These structures have siphoned off resources required by underdeveloped nations for their advancement. They have shaped and moulded Third World economies to meet northern needs for raw materials, markets and investment opportunities instead of meeting the most basic needs of local peoples. In calling for the maintenance of these structures, and bigger doses of western inputs through them, development theorists are perpetuating poverty. When aid giving is planned within this framework, it is pursuing development down a dead-end street.

A second and related atavism afflicting aid donors is the view that development is essentially an economic and technical problem. Economic formulae, mechanical measurements of progress and short-lived aid fads all avoid the central issue: development is fundamentally a political process. It is a question of political power. The mechanisms of underdevelopment are neither natural nor neutral — they serve and are sustained by elitist classes, in both North and South, which exploit and repress the majority. And while the unjust structures which perpetuate underdevelopment among nations are significant causes of underdevelopment, real development is firstly a question of political change *within* nations. Changes in the international arena — important as they are to the full liberation of the Third World — cannot initiate the transformation of domestic political structures. The first necessity is a political transformation within Third World countries — a matter of replacing the current political leadership and structures with a new leadership and structure so that development which benefits the whole people can be initiated. To be authentic, this kind of development strives to distribute justly the benefits of economic growth by meeting the basic needs for food, housing, health and education of the majority. But it is more than a list of benefits. It is an integral process, encompassing not only economic progress but also respecting cultural values and promoting the ability of people and nations to master their own destiny. Therefore, it seeks to reduce dependency and promote self-

reliant economic growth. It is an historical process which democ-
ratizes and reorganizes the ownership of the means of production. It
expands and dynamizes popular participation in the political life of
the country. This is obviously a political process.

The consequence of ditching input-deficiency and economistic
notions of development in favour of a more integral, self-reliant,
and political concept raises a pivotal question: *who* should donor
states aid? If a Third World regime ignores, exploits and represses
its poor, even the best concepts and forms of aid can be diverted or
coopted to strengthen and perpetuate class divisions and oppres-
sion. Further underdevelopment, not development, is the result. In
contrast, if a Third World government acts to promote self-reliance
and rules in the interest of its poor — if the government and the
people are as close as possible to being the same thing — then aid
may be able to make a positive contribution, depending on its orientation and quality. But the determination of an underdeveloped
country to achieve authentic development is the first requisite of
whether such development occurs and whether foreign aid works.
Canadian aid, however, scattered over 90 countries for political and
commercial reasons, reinforcing entrenched elites from Bangladesh
to Kenya, and supporting gross violators of human rights from
Indonesia to Guatemala, seems oblivious to this common sense.

The Ties That Bind

Incorrect concepts of development and the misallocation of aid to
regressive recipients are two of the primary reasons why foreign aid
has failed to bring development in so many places for so many
years. Other factors also operate to subvert the donor's ostensible
intent. Restrictions, regulations and policies governing what agencies like CIDA give and how they give it, further limit and even work
against the supposed purposes of development assistance.

The tying of bilateral aid is one such policy. As an example of
how the self-interest of donors diminishes the value of aid, tying is
the practice most commonly cited by aid critics. And while other
issues may be more or equally important, tying deserves all the bad
press it gets.

Tying aid is simply the insistence of aid agencies that the money
they grant or lend bilaterally to underdeveloped countries be spent
on products and services from the donor country. Canada practised
tying from the start of its assistance program in 1951. But the practice became more generalized after 1959 when the United States and
other donors began to tie more and more of their allocations in an
attempt to use aid to balance their trade deficits. For donors, tying
minimizes the real cost of aid while assuring that goods bought with
aid are *additional* to the normal exports of donors to Third World
countries.

Through the sixties, strong export lobbies in the developed countries pressured their governments to use aid grants and credits to dispose of surplus stocks of food or other commodities and for the explicit purpose of promoting exports from sagging domestic industries. Governments willingly succumbed to the pressure because tying seemed to generate public support, at least in the business community, for development assistance and because it allowed the donor government to relate to particular recipients in a politically identifiable way. By 1969, the Pearson Report noted that tied aid had "spread in a contagious fashion . . . and untied aid is now the exception rather than the rule."[27]

The tying of Canadian aid reached its zenith in 1967, and although some liberalization of restrictions has since occurred, Canadian assistance still remains substantially tied. Originally, all bilateral aid disbursements had to be spent on Canadian goods supplied by majority-owned Canadian companies and containing at least 80% value added in Canada (i.e., only 20% of the total value of a tied aid product, a vehicle for example, could originate in other countries — the rest of the total value of the product had to be made or added in Canada). In 1968, Ottawa eased its value added restriction to two-thirds of the total, but not for the purpose of untying aid. Instead, the lower value added requirement allowed more Canadian-based companies, usually branch plants of American firms producing with a large amount of foreign components in their products, to share in the aid gravy. In 1970, CIDA decided to cover the shipping costs of aid-funded goods; formerly these had been paid by the recipient. In the same year, the government completely untied 20% of its bilateral budget for purchases of high priority projects, usually to cover recipient funding of local costs. For the last decade, Canada has not budged from this 80% tying restriction despite repeated promises for more liberalization.[28]

The Pearson Report called the tying of aid the most serious of all the limitations placed on the flexibility of assistance. The practice saddles the aid recipient with both direct and indirect costs which greatly reduce the real value of the aid. Pearson conservatively estimated in 1969 that the direct cost of tying aid exceeded 20% of the competitive international price for goods and services.[29] CIDA's first president, Maurice Strong, put the figure for CIDA's aid as high as 25%.[30] These added costs generally occur in two ways. Firstly, suppliers in Canada charge monopoly prices for goods sold under the aid program because they realize that aid-receiving countries have no choice but to make this purchase with aid funds. A second way in which costs are added to the aid recipient is the result of higher costs of producing these goods in the donor country than in other countries.

In a hypothetical example, a Third World country can use a

$100,000 credit from CIDA to buy 100 widgits at $1,000 each from a Canadian widgit-maker. But if the same widgits are manufactured in other countries and sell for $800 each, the Third World country could have purchased 125 units had the Canadian aid been untied. If the problem is not one of the difference in production costs between Canada and other suppliers of widgits, but rather one of the Canadian producer charging monopoly prices — charging $1,000 per widgit instead of the normal price of $800 — then the recipient is similarly shortchanged of 20% of the aid allocation's value and the Canadian company pockets the profitable difference.

Instead of paying these tying costs, the Canadian taxpayer could hypothetically save $200 million or more a year of the aid budget and still give the same amount in physical terms if CIDA allowed recipients to buy from the cheapest source. The difference between the price of Canadian goods supplied by tied aid and cheaper international products represents an export subsidy paid by the taxpayer, and endured by the recipient, to exporting companies in Canada.

But for the recipient, the problem is not hypothetical. In the case of the CIDA-sponsored bakery in Tanzania discussed at the beginning of the chapter, it seems that even if the sole supplier of the equipment in Canada did not charge monopoly prices, the cost to Tanzania of the design and equipment was higher than quotations from other countries. Tying regulations not only diminished Canada's contribution but, in a perversion of the theory being employed, may even have caused a drain on savings. The capital Tanzania theoretically "saved" by the CIDA loan is firstly reduced in value by the amount that will have to be repaid to Canada in the future. But, more importantly, the bakery project diverts potential savings in two ways: firstly, consumers spend their money on a luxury project instead of saving or buying more basic goods; and secondly, the government has to allocate precious foreign exchange to import foreign fuel, wheat and spare parts for the bakery.

Indirect costs of tying aid are added by the additional time and money spent to formulate and administer tied-aid programs in both the donor and recipient country. An example of these costs can be found on the Pacific coast of Colombia where CIDA sent six Canadian experts in 1974 to study the region's forestry potential. The team of highly-paid economists, marketing specialists and forestry experts on contract from Reed, Collins and Associates needed small boats to get along the coast to take a forest inventory. The boats could have been purchased in the Colombian city of Medellin for half the price of Canadian boats. But, according to the project director Earl Hindley, CIDA's bureaucracy and tying regulations would not permit expedient local purchasing. Once CIDA in Ottawa received and approved the request for the boats, the Agency had to pass the order to the Canadian Commercial Corporation, a Crown company that handles government procurement. Notorious for its plodding, the CCC then had to purchase the boats from a Canadian supplier, freight them to the east coast of Canada and ship them through the Panama Canal to a Colombian port. Not only were direct costs added by Canadian procurement, but the months of delay caused indirect costs to the Canadian taxpayer and to Colombia as professional staff were left idle in Colombia.[31]

Tying also means that what Canada provides the Third World may be inappropriate and far from a priority for development. This leads to a misallocation of resources for both the donor and recipient.

Bangladesh is a case in point. The best-known Canadian aid project in the country is not the mountain of food aid to feed the hungry but the Bangladesh Earth Satellite Station. Built through an $8 million CIDA loan, the station was originally designed to provide a communications link between West and East Pakistan. But since the 1971 war which created the state of Bangladesh, it has been used for international telephone communications and the reception of global television for the country's meagre stock of 30,000 television sets. In a country where hundreds of thousands of children die in the best of years, such a prestigious project prompted Conservative MP Douglas Roche to dub it the "top-down development model gone mad."[32] CIDA claims that such a project would not be approved today, but the Agency is still providing half a million dollars a year to maintain technical servicing.

Another example of inappropriate aid to non-priority development schemes can be found in the southern African country of Botswana. When two giant mining companies, Anglo American and AMAX, decided to exploit the Selebi-Pickwe copper-nickel deposit in northeast Botswana, the impoverished Botswana government went looking for foreign aid to finance the building of associated infrastructure. Botswana got the World Bank to assume the role of coordinating international financing and the Bank then approached CIDA after Sweden decided not to participate because Anglo American is based in racist South Africa. In 1972 CIDA decided to buy into the project with a $30 million loan for the construction of a coal-burning power plant and related transmission systems.

Secretary of State for External Affairs Allen MacEachen later claimed that "CIDA's participation in developing countries such as Botswana is not predicated on the advantage that might or might not directly accrue to Canada."[33] The Minister was being less than candid, however. Based on poor planning and faulty execution, Canada's aid to the project seems to have been predicated on little more than Canadian advantage.

According to the World Bank, which had hoped that the infrastructure would be financed on an untied basis, CIDA's tying regulations added about 25% to the cost of the power project over and above what it would have cost had it been put out to international bidding. Canadian tying also required the shipping of redwood power poles half way around the world from British Columbia to Botswana. A supply of cheaper eucalyptus trees was available in nearby Swaziland but tying denied this spin-off benefit to a neighbouring economy. Meanwhile, when the "Canadian" boilers for the power plant (made by a subsidiary of the US-owned Babcock & Wilcox Corporation) arrived, it turned out they could not burn the type of coal found in Botswana. Botswana, which wanted to use its own coal supplies to avoid being hostage to imports from Rhodesia or South Africa, had to import Rhodesian coal for 18 months and share the tab with Babcock & Wilcox for converting the boilers to use local fuel.

The negative effects of CIDA's contribution were softened when Ottawa decided in 1977 to forgive Botswana's debts to the Agency. But the contribution of the project to Botswana's overall development is still in question. The capital-intensive mining investment created fewer jobs than possible in other sectors, and even the jobs created were at wages well below those provided in bordering South Africa. The project reinforced Botswana's dual economy, symbolized by the shantytowns which sprang up around the mine site as thousands of peasants converged on Selebi-Pickwe with false hopes of sharing the mineral wealth. And while tax concessions and debt repayments mean that the mining venture has returned little income to the Botswana government, the country has become dependent on a resource-export model of development. As Canadian university professor Linda Freeman concludes in her study of the project:

Export-oriented development for a resource-rich, but otherwise poor, country is irresistibly attractive. Once launched, mining schemes bind the country into a web of unequal relationships with large multinationals and international price and marketing arrangements. In this case, the development at Selebi-Pickwe became another outpost for the Anglo American empire, serving to integrate Botswana more tightly into the mini-centre of South African capitalism and the larger metropoles of the United States and Europe.[34]

Understandably, some CIDA officials were less than enthusiastic about providing low cost financing from the aid program for infrastructure for a project owned by two of the world's richest multinational mining corporations. They quietly grumbled that funding of such a capital-intensive industrial project meant foregoing direct assistance to the poor of Botswana.

Another aspect of the problem of tied aid is found in Canada's technical assistance program. The Agency spends over $50 million annually to send Canadian technical advisors and teachers overseas and to train Third World students in Canada. Rooted firmly in the input-deficiency analysis of underdevelopment, Canadian technical assistance assumes that what Third World countries need to know, First World professionals can impart, and that Canadian professionals are as good as any. CIDA also finds it an indirect way to peddle Canadian exports since Canadian experts working on development projects in the Third World are likely to recommend the purchase of Canadian products or brands with which they are familiar. Sending Canadians to advise underdeveloped countries also ostensibly deepens our national understanding of development problems while generating support for the aid program from another sector of the Canadian population.

No doubt it does the latter, if only because it offers generous perks to Canadian academics. Testifying before the British House of Commons in the early 1970s, one Canadian professor lambasted the motives of his colleagues.

In Canada, for example, they are very keen on technical assistance because, essentially, it is a way by which Canadian professors get to travel to foreign parts at salaries higher than they earn at home. I would regard that kind of thing as being technical assistance for Canadian professors rather than for the developing country.[35]

Critical comments from returning experts are understandably hushed by comfortable financial gags, but just to be sure CIDA puts a two-year legal restriction on its overseas consultants not to discuss publicly any aspect of projects they worked on.

At the other end of the technical assistance pipeline aid recipients get Canadian experts just as they get Canadian equipment — on the donor's terms. A tied, technical assistance grant obliges recipient countries to pay Canadian advisors and teachers at Canadian rates. The result is an embarrassing discrepancy between the income and lifestyle of Canadian experts and their local colleagues. Canadian experts are usually not as expensive as advisors from multilateral institutions like the World Bank — where $300 a day plus expenses is the going rate — but they don't come cheap. With salaries, living expenses, trips home, and other perks, it costs CIDA up to $90,000 to keep a consultant in the field; in contrast, volunteers with CUSO cost about $15,000 annually. As a result, underdeveloped countries get only one Canadian expert for the price of two people from Europe or three from another part of the Third World.[36] And aid recipients claim that no more than 50% of the aid-financed experts, advisors, consultants and teachers they receive will "produce" more than their local costs (housing, support staff, travel, etc.); in other words, such foreign aid carries a value to the recipient of less than zero.[37]

Theoretically, technical assistance constitutes a "holding operation"; once local people are trained, recipient governments say, it won't be needed. But knowledge has a built-in obsolescence. Development fashions change fast, technology faster, and foreign experts, with their international experience and First World citizenship, are hard to replace unless a Third World government is deeply committed to self-reliance. The magazine *African Development* explains the perpetuation of dependency on foreign experts in English- and French-speaking Africa where there are now at least twice as many technical experts as formerly there were colonial administrators:

The fact is that like a sort of geometrically progressing Parkinson's law aid begets more aid and technical assistance personnel spawn ever more of their kind so that despite brave attempts at self-reliance most African states are becoming more rather than less dependent upon some form of assistance from outside.[38]

The foreign expert, sought-after as he or she may be, is one of the northern world's most effective agents for extending throughout the Third World a cultural sameness born of western technology which carries with it the introduction of inappropriate technologies in underdeveloped countries. The imposition of northern ways on southern societies is often due to the foreign advisor's isolation from the real needs of local people. He or she is divorced from the poor once by profession, twice by culture and a third time by the rules of the tied aid game. When these emissaries of Canadian aid are insensitive to different cultures, indifferent to the opinions of local people, and living in cloistered, affluent, expatriate colonies, they cancel out their potential contribution and with it a substantial part of Canada's image abroad.

Thus, the ties that bind underdeveloped countries to aid donors cause more than extra costs to aid recipients, misorienting the selection and execution of aid projects in equally, if less quantifiable ways. The problem starts when a Third World development planner begins to think about requesting aid from agencies like CIDA. He knows that the kind of projects poor citizens are interested in — land reform and related rural development efforts, for example — are not only politically suspect in the eyes of local elites but also require a lot of local spending on labour, local goods and services. He also knows that it will be very difficult to get a project through CIDA if it has 80% local costs. So, right from the start, he shapes a funding request to fit CIDA's tying regulations. Some alternatives are discarded from the outset and development projects get designed and distorted by CIDA's concepts and criteria, not by objective development needs.

According to a McGill University study based on interviews with CIDA officials, about 30% of all projects considered by CIDA's bilateral division are initiated by requesting countries in a form acceptable to the Agency.[39] Another 30% arrive in CIDA's hands in unacceptable form and require substantial modification to conform to the Agency's policies and standards. In the process of approving or redrafting these project submissions, such CIDA policies are too often the predominant consideration. Negotiations between CIDA and a Third World government then take on the characteristics of unequal bargaining between a weak trade union and a powerful management. The Third World nation has a request, already reduced from maximum wishes to suit CIDA, and the weight of moral persuasion. But CIDA, in the management seat, has considerably more in its bargaining hand — administrative capacity, technology, access to the files of multilateral institutions on the requesting country, the knowledge that other supplicants are lining up outside its door, and finally, money.

When CIDA wishes to alter development projects to fit its policies, aid recipients can either accept the changes — and the problems they carry with them — or forget about funding. But conditions of poverty, dependent economic structures, and large foreign debts force even progressive underdeveloped countries to seek international financing; many will accept even traditional forms of aid with their tying restrictions — hoping to make the best of it — rather than mortgage themselves more than they already are to the higher cost money and sometimes more stringent conditions of commercial lenders. Regressive governments seek concessional aid for the same reasons but object less to the problems presented by tying because their elite classes benefit from the top-down, dualistic and donor-dependent models of development that tied aid brings. In a nutshell, this is why, despite the numerous problems with tied aid, its conceptual foundations and its delivery methods, tied aid is still sought by so many nations of the Third World.

Donor tying finally means that development efforts with a high demand for local spending don't get the attention they deserve. In her study of Canadian aid in southern Africa, Linda Freeman concluded that tying limits Canadian aid to "urban, capital intensive, high technology projects, usually with an emphasis on capital assistance to infrastructure and technical assistance to senior levels of national institutions."[40] As long as CIDA is harnessed by tying regulations, Canadian aid will be unable to make significant contributions to the very types of development programs — basic needs and rural development efforts that empower local peoples — which the Agency has set as its first priority.[41]

Despite the lengthy litany of complaints against it, CIDA remains staunchly committed to tying. The Agency's new president, Marcel Masse, says he wants to spend more of the bilateral aid budget on people-serving, social programs like rural development and health instead of large infrastructure projects.[42] Such a shift in spending implies significant untying of aid, but neither Masse nor his Agency are making any concrete moves in this direction. CIDA hasn't even fully utilized its authority to untie 20% of bilateral funds.

In fact, Masse's boss, External Affairs Minister Mark Mac-Guigan, seems to be going in the opposite direction, as seen in his testimony before the Parliamentary Standing Committee on External Affairs and National Defence in the Spring of 1981:

With respect to tied aid, we are not moving away from tied aid. We have a fairly flexible system there and I must say that I consider the issue of whether aid is tied or not to be a rather minor league issue. I do not think it is of substantial importance in this field at all.

And later in the same testimony:

Tied aid really is a red herring. . . . I am not only not opposed to tied aid, I think aid is an important protection for our citizens, as long as it does not interfere with or inflate the cost of development in developing countries, I think it is something we can really justify.[43]

MacGuigan's position conforms to another recent attempt to deal with the tying problem by downplaying its importance. In its main report published in 1980, the Parliamentary Task Force on North-South Relations failed to bring forward any specific recommendation on untying, sidestepping the issue by musing that a significant portion of aid *should* be spent in Canada "consistent with development assistance objectives".[44]

The primary reason why Canadian government leaders refuse to untie aid — or for that matter to change their concepts of development — is their dedication to using aid as a tool to help the domestic economy, to develop Canada, in other words, through the promotion of the exports of private companies.

The Development Business

An internal directive issued by Michel Dupuy when he took the helm of CIDA in 1977 signalled a new emphasis in the Agency's programs. Canada's sagging economic growth and its prospects for more of the same, Dupuy explained, "require that CIDA strive to ensure that its activities maintain or generate employment and economic benefits in our own country."[45] Turning foreign aid towards domestic economic problems was not to be achieved at the expense of CIDA's "development" mandate, Dupuy said in the same directive. But at the same time, he told his staff that the Agency's 1975 *Strategy* paper, the basis for this development mandate, was not "cast in stone", a phrase which ensured immediate consignment of the document to the archives. Instead, as Dupuy later told Parliament, "our first priority is to look at the resources Canada can make available."[46]

Dupuy was publicly articulating an assumption which has

always been implicit in Canadian aid-giving: that development assistance can simultaneously develop both "them" and "us".[47] This "mutual benefits" assumption directly contradicts the conservative critique that aid is a massive give-away. If aid really bolsters Canada's economy, it cannot at the same time be a drain on national resources.

Indeed it is not. If all Canadian aid were simply transferred to the Third World as a kind of equalization payment with no strings attached, the figures in CIDA's annual reports would be an accurate record of the cost of development assistance to the Canadian economy. But most of the disbursements chalked up by CIDA never actually leave the country. To take a different example in another area of government spending, most of the money spent on national defence — $3.8 billion in the 1977-78 fiscal year — stays in Canada for wage payments and equipment, supplies and services purchases. In this way the defence budget helps stimulate the economy. In the same way, the portion of CIDA's budget spent in Canada is not a loss, but rather a recirculation or reallocation of money within the domestic economy.

Past CIDA presidents have gone out of their way to advertise this fact — especially before business audiences. Paul Gerin-Lajoie told the Montreal Board of Trade in 1973 how companies benefit from CIDA spending:

We know that 80 to 90 per cent of this money is currently being spent in Canada on Canadian goods, commodities and services... 7,564 contracts have been placed with Canadian firms in the past three years... a recent study has indicated that CIDA will be responsible for the maintenance of over 48,000 man-years in the '73-'74 fiscal year.[48]

Four years later, in a comparable speech to the prestigious Empire Club of Toronto, Michel Dupuy reported that $650 million, or 60% of the CIDA budget, was being spent in Canada each year and that the number of jobs generated had jumped to 100,000.[49]

Dupuy's figures were guesstimates of the amount of aid funds recouped by Canadian enterprises after a paper transfer to the Third World. They can be calculated by some simple deductions from the stated amount of annual aid-giving. During the government's 1977-78 fiscal year, for example, CIDA claimed that total official development assistance (ODA) totalled $1,277 million, its best year to that date. This amount is the cost of development assistance to the Canadian taxpayer — $220 per family.

Some of this money goes to pay Canadians to administer the aid budget at home and overseas. Although CIDA's administration budget ($30 million) is not included in the ODA total, some experts estimate that there is an additional administrative cost of $10 million hidden within the aid program.[50] Deduct $10 million from the 1977-78 aid allocation.

Next, allowance must be made for a major item in the CIDA figures peculiar to the 1977-78 fiscal year — the forgiveness of $232
million worth of debts owed by the Third World to Canada. While
this amount is registered as a contribution, it represents no new
aid giving. CIDA's debt forgiveness was an important gesture
towards the Third World's debt problem, but it cost the Canadian
economy nothing in 1977-78. It merely transformed loans extended
in previous years into grants; it increased the amount of earlier
grants and decreased the amount of earlier loans.[51] For gauging the
cost of aid to the economy, this one-time measure should be
removed from the 1977-78 calculations.

Table 4-X

Calculating the Real Cost of Aid to Canada's Economy
(fy 1977-78, millions of $)

1. Stated Official Development Assistance		$1,277
2. Deductions of amount spent in Canada:		
Hidden administration costs	$ 10	
Debt forgiveness	232	
Food Aid	232	
Debt payments received	4	
Non-grant element of loans	33	
Tied bilateral aid	331	
Canadian procurement under multilateral	159	
Other program spending in Canada	21	
	1,022	
3. Real Cost of Aid to Canada's Economy		$ 255

One of the largest elements of the remaining foreign aid allotment, accounting for almost a quarter of the total, is food aid. In
1977-78, CIDA spent $232 million to send Canadian agricultural
products to the Third World. These funds never left Canada. Wheat,
rapeseed, milk powder and other food products which Canadians
could neither eat nor sell commercially were bought up by CIDA and
shipped abroad. This $232 million represents a transfer payment
from the general taxpayer to Canada's rural economy. Because our
food aid more often than not is a way to dispose of surplus food, it is
not a real cost to Canada. The Pearson Report of 1969 explains:

If there is any reason to believe that goods devoted to foreign aid would
otherwise have gone to waste, their real cost to the supplier would be nil.
This may have been the case with some of the aid in the form of surplus
food.[52]

Deduct $232 million in food aid.

Although much of Canadian bilateral aid is provided in the form
of grants, about 40% is made up of loans. Loans have to be paid

back with interest, but since Canada's aid loans have been made at concessional terms (low or zero rates with a long pay-back period), CIDA's income from past loans was only $4 million in 1977-78. But this amount should be deducted from the stated disbursements. The real cost of current loans is only the difference between CIDA's concessional rates and the cost of money on commercial markets (i.e., what CIDA could be making by investing its loan funds commercially compared with its actual return on aid loans). According to CIDA publications, the level of concessionality of its loans in 1977-78 was about 85% of their face value. Thus, the amount extended in loans — $220 million — can be reduced by the 15% non-grant element.[53] Deduct $33 million more.

Next, most bilateral aid is tied to the purchase of Canadian goods and services. Once again, such aid never leaves the domestic economy. Pearson comments:

The fact that most bilateral aid is tied to purchases in the supplying country and helps to promote more production and exports, the real burden of aid must be less than the fact value of the resources which are transferred.[54]

In 1977-78, non-food bilateral aid amounted to about $414 million. According to a Treasury Board study, about four-fifths of this aid is still tied to procurement in Canada. Using this as a rule of thumb, deduct $331 million to allow for tied aid.

Of the remainder, $319 million is non-food multilateral aid. About two-thirds of this amount is in the form of loans or advances to multilateral institutions. Although it may not be expected that these funds will ever be paid back, they are still considered loans or assets on Canada's books and could be accordingly devalued. But let us generously treat all multilateral allocations as grants. By virtue of Canadian membership in international financial institutions such as the World Bank, Canadian enterprises can compete for contracts under the procurement processes of these agencies. According to one study of Canadian procurement from World Bank spending, Canadian companies win contracts worth over 50% of the amount of money CIDA contributes.[55] If this level is taken as a bench-mark — 50 cents on the dollar — of the return to the domestic economy from multilateral aid, then the stated value of that aid can be cut in half. Deduct another $159 million.

Finally, an allowance should be made for the portion of aid allocated to non-governmental organizations and special programs which stays in Canada. This includes the administration expenses and education costs of NGOs, some of the research of the IDRC, support to Canadian businesses through investment and export incentives, and Canadian products and services purchased by all these entities. While it is hard to put a concrete figure on the value of this spending in Canada, a ballpark portion of 25% of the special programs budget of CIDA might be a conservative approximation. And so another $21 million can be subtracted.

After all these calculations, the real cost of aid to the Canadian economy in the 1977-78 fiscal year was $255 million, or only 20% of the amount stated as Canada's contribution. The rest is theoretically a boon to our economy because, with both employment and production at less than maximum levels, the aid program does not compete for already-employed human and physical resources. Instead, with unemployment well over 7% and productive capacity underutilized during 1977 and 1978, the portion of foreign aid that stayed in Canada could be considered a stimulus to production, employment, profits, incomes and even government tax revenues. In fact, if the aid program did not exist, unemployment would be somewhat higher and the government would have to make higher payments for unemployment insurance and welfare.

But if aid is not a great cost to the Canadian economy, does it really generate significant domestic employment and other economic benefits? There is, after all, no shortage of critics who frequently question the contribution to the general welfare made by other government expenditures — including defence spending, debt repayments, and politicians' salaries to name but a few. In tying aid to Canadian economic needs are Canadians really developing themselves, or fooling themselves?

When the domestic impact of aid spending is analyzed, it immediately becomes apparent that aid has never been conscientiously applied to solve Canadian economic and social problems, and that it is a blunt, if not near-useless, instrument for such a job. Beyond generalities about economic stimulation, no CIDA official dares claim that the Agency makes careful use of aid to advance national objectives such as overcoming regional disparities, increasing employment in labour-intensive industries, supporting the diversification of the economy toward manufacturing, or developing research and technological capabilities. CIDA spending is simply not aimed at these targets — either because other programs can better address them, unencumbered by an overseas development mandate, or because the Agency as yet hasn't figured out how to do it, and justify it.

Instead, patterns of aid spending seem to fortify regional inequalities. According to a study prepared for the Economic Council of Canada by Carleton University economist Keith Hay, four-fifths of all capital goods procured by CIDA in 1974-75 came from Ontario and Quebec. And while food aid originates from the Prairies, and British Columbia contributes to commodity aid, the Atlantic provinces are virtually excluded. The four eastern provinces, supposedly the prime target for development programs within Canada, supplied only 2.2% of all goods procured under the tied portion of the 1974-75 aid budget.[56] The same pattern shows up in a review of all of CIDA's active contracts in February 1981; 75% of them were with companies based in industrial and financial centres of Quebec and Ontario.[57] Untying aid, in other words, would affect those regions most able to afford the loss.

CIDA's impact on employment is also greatly exaggerated. While Dupuy claimed that 100,000 jobs depended on the aid program, Professor Hay's independent study showed that it supported no more than ten to twenty thousand jobs annually. Most of these jobs would probably still exist without aid because, except for some manufactured products, Canadian goods are internationally competitive.[58]

Although it provides little relief to immediate domestic problems, aid is still supposed to excel in the fostering of medium- and long-term economic gain for Canada by expanding our exports. As former CIDA president Michel Dupuy boasted to the Empire Club in 1977:

The bilateral aid programs provide foreign markets for key Canadian industries and may sometimes represent a major source of contracts. . . . By establishing Canadian technology and expertise in the developing countries on whatever terms we grant them, we are laying the groundwork for repeat business and for expansion of Canadian trade in the future.[59]

Dupuy's claim is that aid's giveaway samples, or loss leaders, entice potential customers to make larger buys with hard cash. Canadian consultants are supported by aid because they act as promoters of Canadian exports in new markets, encouraging Third World states to purchase Canadian goods many times the cost of an aid-supported consultant.[60] CIDA's support for Canadian foreign investment in the Third World (through its Industrial Cooperation Program) is deemed positive for the Canadian economy since these investments will return profits from overseas. But foreign investments are also considered part of export promotion because "companies taking advantage of the program view it as a marketing tool whereby a branch facility is established in a developing country for final assembly, with key components coming from Canada."[61]

But the logic of CIDA's justification of its export objective is as flimsy as its results are ephemeral. Aid may boost exports today, but it's incapable of changing Canada's export future. One of the reasons is that aid-financed exporting is only a minute percentage of the whole. According to Conservative MP Douglas Roche, CIDA's tied aid represents only .23% of the Canadian GNP.[62] Aid-supported exports of goods and services through both bilateral and multilateral channels amount to only about one percent of our annual total exports. The tied aid impact on the overall Canadian trade picture is so small, according to the Economic Council of Canada, that "moving from the present level of bilateral aid-tying [about 85%] to a level as low as 40 per cent would not have a noticeable impact on the Canadian balance of payments."[63]

But the fundamental reason why aid can't generate long-term trade is explained by former CIDA president Maurice Strong. Interviewed on the CBC's *Fifth Estate* television program, Strong rejected Dupuy's claim that aid lays the groundwork for repeat trade. "That argument is not true in basic economic terms," he pointed out, "because you don't really open up markets by requiring people to buy things from you that they're not going to buy when they're free to choose for themselves."[64] If Canadian goods and services are uncompetitive internationally, they will only be taken by the Third World when given as aid. As the CIDA bureaucrat jokes, these Canadian goods are only fit to be tied. On the other hand, Canadian goods and services that are internationally competitive, and some certainly are, will be bought by the Third World at their own discretion. Aid should simply not be needed to introduce and sustain the sale of these goods to the Third World — unless, of course, Canadian entrepreneurs fail to do their hustling or prefer to pocket a government subsidy whether their product is competitive or not.

But to Canadian free enterprisers whose diatribes against Ottawa's lavish spending habits never cease, talk of subsidies is embarrassing. Business lobbies, like the Canadian Export Association, deny that they are the beneficiaries of subsidies and use a different vocabulary to justify tied aid as a necessary export promotion vehicle.[65] One argument is that recipient countries can go to any one of a variety of donors and that when they choose Canada they should expect to take Canadian products. But Third World countries do not have this range of options. The international aid scene, after all, is not characterized by a multiplicity of donors anxiously competing to aid a few poor nations; in fact, the reverse is true. A related argument is that Canadian assistance is only utilized in sectors where Canadian expertise and goods are internationally competitive. If this were the case it would be a good argument for untying, because again, tied-aid penetration of markets wouldn't be necessary.

Business executives also argue that Canada has to tie its assistance because other donors do it. If CIDA were to unilaterally untie aid, business representatives say, Canadian aid funds would be spent by recipients in western Europe, Japan and the United States instead of Canada; why should the Canadian taxpayer help expand the exports of Canada's commercial competitors?[66] As the most dogged defender of tied aid, the CEA accuses countries like France and Japan of using aid mixed with more commercial export financing to secure export deals that Canada can't match because Ottawa will not permit this kind of credit blending, or *credit mixte*, of CIDA and EDC funds.[67] Canada is already at a disadvantage in world trade because it is not a former colonial power, business leaders say, and releasing aid from its export promotion role would put us at a greater disadvantage.

This set of arguments is contradictory. Corporate executives are protesting that tied aid practised by Canada is not a subsidy to private enterprise, but *is* a subsidy when practised by other donors. When business admits that it would lose sales to other donors if Canadian aid was untied, it is also conceding that aid hasn't succeeded in establishing permanent export markets. Tied aid is portrayed not as a positive vehicle for export promotion, but as a defensive measure to prevent Canada from losing out in the cutthroat export subsidy war now raging among donor nations. This is a kind of competition not only far removed from development goals but even at loggerheads with them. It provides no net benefit to Third World countries because the other side of the donors' export subsidy competition is their increasing use of trade protectionism which excludes Third World exports from donor markets. In trade wars, the weakest nations invariably lose. Donor competition in aid subsidies for exports appears to offer underdeveloped countries greater choice among northern suppliers, but it's a choice restricted to only a few southern countries and selected northern inputs that donors are desperate to sell — not what Third World countries most need for development. Unilateral untying of Canadian aid might mean that more Canadian assistance would be spent in other industrialized countries — unless untied Canadian aid were directed where it should be in the first place: toward the kind of grassroots-oriented, self-reliant, local spending projects which don't require northern inputs. Such aid wouldn't be an export subsidy but, to salve the worries of business leaders, neither would Canada be taken advantage of by other donors.

Whatever their arguments, Canadian private exporters are unable to prove tying aid is an irreplaceable and successful way to introduce Canadian goods and services into unfamiliar markets and thereby build long-term trade relationships. Businessmen like J.H. Whelan, who doubles as Chairman of the CEA and of the International Paper Sales Company, usually rely on selected anecdotes to sell their case. Addressing the House of Commons Task Force on North-South Relations in late 1980, Whelan cited the case of how his own industry broke into India's market for newsprint because of the introduction of the Canadian product through several years of newsprint aid grants from CIDA. But when MP Doug Roche challenged the CEA to back up its strongly pro-export position with more than anecdotes, Whelan was unable to supply concrete data. After asking no less than seven times for evidence to support the CEA brief, Roche finally secured a frank answer. "We have no published evidence in this area," the CEA conceded.[68]

As a result, journalists like the *Financial Post*'s Sheldon Gordon dismiss the business arguments and conclude that the foreign aid program is "Ottawa's costliest subsidy to Canadian private enterprise."[69] And this subsidy accrues not to the Canadian economy as a whole but to a small group of private companies. A still classified Treasury Board study on aid tying, using the sample year of 1974-75, provides a fascinating profile of who benefits from tied aid.[70]

Canada's bilateral aid program in the 1974-75 fiscal year totalled $496 million, of which 80.8% was tied, 10.8% untied, and 8.4% allocated to cover transportation costs. Predictably, tied aid procurement of goods and services — food and commodities from the western provinces, consultants and manufactured goods from Ontario and Quebec — reflected the distribution of economic activity in Canada and thus did not correct or reduce regional disparities or regional economic inequalities. Exports of Canadian equipment under tied aid, the type of manufactured goods most frequently the subject of Ottawa's export promotion schemes, totalled $94.5 million and the Treasury Board estimated that the tying cost to recipients of these equipment supplies, as well as consultant services, was about 25% of their value.

According to the study, a mere 23 firms accounted for over 60% of these equipment shipments under tied aid. (See Table 4-XI.) All but two of these equipment-makers were located in Quebec and Ontario. Most of them were among the largest 400 corporations in Canada. And over half of them were Canadian subsidiaries of foreign parent firms — begging the question whether aid helps "Canadian" companies as much as it bloats the balance sheets of foreign multinationals.

Because more than half of these 23 firms were less than optimally competitive in international markets, the Treasury Board concluded that tied aid — while not a significant tool for breaking into limited market nations where Canadian aid is directed — was of some importance to a small number of large enterprises. For example, one of these companies, the Montreal-based locomotives maker Bombardier Inc. (formerly MLW Worthington), was listed by the Treasury Board as only moderately competitive. Bombardier's vice-president, Henry Valle (who is also the chairman of the CEA's Development Aid Committee), told the *Fifth Estate* in 1978 that the company would find it very difficult to survive without help from CIDA because "CIDA's business over the last eight or nine years has probably represented maybe one-third of our business."[71]

But an alternative source of export financing was available for Bombardier as for other companies on the select list of manufacturers benefitting from aid. While CIDA provided $58 million to the top 23 suppliers during 1974-75, seven of the same companies won

Table 4-XI

Principal Suppliers of Equipment Goods Under Tied Aid Procurement, 1974-75

Company	Cdn Headquarters	Nationality of Ownership
Alcan Aluminium Ltd.	Que	Cdn/US
Allis Chalmer Corp.	Que	US
ASEA Ltd.	Que	W. European
Canadian General Electric Co.	Ont	US
Canadian Ingersoll-Rand Co.	Que	US
Canadian Mannex Corp.	Ont	W. Germany
Canron Ltd.	Ont	Cdn
de Havilland Aircraft Ltd.	Ont	Cdn
Dominion Road Machinery Co.*	Ont	Cdn
Dynamic Industries Inc.	Que	Cdn
E.B. Eddy	Ont	Cdn
General Manufacturing Co.	Que	Cdn
GTE Lenkurt	B.C.	US
Hawker-Siddeley Canada Ltd.	Ont	UK
International Harvester Co.	Ont	US
MLW Worthington Ltd.**	Que	Cdn
Northern Telecom	Que	Cdn
Pirelli Cables Ltd.	Que	Switz.
Raytheon Canada Ltd.	Ont	US
RCA Ltd.	Ont	US
Royal Mint	Ont	Cdn
Versatile Manufacturing	Man	Cdn
Westinghouse Canada Ltd.	Ont	US

* Name changed in 1977 to Champion Road Machinery Ltd.
** Name changed in 1976 to Bombardier-MLW Ltd., and currently known as Bombardier Inc.

Sources: Government of Canada, Treasury Board, "l'étude sur les effets de délier à la source et sans restrictions le programme canadien d'aide bilatérale, 1975". Financial Post, **Survey of Industrials** (various years). Statistics Canada, **Inter-Corporate Ownership 1975.**

export orders abroad with the help of $215 million in export financing courtesy of the Crown-owned Export Development Corporation (EDC).[72] In other words, if Canadian-made products are internationally competitive and commercially desired by Third World nations, there are other vehicles more appropriately designed for export financing than the aid program.

The conclusions of the Treasury Board study suggest why the government has been hiding it from public scrutiny. On the export front, aid shows itself to be not only a small and ineffective tool for trade promotion but also a replaceable form of export subsidy benefitting a very small number of favoured firms. It is hard to understand why national business lobbies representing thousands of companies that aren't aided by aid so vehemently resist even the most modest proposals for untying. One explanation, of course, is the private sector's unconcealed appetite for state subsidies that come their way — grab and gobble up whatever you can get.

But it also appears that the small number of companies which do benefit from the taxpayer's largesse toward the Third World are able to mobilize the corporate solidarity of their free enterprise colleagues in lobbying the federal government. Most Canadian enterprises of any size are members of one or more business associations or lobby groups. To coordinate lobbying approaches to international business matters, Canadian companies set up an umbrella group in 1977, the Canadian Business and Industry International Advisory Committee (CBIIAC), whose members include the most important and strongest business associations concerned with foreign trade (the Canadian Association-Latin America and the Caribbean, the Canadian Chamber of Commerce, the Canadian Committee of the International Chamber of Commerce, the Canadian Committee of the Pacific Basin Economic Council, the Canadian Export Association, and the Canadian Manufacturing Association).[73]

As individual companies, or as members of business associations, the business sector regularly converges on Ottawa to press its views. With their substantial financial and professional resources, businessmen can mount lobbies in a variety of ways: they serve on government advisory boards and task forces; many of their associations have yearly consultations with the federal Cabinet; they often are requested to comment on proposed legislation; they present briefs to parliamentary committees; they have both informal and formal links with the bureaucracy (such as the CEA's twice yearly meetings with the President of CIDA); and many have the resources to employ full-time government relations officers (lobbyists).

When business presses Ottawa on the aid theme it argues that without corporate support — meaning if aid was untied from its export function — the whole aid program, not just tied aid, would be in jeopardy of losing its political support.[74] Such an argument is not supported by public opinion polls showing that the vast majority of Canadians feel aid should be given for reasons other than Canada's economic benefit.[75] But the large corporations, as Prime Minister Trudeau once remarked, are among the vested interests "whose voice is louder than others" in the Canadian democracy.[76] Elections, after all, are not fought and governments are not turned out over the issue of foreign aid. So, despite the unrepresentivity of its views, business holds the whole aid program hostage to the export promotion shibboleth.

But federal policy makers are not just cajoled by business. They also fervently share the business belief that exports must expand if Canada is to prosper. Private corporations are the lead actors in their export-led economic strategy, and the aid program is one of several supporting roles played by the state. This is a weak drama, however, not only because the actors are unconvincing in their parts but also because the central plot doesn't work.

The historical development of Canada's political economy has set a difficult scene for Ottawa's economic policy scriptwriters. Since the end of World War II, the federal government has depended on two major engines to propel the national economy: export trade and foreign investment. As a result, Canada's economy today is one of the most dependent in the world, more vulnerable to the buffetings of the international marketplace than any other industrialized country and even more so than many Third World nations.[77] Twenty-seven percent of our total output of goods and services is exported to other nations; or, expressed another way, we sell abroad over three-quarters of the Gross National Product originating in the goods-producing sector. Over two-thirds of this trade is with a single trade partner — the United States.

Meanwhile, foreign investment in Canada, also primarily from the United States, has made us the host of more foreign investment capital than any other single nation in the world. By the end of 1977, foreign corporations owned $47 billion worth of Canadian investments or just over one-third of all of Canada's non-financial industries. In acquiring this control, these corporations have been instrumental in shaping and defining the nature of the Canadian economy. Viewing Canada as a resource colony, a supplier of raw materials and a consumer of finished products, our absentee landlords have oriented the economy disproportionately toward the production and export of raw materials and semi-processed resources — what Ottawa bureaucrats call "rocks and logs" — and away from the development of a mature manufacturing sector.

In the manufacturing sector, where non-residents control about 55% of all capital employed, the foreign transnationals have ordained that their subsidiary branch plants shall produce only, or essentially, for the domestic market, leaving international sales to other, more profitable, or home-based subsidiaries. Consequently, Canada traditionally registers a trade surplus in agricultural commodities, raw materials and semi-processed goods due to a small list of products we are eminently good at producing for export (forest products, minerals and grains). But at the same time, we record large deficits in trade in finished products — $16 billion in 1980. Manufactured goods that are imported instead of fabricated at home represent the foregoing of employment for an estimated 200,000 Canadians. And the problem is getting worse. The Science Council of Canada reported in a 1979 study that Canada's share of world trade in manufactures is steadily falling and that "in terms of trade and employment trends, Canada seems to be in a process of de-industrialization."[78]

Meanwhile, there are also serious problems in Canada's service trade account which tabulates payments and receipts for services such as travel, interest payments, profit remittances, royalties and transportation costs. For most of the past decade, Canada's traditional deficit on the service trade account has grown faster than our surplus in merchandise trade. By 1980, this net service trade deficit reached $10.7 billion. Of this amount fully half was due to the outflow of capital to pay interest charges on our foreign debt (Canada's net external debt in 1980 was about $73 billion, or about $12,000 per Canadian family) and to pay dividends to the parent companies of Canadian-based subsidiaries. When our surplus in trade in goods is combined with this deficit in trade in services, the result is a significant and recurring current account deficit — a red flag on Canada's international financial ledger or balance of payments. [79]

These problems in the Canadian balance of payments ledger are strikingly similar to those experienced by many Third World countries. So are Ottawa's responses. Two possible solutions — the attraction of more foreign investment capital and borrowing more abroad — are currently being pursued by Ottawa but with some (though not enough) reservation. Both put the nation's economy on a dangerous treadmill. They are short-term remedies which require the later payment of interest, amortization, and dividends for each dollar received today. Such measures deepen Canada's indebtedness and with it our dependency on the owners of foreign capital.

The other way Ottawa hopes to solve the balance of payments dilemma — or at least keep the wolves from the door — is the export-led growth strategy. An export imperative now permeates much of Ottawa's fiscal, monetary and industrial policy as well as foreign policy, and of course, aid giving. Federal policy makers set their export strategy sights at 1) reducing the current account deficit by increasing exports of all kinds; 2) diversifying the country's trade dependency on the US by promoting exports to western Europe, Japan and the Third World — the so-called "third option"* — and 3) supporting the growth of selected export-oriented manufacturing industries in order to reduce the trade deficit in these products.

This proposed solution is both flawed and misguided. Because of the structure of the Canadian economy, the export drive is notably successful only in the sale of raw materials and semi-processed resources. This runs the risk of perpetuating our national economic status as "hewers of wood and drawers of water" while depleting our non-renewable resources, continuing technological dependency and providing less than optimal job-creation based on our natural resource heritage.

Relying on export-led growth also bypasses the structural problems at the core of the Canadian political economy. As long as for-

* The options, as set forth by External Affairs Minister Mitchell Sharp in 1972, were (a) ultimate absorption by the US, (b) maintaining the status quo, and (c) the third option, aggressively diversifying and deepening Canada's trade ties outside of North America.

eign control of the economy continues to expand, each increase in Canadian merchandise export surpluses will be cancelled out by the ever increasing outflow of interest and dividend payments related to foreign investments. And, as we have already seen, the tools that Ottawa is wielding to promote exports often benefit foreign-owned subsidiaries in Canada, thus reinforcing one of the problems at the root of our trade imbalances.[80]

No amount of export boosterism will diversify trade away from the United States or correct the current account deficit as long as US-based corporations continue to expand their ownership of Canadian assets. Two-thirds of all Canadian exports are accounted for by a mere 173 firms, many of them US-owned, and some 40% of all Canada-US trade is really intra-company exchanges between US parent companies and their Canadian subsidiaries.[81] Canada's trade patterns thus reflect patterns of foreign investment. The fallacy in trying to expand and improve the content of "Canadian" exports is that so much of our trade is regulated by foreign transnationals. And these transnationals have the ability to utilize Ottawa's export promotion subsidies in opportunistic ways. According to the *Financial Post*, federal trade officials are frustrated by foreign-owned subsidiaries that will export only when Ottawa offers special export financing or assistance from the Export Development Corporation or CIDA.[82] But no amount of subsidization is going to generate longer-term export capability as long as the marching orders of foreign headquarters forbid it.[83]

Because of these fundamentals, the "third option" has failed to diversify Canadian trade patterns. Throughout the seventies, the share of total Canadian trade accounted for by Canada-US exchanges remained the same.[84] If anything, the third option just prevented it from growing larger.

Canadian aid undoubtedly accounts for an important portion of each year's exports to some aid recipients; for a handful of Third World countries, aid-funded exports are virtually the only Canadian goods they import. From the policy maker's point of view, aid may not be an effective promoter of permanent trade but it sustains a visible Canadian presence in foreign markets and an unfounded but everlasting hope for major trade breakthroughs.

Comparing the Treasury Board's figures for Canadian goods exported under tied aid with total 1975 exports to most aid recipients, aid-financed goods exports accounted for less than 20% of total exports. More specifically, Canadian exports of finished products under the aid program accounted for only 7.5% of all such exports to the Third World — or less than 1% to all world markets.[85] And in the wider picture, all categories of Canadian exports to the Third World account for only 8% of Canada's world trade compared to 34% of US exports, 17% for the European Economic Community, and 46% for Japan.[86]

If Canada is to climb out of its balance of payments hold, Ottawa must obviously focus its attention on the primary, not the peripheral, issues. At the heart of the matter is the dominant Canada-US trade relationship and the fundamental problem of foreign economic domination. Using foreign aid to attempt to repair the effects of Canada's economic dependency shifts some of the burden of these problems, through the vehicle of costly and inappropriate tied aid, to underdeveloped countries. It's an attempt to transfer not real assistance, but part of our own maldevelopment. In doing so the tied aid band-aid can also harm the donor because, as the Pearson Report noted, "foreign trade patterns are distorted, markets disrupted and inefficient industries bolstered. A country's own reputation for competitiveness is undermined by its resort to tying."[87]

Getting at the heart of the matter also means questioning the efficacy of export-led models of development. The prevailing wisdom of Ottawa policy-makers, as Marcel Masse explained to Toronto's Canadian Club, is that "trade has been the engine of growth for Canada and must become so for the developing countries."[88] Export-led models are similarly the current fashion in underdeveloped countries, adopted because of critical debt problems and the aggressive advertising of the export elixir by northern nations eager for more trade with the South to overcome their own economic malaise.

But relying on trade to bring development is like betting on a game of chance you know is rigged against you with the weekly household funds. It means relying on a system of unequal international exchange set up and regulated by the largest economic powers to their own advantage. It means structuring the national economy to serve international demand instead of national priorities. The nations of western Europe, the United States, Japan, the USSR and China, in contrast, all got development to take hold in their economies by meeting domestic needs first and later expanding into international trade and investment to sustain growth. Both Canada and Third World nations should ponder long on this historical experience before equating the achievement of export targets, instead of the fulfillment of basic human needs and domestic priorities, with development.

Ottawa, however, does not appear ready to explore self-reliant models of development or to confront Canada's central problems of structured dependency. If the aid program is any measure, our federal policy makers are now more than ever committed to pursuing export-led growth by expanding subsidies to private corporations. Recent program innovations and policy trends at CIDA are direct responses to the current agenda of the business community.

Several recent reports and briefs to government by corporate executives and their business associations detail what the private sector wants out of foreign policy and the aid program in the eighties.[89] Representative of their position is the 1979 report of the Export Promotion Review Committee (the Hatch Report), a grouping of senior business leaders set up by the Department of Industry, Trade and Commerce to recommend changes in government export promotion and support services. Arguing that state subsidies and supports are now "an integral element of export financing", and chiding CIDA for taking an "overly philanthropic giveaway approach to aid", the report says "aid policy should be more closely integrated with Canada's trade strategy." Among the specific recommendations suggested by this report and other business briefs are the following:

• the amount of aid sent to multilateral institutions should be reduced as Canadian firms are unable to win sufficient contracts for multilateral aid projects;

• an increasing percentage of aid should be channelled on a bilateral basis;

• less bilateral aid should go to the poorest countries because they "are too undeveloped for much meaningful trade to result." Instead, CIDA should concentrate on fewer countries, especially the newly industrializing countries (or NICs in development parlance) or middle income countries "with whom there is trade potential";

• CIDA should expand its practice of offering parallel financing for projects supported by the Export Development Corporation. The EDC itself should provide more competitive financing, including the type of *credit mixte* practised by other industrialized countries;

• CIDA programs for promoting commercial sales and private investments in the Third World (the Industrial Cooperation Program) should be applauded and expanded.

External Affairs Minister Mark MacGuigan was quick to respond to this business overture. In a mid-1980 speech, he signalled to the business community that in the arena of international relations, the ship of state would work more closely with them:

It is the role of the private sector to inject life and substance into economic relationships, and for this reason the Canadian government is encouraging a more explicit role for businessmen and business associations in shaping relationships and in influencing the form and conduct of foreign policy.[90]

Later, in early 1981, MacGuigan unveiled his first contribution to Canadian foreign policy — a copy, like much of his foreign affairs captaincy, of thrusts of the Reagan Administration in the US — "bilateralism".[91] Canada's commercial and political relationships with other countries, MacGuigan announced, will be concentrated on bilateral links with a selected number of countries. Applied to the

Third World, bilateralism gives business its wish by establishing priority relationships with NICs such as Mexico, Brazil, Venezuela, South Korea, Singapore, Indonesia, Nigeria and others.

CIDA is now working through the implications of this bilateralist foreign policy. Already Canadian aid officials privately talk of reducing the multilateral share of the Agency's budget to less than 20% of total non-food aid from the 35-40% level it achieved in recent years.[92] MacGuigan still remains committed, however, to the "use of multilateral instruments to try to ensure the stability and growth of the world", and so a dramatic drop in multilateral involvement should not be expected.[93]

In response to the private sector's pressure to send more aid to the NICs, CIDA is expanding or creating new programs to aid corporate involvement in these countries rather than shifting bilateral disbursements away from the poorest.[94] Already, the Agency has announced the doubling of its Industrial Cooperation division budget from $9 million in the 1980-81 fiscal year to $18 million for 1981-82.[95] The division has also unveiled a new facility to help Canadian consultants win contracts for major capital investment schemes overseas, another new program to assist Canadian manufacturers in adapting their technology for sale to the Third World, and Marcel Masse says he has several other schemes in the works to help the private sector.[96]

Masse has expressed interest in directing more bilateral aid money towards social projects which could be implemented and administered by non-governmental organizations, a move designed to get around CIDA's staffing limitations and its incompetency in these fields.[97] For NGOs the availability of bilateral money is tempting, but the concept threatens to debase NGO development objectives and make them appendages of the state. For CIDA, however, the idea is a convenient way to improve the Agency's "soft" image while continuing support for traditional infrastructure projects under the bilateral division and constructing hard-nosed export and investment programs in other divisions.

But for the business community, these sops are not enough. The private sector's government voicepiece, the Department of Industry, Trade and Commerce, wants a bigger share of the bilateral budget to promote trade with the NICs. Trade Minister Herb Gray told the Parliamentary Task Force on North-South Relations in late 1980 that his department generally favours "deployment of our own limited foreign-aid resources to a greater extent than is currently the case into product and market areas which can lead to increased business for Canadian manufacturers."[98]

Meanwhile, business has won concessions on other aid-related fronts. In January of 1981, the Department of Industry, Trade and Commerce announced the initiation of a *credit mixte* facility, whereby the EDC will offer loans at concessional rates, subsidized by the government, to match those offered by other industrialized nations to Third World buyers. Although this $900 million subsidization program does not directly affect CIDA's budget, the portion of the EDC's financing under its *credit mixte* facility, when applied to countries on CIDA's list of aid recipients, will count as part of Canada's official development assistance contribution.[99] Similarly, countries' search for oil with the help of Petro-Canada International (and other Canadian suppliers and consultants) will be chalked up as ODA.[100] In other words, a significant portion of MacGuigan's promised increase in ODA over the next decade will be accounted for by export and investment promotion programs directed by business-oriented arms of the government that are unrestricted by mandates to develop Third World countries.

The federal government's regular capitulation to business pressures can be explained as an expression of the nature of the state in the Canadian political economy. The state (not just Parliament but all parts of the government and its dependent agencies and institutions) acts to mediate the conflicting interests of different social classes in such a way as to ensure the continuation of existing class relations of power.[101] This doesn't mean that the state satisfies every whim of the dominant business class — the system is more complicated. In Canada, the role of the state is particularly complicated by the fact that the dominant corporate class is not Canadian, but foreign, largely American. But by helping private enterprise accumulate, by containing or resolving social conflicts, by granting the system as a whole a mantle of legitimacy, the state works for the general political and economic interests of this dominant class. It's not so much that business bosses the government, but as Douglas Roche puts it, that "a business ethic forms the basis of government decisions."[102]

Within the context of the largely US-defined interests of the West, Canadian aid giving was initiated as an anti-communist weapon in the Cold War. It continued as an established pattern of international relations, providing a mechanism through which Canada could gain prestige and influence. But as the size of the aid program grew, and because national and international economic problems caused the needs of Canadian-based corporations to increase, CIDA has been increasingly pressured towards the promotion of Canadian exports and therefore the accumulation of private profits.

Some aspects of the aid program, however, are defined by the political needs of the state itself, by its long-range assessment of the needs of the status quo, by other national and international interests, and even by the philanthropic nudges of the Canadian public. In its efforts to juggle these interests an agency like CIDA maintains a mix of programs with, it hopes, something for everyone. From time to time, the Agency will even entertain reforms and publicly ponder its purposes and goals. This helps sustain its legitimacy, as does the Agency's perpetuation of the blatant hypocrisy of calling subsidies to private exports, development assistance.

But, tied to the Canadian state's leash, CIDA remains most loyal to its big business master. And the master knows that CIDA's business is not so much "development", as the development of business.

Food Aid:

Blessed Are the

5   Givers

When the Allied forces liberated Nazi concentration camps at the end of World War II, they were unprepared for the discovery that awaited them. There, in an emaciated state, they found thousands of people in the last stages of starvation. Allied medical teams did not know what to do. It took time and the sacrifice of many lives to learn that the best nourishment for such cases was a diet of skim milk. The civilization that could split the atom had only begun to learn about human hunger.[1]

We're still learning. The difference today is that the sight of human hunger is no longer unfamiliar. When twenty million people died in India during the last thirty years of the nineteenth century, few people in the West were even aware of the disaster. But television has brought the spectacle of famine and death into the daily lives of North Americans and Europeans. It has hit us squarely in the gut with images of bloated bellies and protruding ribs. Massive global hunger has been engendered by natural disasters, economic exploitation and political repression.

But the West is better at pulling together reports on starvation than at developing solutions. Food aid has been the primary response of western countries to famine in McLuhan's electronic age of the "global village". Canada alone has shipped over $2 billion worth of food to the Third World, fully one-fifth of all the aid ever provided by CIDA and its predecessors. But after three decades of

massive food transfusions, there are still 70 million seriously malnourished and perhaps another 500 million chronically hungry people in the world today. Food aid is the most dramatic failure among
our aid programs.

Canada's Tutor

The pre-eminent practitioner of self-interest in food aid, and Canada's natural tutor in the subject, is the United States. If food aid has
a bad name today it is largely because of Washington's use of food
transfers to promote its own foreign policy objectives.

Shortly after World War I, soon-to-be-president Herbert Hoover
directed a food relief program developed to support anti-communist
movements in eastern Europe. Food aid, reasoned Hoover, could
effectively combat the spread of communism at a far lower price
than costly military invasions.[2] A quarter of a century later the practice and thinking were much the same. In the aftermath of World
War II, Washington shipped large quantities of foodstuffs to fascist
forces in Greece, to Chiang Kai-shek fighting Mao's liberation army
in China, and to Italy and France in an effort to woo voters away
from their increasingly leftward tendencies and to undercut trade
union militancy. "Food is a vital factor in our foreign policy,"
explained Secretary of State George Marshall to justify the massive
food consignments sent to Europe as components of the Marshall
Plan of post-war reconstruction.[3]

In 1951, India's request for US grain to stave off famine alerted
Washington to new uses for food aid. The US agreed to India's
emergency request on the condition that it relax its embargo on the
export of thorium, an element essential to American nuclear energy
production. India capitulated and the US grain was shipped.

Washington formalized its ad hoc food giving with the 1954 pas-
sage of the Agricultural Trade Development Assistance Act, more
commonly known as PL 480. With barely a mention of altruistic
goals, the act commandeered food aid for the service of American
"national security" objectives. It would be used to secure supplies
of strategic raw materials. It would dispose of price-depressing
surpluses of American food products and keep farm incomes and
agribusiness profits high and stable. It would expand US agricultural trade, create new markets and function as a vehicle for pursuit
of political objectives. Despite its avowedly self-serving goals, the PL
480 program was deceitfully dubbed "Food for Peace".[4]

Since its inception, PL 480 has sold or donated over $25 billion
worth of US food products. By offering concessional food aid to its
allies, denying it to "unfriendly" governments, and threatening
poor non-aligned nations with a boycott if they behave badly, Washington has wielded PL 480 as an effective foreign policy tool to keep

nations and regions within the US sphere of influence. As Senator Hubert Humphrey explained in 1957:

... if you are looking for a way to get people to lean on you and to be dependent on you, in terms of their cooperation with you, it seems to me that food dependence would be terrific.[5]

Food dependence means using food as a weapon. In 1974, for example, the United States told Bangladesh that it would not be eligible for any more food aid until it stopped exporting locally-made gunny sacks to Cuba. Suffering one of its worse famines, Bangladesh succumbed, cut its Cuba ties and "qualified".[6] When Chile elected a socialist government in 1970, Washington cut off its traditional food transfer program. It even refused to accept hard cash from Chile for food. But after the military mounted a bloody coup d'etat in 1973, food-laden ships immediately set out to aid the new right-wing regime of General Pinochet. By 1975, Chile's junta was receiving more food aid than the rest of Latin America combined.

The deployment of food aid in Vietnam shows its military applications. In 1973, almost half of all PL 480 food went to Cambodia (now Kampuchea) and South Vietnam. The latter received twenty times more than the five African countries most seriously affected by drought. The following year, South Vietnam and Cambodia absorbed $499 million in US food credits while famine-stricken Bangladesh (even after its gunny sack submission) got only $41 million. Part of the PL 480 program allowed the regime in South Vietnam to resell food aid locally and use the funds for other expenditures, including military hardware. The military use of these "counterpart" funds became important when Congress restricted appropriations for direct military aid to the Thieu regime. The State Department was able to use the food aid mechanism to get around the legislators and increase support for South Vietnam. Understandably the Pentagon expressed unbridled enthusiasm throughout the war years for food aid to South Vietnam, Cambodia and South Korea. So goes the transformation of butter into bullets. Between 1946 and 1975, the resale of US food aid in the Third World contributed a whopping $6 billion in local currencies to the military ambitions of consistently repressive and elitist governments.

Charity Begins at Home

Just as our foreign policy follows an American lead, the use of Canadian food aid has been generally consonant with US strategies to reward friends, punish enemies and court those in between.[7] Unlike the American plan, however, Canada's food aid program has never been so integrally part of specific foreign policy ambitions. But Canada has completely copied US practice in its adoption of food aid as a means of "surplus disposal" for the benefit of the domestic economy.

Canada first ventured into food aid in 1951 — the same year Washington was arranging its thorium deal — with a $10 million shipment of Canadian wheat to India under the Colombo Plan. The hope was that hungry men would listen to those with bread — forgetting, for a moment at least, that most Asians prefer rice and that hungry men also listen to revolutionaries.

Looking back on that first wheat shipment, CIDA today confesses that "Canadians' humanitarian response to the needs of Asian development was eased by large agricultural surplus."[8] In fact, food aid could not have been discovered at a better time. Food production was on the rise in North America while markets were declining in Europe as those economies recovered from the war. Both factors contributed to Canada's "large agricultural surplus".

Enthusiasm for food aid soared after the 1957 election of John Diefenbaker, a leader deeply committed to the fortunes of western agriculture. The new Conservative government immediately boosted aid allocations for foodstuffs from the $645,000 spent during the last year of the St. Laurent government (1.9% of the total bilateral aid budget) to $5 million (29.6% of bilateral spending). By 1959, food aid disbursements totalled $12.5 million.

Diefenbaker had no qualms about demanding help from the supposed beneficiaries of Canadian largesse. When the Prime Minister toured the Asian Commonwealth in 1958, a Lahore newspaper, *The Civil and Military Gazette*, reported his perspective on the Canadian quandary:

In view of the fact that we have in Canada a tremendous surplus of wheat, we would naturally hope, if not expect, that these countries would take a large share of wheat and flour under the Colombo Plan. It is our hope that in the next few years a substantial portion of our contribution will be made up of wheat.[9]

According to the *Gazette*, Diefenbaker also "took the view that the Asian countries, as fellow Commonwealth members, should be willing to help Canada's problems as well as their own."

But two of the recipients, India and Pakistan, didn't share the Prime Minister's view of Commonwealth solidarity. They noted that, since the United States consolidated its food aid program in 1954, the Canadian package had lost some of its attractiveness. The US paid all or part of the shipping charges for its food aid while recipients of Canadian food had to use their own foreign exchange savings to pay freight costs. Even though Canadian food aid was given as a grant rather than a loan for food purchase, it proved more costly to the recipients in terms of precious foreign exchange. In these circumstances, Canada's insistence on allocating development funds to food aid "caused the Indian and Pakistani governments to react privately with dismay and resentment."[10]

In 1963, the new Liberal government made some cosmetic adjustments to Diefenbaker's enlarged food aid program. Minister of Trade and Commerce Mitchell Sharp promised in July of that year that expenditures for food transfers would rise quickly to $40 million annually. Obliquely acknowledging that food aid doesn't really advance Third World development, Sharp announced that future food appropriations would be considered distinct from development assistance programs. Two and a half months later, however, Sharp was retreating from his food aid pledges. In the interim, large quantities of wheat had been sold to the Soviet Union. The Minister speculated that "It might take a little longer to build up to the $40 million which was mentioned." The idea of removing food aid from total development assistance figures was conveniently forgotten and foodstuffs continue to bloat the real value of Canadian foreign aid.

The $40 million target was finally reached in the 1966-67 fiscal year when famine once again swept through India. In the following years, food aid commitments continued to grow until in 1971 CIDA could boast that it was the main cash customer of the Canadian Wheat Board. Throughout the 1970s, CIDA supplied almost 10% of all food aid in the forms of cereals received by underdeveloped countries. CIDA's food aid disbursements peaked at $237.51 million during the 1976-77 fiscal year; 63% of the total went through bilateral channels and the rest through multilateral plans such as the UN World Food Program. (See Table 5-XII.)

Table 5-XII
Canada's Food Aid Disbursements, 1971-1980

fiscal year ending March 31	Total Food Aid* ($ millions)	Food Aid as Percentage of Total ODA
1971	104.16	30%
1972	80.50	20%
1973	112.41	22%
1974	115.21	20%
1975	174.57	23%
1976	222.54	25%
1977	237.51	25%
1978	232.52	22%
1979	194.44	17%
1980	187.71	15%
Total 1971-1980	1,661.57	21%

* Bilateral and Multilateral included.

Sources: CIDA, **Annual Reports**, (various years); CIDA, **Strategy for International Development Cooperation 1975-1980**, (Ottawa, 1975).

Wheat Aid — Taking A Backseat to the Marketplace

Wheat and wheat products make up most of Canada's food aid packages. The disposition of this commodity, in the marketplace and in government policy during the early seventies, clearly demonstrated that food aid takes a backseat to commercial food exports. Throughout the last two decades, Canada has been an important producer and even more important exporter of wheat. Canadian wheat farmers produce about 10% of world output and account for more than 20% of world wheat trade. In some years, the figure is as high as 40%. Together, the United States and Canada control a larger share of the world's exportable surplus of grains than the Middle East does of world oil exports.

But by the mid-1960s, competition between the two North American neighbours for international commercial wheat sales had created problems. Using sophisticated farming techniques and machinery, both had been increasing output steadily since World War II. By the mid-sixties, their carry-over surpluses (reserves in storage at the time new crops begin to come in) were rising without a parallel expansion of markets.

Then in 1966, Washington adopted a more aggressive sales strategy to correct growing trade deficits. The following year, the International Grains Agreement collapsed and Canada joined the US, France and Australia in a wheat price war. American inroads into traditional Canadian wheat markets in Europe pushed Canadian inventories up to an all-time high of 1,008 million bushels in 1971.

Throughout the 1960s, with wheat in surplus, demand slack and prices depressed, both US and Canadian food aid programs unloaded large quantities of the grain in the Third World. The wheat-centred PL 480 program regularly absorbed between 25 and 30% of total US agricultural exports. In Canada, food aid shipments of wheat accounted for 10% of all wheat exports by the end of the decade.

But after 1971 the trends were reversed. The soft market turned rigid. Carry-over stocks fell dramatically. International wheat prices skyrocketed. As a direct result, PL 480 food aid was cut back to only 4% of agricultural exports by 1973. Between 1971 and 1973, Canadian wheat food aid was cut in half. In the midst of these apparent vagaries of the free market and vacillations of food aid programs, arose the spectre of massive starvation in the Third World — the "food crisis".[11]

What had happened? At the highpoint of Canadian surplus stocks of wheat in 1971, Ottawa applied a traditional economic instrument, "supply management", to protect the incomes of Canadian producers. The Lower Inventories for Tomorrow (LIFT) program was created. Analogous to the 1930s practice of paying farmers not to grow certain products, LIFT aimed to reduce wheat acreage with the expectation that lower future production would tighten the oversupply situation and raise prices. Washington had adopted similar agricultural management policies earlier.

As LIFT reduced wheat production and markets improved, surpluses declined and consequently food aid shipments felt the impact. Between 1971 and 1972, Canadian food aid in wheat, flour and semolina decreased by 15% in volume.[12] The next year, as more North American cropland was taken out of wheat production, the Soviet Union made a massive purchase of American wheat. International markets suddenly tightened. Weather-inflicted damage to harvests in other countries further closed the vise. World stocks of

Table 5-XIII

The Relationship of Wheat Stocks, Exports and Food Aid, 1968-1976

Year	Carry-over stocks of wheat in Canada* (000's of bushels)	Total exports of wheat and flour** (000's of tonnes)	Food aid in wheat, flour and semolina (000's of tonnes)	Wheat, flour & semolina food aid expressed as percentage of exports
1968-69	672,510	8,322	785	9.4%
1969-70	851,828	9,430	834	8.8%
1970-71	1,008,690	11,844	1,254	10.6%
1971-72	734,154	13,714	1,051	7.6%
1972-73	583,757	15,693	657	4.1%
1973-74	365,401	11,414	606	5.3%
1974-75	370,704	10,728	560	5.2%
1975-76	288,114†	NA	NA	NA

† preliminary data
* carry-over stocks are calculated by calendar year
** exports of flour are expressed in terms of wheat
Sources: CIDA, **Annual Reports** (1969-70 to 1975-76); Theodore Cohn, "Food Surpluses and Canadian Food Aid", mimeo, June 1976; **Strategy for International Development Cooperation,** (CIDA, 1976)

grain fell to a low of thirty days supply, and international wheat prices tripled within a year and a half.

Once again Canadian food aid moved in lock step with the marketplace. In the 1972-73 fiscal year Canadian volumes of wheat aid fell a further 37%. Wheat and its related products, as a percentage of all food aid, declined for the first time since 1951 — from a traditional average of over 90% of all food aid to a 1972-73 low of 70.3%. As less wheat was produced in the early 1970s and more sold on commercial markets, aid-supported exports of wheat products declined from 10.6% of total exports in 1970 to a level of 4.1% in the tight-market, "food crisis" years of 1972-73. (See Table 5-XIII.)

Because many underdeveloped countries were unable to purchase foodgrains for human consumption, even on commercial terms, in 1972-73, CIDA president Paul Gerin-Lajoie later proposed that in the future Third World countries be given the "right of first refusal" to buy a certain portion of grain on a commercial basis. This would prevent the wealthiest countries like the Soviet Union, Britain and Japan from capturing the entire market in shortage years for the purpose of feeding livestock. But the Canadian business community emphatically rejected the idea maintaining that it would disrupt Canada's export business with its regular customers.

Table 5-XIIIa

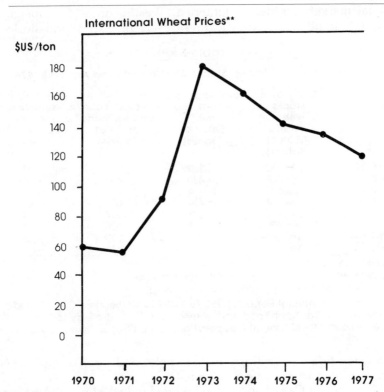

International Wheat Prices**

**FOB US Gulf, no. 2 Hard Winter (Ord.)
Source: UN World Food Council, Food Aid (WFC/38), March 24, 1977, pp. 3-4.

Leftover Give-aways

The dollar value of all Canadian food aid did not slump in tandem with the fall in the volume of wheat aid in the early 1970s. Higher wheat prices compensated for its smaller amount, and at the same time CIDA introduced new products to its food aid package — milk powder, rapeseed, rapeseed oil, cheese, fish and egg powder.

Table 5-XIIIb

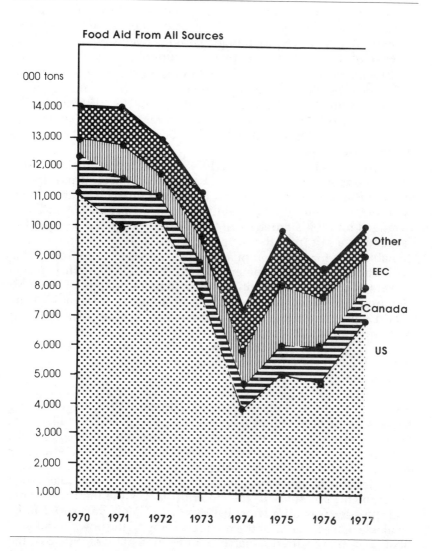

Food Aid From All Sources

The inclusion of rapeseed illustrates a further commercial pressure on the program. CIDA has usually preferred to send food aid in a relatively unprocessed state; the product is easier to transport and Third World processing generates employment and income in the recipient country. But with rapeseed, Canadian businessmen and their allies in the Department of Industry, Trade and Commerce were quick to see new commercial possibilities in the development assistance field. Companies involved in the processing of rapeseed into rapeseed oil lobbied for more processing in Canada before food aid exports left the country. Industry, Trade and Commerce put its weight behind the companies. As a result, the amount of rapeseed oil exported in CIDA's program increased between 1972 and 1974, as it replaced the amount formerly sent in unprocessed rapeseed.

The inclusion of non-grain food in the Canadian aid basket has been sporadic, ill-planned and usually linked to the sudden development of surpluses. It creates absurdities like the 1959 contribution of $60,000 worth of surplus Canadian butter to South Vietnam — a contribution of doubtful development benefit or palatability to the Vietnamese people.

More recently, in the fall of 1974, Agriculture Minister Eugene Whelan was searching around for a solution to a beef surplus he had on hand as a result of conflicts between Canada and the United States.[13] The answer: beef aid. The Department of Agriculture arranged for CIDA's purchase of "Beef Loaf", a canned beef product labelled as a gift from the people of Canada. It was a highly questionable item for inclusion in an aid program that supposedly deals with Third World development. Beef cattle are very inefficient converters of grain into protein — more than 14 pounds of grain are required to produce each pound of beef. In urban areas of the Third World where most food aid is consumed, such aid diverts public tastes from traditional, locally-grown foods to imported ones. City residents become dependent on expensive imports, demand for domestic products shrinks and the underdeveloped nation's agricultural economy suffers.

CIDA has also added egg and milk powder to its shopping list, especially when stockpiles were rising. In early 1976, Eugene Whelan was trying hard to find ways of giving part of a $200 million milk powder surplus to underdeveloped countries. CIDA helped to make a small dent in the inventory with a $700,000 gift of milk powder to the victims of the February earthquake in Guatemala. Canadian officials claim the shipment was made at the request of the Guatemalan government, but study of the aid effort leaves the impression that milk powder was on a short list of what Canada advertised to be available. Large sectors of the population found the powder indigestible, and many suffered diarrhea and serious illness. Some of the milk, labelled a gift from the people of Canada, ended up on the shelves of corner grocery stores in middle-class districts of Guatemala City relatively untouched by the earthquake.[14] The milk powder problem is not peculiar to Guatemala: an estimated 60 to 90% of the Third World's population lacks the enzymes necessary to digest the lactose in cow's milk. Milk powder requires the added ingredient of clean drinking water — an element sadly lacking in the Third World and especially so in disaster situations. Milk powder should probably not even be considered for food aid packages in many situations. CIDA admits, but discounts, the lactose deficiency and water supply problems and, bolstered by Canadian self-interest, still retains its faith in milk powder aid.[15]

Help or Hindrance?

Food aid is so obviously a form of surplus disposal that aid administrators go out of their way to convince their constituencies that it also has a developmental value. Experts at CIDA argue that grants of food not only feed hungry people but generate counterpart funds as well. These counterpart funds, collected by the recipient government from the local sale of Canadian food aid, can then be applied to other projects. In this way, food aid is transformed from *relief* into real *development*, CIDA claims. Food aid programs also release valuable foreign exchange earnings for Third World governments to use for purchase of essential imports — including food — on world markets.

Aside from its apparent benefit for the Canadian economy, however, does food aid really accomplish all that it claims?

It would seem obvious that by its very nature food aid has limitations: it can keep some hungry people alive but cannot, in itself, solve their search for daily bread. It does not address — and so may divert attention from — the central issues of food production and distribution, of economic systems, and of class structures and politics. Food transfers to the Third World often help to stave off urgent agrarian reforms, supplying a meal for a day while the planning of food production for tomorrow is overlooked by governments intent on following a more glamorous, western-inspired model of development through industrialization.[16]

Because Canadian food aid is usually sold in commercial markets — by local intermediaries or government agencies — much of it may never reach the people who need it most. Those with the ability to pay, get; those lacking cash, stay hungry. In some countries, food aid distribution systems are prey to smuggling, pilfering and profiteering by local officials and middlemen. (Such "leakages", as CIDA euphemistically calls them, in turn arouse indignation among Canadians — for some reason our domestic corruption and mismanagement is perceived as less offensive.)

There's yet another Catch 22. Canadian food aid is usually sold at less than prevailing local prices in the recipient nation. Its sudden arrival can undercut the domestic market for the foods of the small local farmer. Unable to get a decent return for his crops, he is forced to sell his land, becoming a landless, and often jobless, labourer in the slums of swelling cities. The free distribution of food aid would obviously aggravate this situation. In the long run, the food gifts of industrialized countries help neither the hungry consumer nor the small struggling farmer.

The situation of Bangladesh, the recipient of $10 billion in food aid since 1979 and Canada's second largest food aid recipient after India, illustrates the dilemma. In 1976, despite record harvests and massive inflows of food aid, 360,000 infants and young children died of malnutrition. Of the 600,000 tons of international food aid shipped to Bangladesh that year, only 19% reached the destitute — orphans, widows, refugee camp residents and the rural unemployed. Fully 90% was pumped into the country's food ration system which gives first priority to the military, police and civil service. Urban centres are on the second rung. According to the British development magazine, *The New Internationalist*, the food ration system functions as "a welfare system for the politically volatile middle class" whose support the government needs to maintain political power.[17] An urban middle class ends up paying low, subsidized prices for food products from abroad (as low as one-third the local market price), while the country's 22 million peasants pay the going domestic rate. And they must pay it with an income that shrinks because of the dumping of Canadian foodstuffs.

In a report on its food aid program in Bangladesh, CIDA concedes the problem:

It is indeed a sad fact that part of our food aid does not reach those for whom it is meant. We know that the existing ration system does not guarantee the just sharing of foodstuffs between rural and urban areas, or between those who need the most and who need the least. . . . It still has a large bias towards serving the urban areas, which by Bangladesh standards are basically middle class.[18]

The report goes on to note that political and economic changes could make Bangladesh self-sufficient in food. For example, land reform is needed to change the current situation wherein 10% of the rural population owns 47% of the land while almost 50% of the rural population is landless.

Meanwhile, counterpart funds generated by the sale of food aid in Bangladesh contribute an estimated 18% of the national government budget, encouraging complacency about the food crisis and reducing pressure on the government to invest in agriculture. Although Canada supposedly controls the earmarking of these counterpart funds for development projects, a recent confidential study by CIDA and the Treasury Board admits that in practice no such control exists.[19]

Western aid agencies claim to have solved many of these problems with food aid by channelling foodstuffs to food-for-work projects. The idea of food-for-work is to use foreign food gifts as payment to jobless people to build infrastructure in Third World rural areas. In this way, food aid supposedly avoids the problem of depressing the prices of local agricultural products while benefitting unemployed workers and the society as a whole through the building of food-for-work roads, water systems or buildings. But society as a whole cannot benefit in countries where wealth and power are tightly held. In these cases, food-for-work ends up building infrastructures to benefit local elites while the administration of such programs also lines the pockets of the wealthy who use the scheme for corruption and patronage. As an AID-sponsored study of rural works projects that use food-for-work aid concluded: "Such projects provide income to rural workers for a specified period, but do nothing generally to change the fundamental economic conditions that produced unemployment in the first place... such projects tend to provide long-term benefits to landlords."[20] As a solution to the problems of traditional food aid, food-for-work projects have been created from the same mould. Their main function is to take the edge off a potentially explosive rural situation by providing a few jobs. But, like traditional food aid, such programs actually strengthen the structures that generate hunger.

The Limits of Food Aid

As counter-productive as most food aid is, it does have one positive application, recognized by both critics and proponents. When countries like Bangladesh are struck by natural disasters, emergency food aid can play a useful, temporary role. In contrast to Canada's usual response to emergencies, however, aid to disaster situations should be well-planned, carefully prepared and disinterested. The best contribution Canada could make in such situations would be a cash transfer to affected countries, allowing for local purchase of food products or for imports from neighbouring nations. Canadian stockpiles of food should only be used when these local supplies are unavailable and when the Canadian substitute is appropriate.

But even emergency food aid is a pitifully inadequate response where social and economic structures underlie the so-called "natural" causes of disasters. The Ethiopian drought of 1974, for example, was not caused so much by an absolute shortage of food as by landowners who forced tenant farmers to pay up to three-quarters of their crops as rent. As crop yields fell because of drought conditions, the peasants were not left with enough to sustain life. An estimated 100,000 died.[21] Similarly, the 1976 earthquake in Guatemala was what one observer termed a "class-quake". Poverty, as much as falling rock and earth, was the villain. An economic system that forced thousands of families to build fragile dwellings on the precarious slopes of ravines and mountainsides exposed many more poor than wealthy to the disaster.

Food aid is a necessary form of relief in such situations. But it should not be considered "development aid". It doesn't facilitate development and in all too many cases actually promotes underdevelopment. It may soothe the consciences of Canadian agricultural planners to know that when Canadian farms produce more than can be consumed domestically or exported commercially, the leftovers can be given away to the Third World instead of destroyed or buried. But burying the surpluses is no more absurd than imposing food aid on underdeveloped countries. If there are problems of oversupply in Canada's profit-centred food system, food aid cannot solve them.

More than most, Canadian farmers readily understand the negative effect of food aid on the Third World. They understand how it bankrupts the small farmer by undercutting his market — a process similar to the impact of low-priced imports which often have the same impact on Canadian farmers. As a result, there is little significant grass roots pressure from farmers for food aid programs. Lobbying for food aid is done by organizations which claim to speak for farmers (quasi-governmental marketing boards and provincial and federal departments of agriculture), as well as corporations involved in the processing of food included in the current food aid program. Corporate lobbyists include organizations such as the Grain Millers' Association and the Rapeseed Crushers' Association, both representing food processors who support food and push for the inclusion of more food products which have been processed in Canada.

Within the government, the Department of Industry, Trade and Commerce and the Department of Agriculture exert strong pro-food aid pressure on CIDA. They expect food aid to contribute to improved trade prospects for Canada although food aid exports to the Third World represent only about 3% of all Canadian agricultural exports. There is also a "bureaucratic" pressure, internal to CIDA and the federal government, which prompts more food aid disbursements. Because large amounts of food can be dispensed with minimal administrative costs, "the decision to employ this form of aid is biased by its great disbursement ease compared with other forms of aid."[22]

The debate even surfaces in Cabinet discussions. In testimony to parliament in 1980, former Trudeau foreign affairs advisor Ivan Head revealed that the Cabinet had been divided when it first considered a proposal to fund the International Rice Research Institute to help underdeveloped countries increase food production. "Those who argued that it was in Canada's interest that the developing countries continue to rely on Canadian wheat and wheat flour argued that it was not in our interest, therefore, to assist them to grow their own food," Head explained.[23]

Because of these pressures, food aid continues to account for up to 20% of CIDA's total annual budget. To distract attention from this traditional form of relief the Agency points to its new programs, aimed at expanding food production in the Third World — a subject dealt with in Chapter 6. But the level of food aid allocations is not likely to diminish as other programs expand. Ottawa's export strategy includes the active promotion of selected grain exports, even at the expense of neglected domestic food production, which is suffering from import competition and reducing Canada's food self-reliance.[24] CIDA also wants to maintain a food aid program because it's a flexible instrument of supplying quick balance of payments support to tottering governments. (Jamaica, Portugal and Turkey have already received such support.) A balance between bilateral and multilateral food aid channels will likely be kept since each offers a particular advantage: multilateral lets CIDA dispatch food quickly without administrative burdens; bilateral can distinctly promote Canadian commercial food exports. For the future CIDA will remain a major customer, dumping ground, and salesman for Canadian food surpluses.

The world now has the economic, human, and technical capacity to nourish and sustain every single person on earth several times over. Food aid itself is an indictment of national and international economic and political systems which do not meet humanity's basic need for food. There may always be a limited role for food aid as a form of emergency relief. But CIDA could significantly improve the quality of its overall development assistance by simply cutting the quantity of the surplus food it dumps on the underdeveloped world.

Harvest of Discontent:

"Basic Needs" Aid to

6   the Rural Poor

Participants at the 1975 Commonwealth Conference on Food and Rural Development were stunned when a government official mentioned that Canada's foreign aid administrators had decided to adopt some of the tactics of the Viet Cong. During the Vietnam war, the official went on to explain, US foreign aid went largely to the middle and upper classes of Vietnamese society. The Viet Cong, on the other hand, worked to gain the support of rural villagers by preventing rich landowners from extracting exorbitant rents for use of land and water. Despite the huge volume of US aid, it was the Viet Cong who, by challenging the power of the rural establishment, won the loyalty of the peasantry.[1]

Make no mistake. CIDA has embraced not the revolutionary cause of Vietnam's liberation movement but a new fad in aid giving — what is now known as "basic needs" aid. It's an attempt to atone for the sins of trickle-down aid giving, which supports the already rich in underdeveloped countries and stimulates the exports of donor nations. The "new aid" hasn't displaced these traditional forms of assistance; they are still central to Canada's aid effort. It has simply been tacked on to the old structures as a fresh program, ostensibly designed for the exclusive benefit of the poor.

In its 1975 policy document, *Strategy for International Development Cooperation 1975-1980*, CIDA announced that Canada would "focus its assistance to a greater extent on the most crucial aspects or problems

of development" — particularly food production and rural development. This focus interprets Canadian aid as a "support and catalyst
to self-reliant efforts" towards meeting "the basic needs" of "the
least privileged sections of the population" in the poorest nations of
the Third World.[2] The Agency later pledged to spend over 33% of its
bilateral aid budget on agricultural and rural development schemes
for the 1977-1982 period, a dramatic leap from 6.3% in 1974.[3]

Basic needs aid, which includes a strong emphasis on what is
called integrated rural development, has now been named as a
priority by the national aid agencies of most western countries. At
first glance, this type of development assistance appears to be
addressing one of the most serious problems of underdevelopment
in a way that avoids the pitfalls of the past. But closer scrutiny of the
new aid shows that the ultimate winners will not be the poor, but
the traditional rural elites, middle-class farmers and western
agribusiness firms.

The Rural Poor

Poverty is overwhelmingly a rural problem. Eighty-five percent of
the world's poor — over 680 million people — live in the Third
World countryside. A third of them are landless rural workers who
depend on insecure employment on large estates to earn what are
often below-subsistence wages. But the majority of the rural poor
are small peasant farmers, tenants, sharecroppers and squatters
eking out an existence on tiny plots of land and paying as much as
60% of their annual harvest in rents to their landlords. They number
over 700 million individuals working on 100 million land holdings of
less than five hectares each (one hectare equals 2.47 acres).[4] And
most of them are women; contrary to common assumptions, according to the UN, women provide the bulk of agricultural labour in the
Third World and are the majority of the world's food producers.

In contrast, the wealthiest 20% of landowners in the Third World
controls between 50 and 60% of all cropland. In Latin America,
where skewed land ownership is most extreme, 7% of the landowners possess a startling 93% of the arable land.[5] Land ownership,
more than any other factor, determines the wealth of the elite
classes and the poverty of the majority throughout the Third World.
It is also the basis of political power. Only countries which have
experienced political and social revolutions, such as China and
Cuba, have effectively broken the Third World pattern of skewed
land ownership through thoroughgoing land reform. Elsewhere,
landed oligarchies wield enormous political and economic power
and resist — often by using violent repression — any attempts to
better the conditions of the peasantry.

Aid programs have only aggravated the problem. According to

World Bank official Leif Christofferson, the 680 million rural poor received little or no benefit from the economic growth and the development programs of the last two decades.[6] Food aid programs had the calculated effect of developing First World tastes among Third World consumers. The dumping of food aid also undercut the local markets for the products of small farmers, forcing an increasing number off the land and onto the roads to the cities. The "green revolution" of the 1960s did increase overall Third World food production but the rich harvested most of the benefits. They alone could afford the expensive miracle seeds and costly fertilizers and equipment the wonder plants required; they alone owned the high quality land that green revolution technology required. The highly touted "revolution" simply enabled the rich to monopolize more land and become richer. During two decades of aid giving, according to the United Nations World Food Council, national average food consumption for the lowest income groups in the Third World deteriorated markedly.

Reform or Revolution

By the early 1970s, unequal distribution of wealth in the countryside, aggravated by western aid programs, had created a potentially explosive crisis. A turning point was reached when, in 1972 and again in 1974, world food production declined and food aid was cut back, precipitating the international "food crisis". Aid administrators were forced to focus their attention not only on emergency aid but also on longer-range solutions.

Robert McNamara — the American Defense Secretary during the buildup of the Vietnam War, born again as the development-prophet president of the World Bank — was the first to articulate the issue and propose a strategy for handling it. An "increasingly inequitable situation will pose a growing threat to political stability," he warned the governors of the World Bank meeting in Nairobi in 1973. Remembering that twentieth century upheavals had frequently grown out of rural unrest, he insisted it was time the World Bank and Third World governments measured the "risks of reform against the risks of revolution."[7]

McNamara's speech is now seen as a landmark — the beginning of what development pundits now call the "basic needs" phase of international aid. The previous phases of "reconstruction" and "development" had bypassed the poor. McNamara explained that traditional aid — the construction of economic infrastructure such as hydro-electric dams, roads, airports and communications systems — had "aimed primarily at accelerating economic growth [which] benefited mainly the upper 40 per cent of the population." In contrast, "basic needs aid" — a term coined by the 1976 International

Labour Office assembly on *Employment, Growth and Basic Needs* —
tries to eliminate "absolute poverty" by meeting the minimum needs
of the most destitute.

In Nairobi, McNamara outlined a five-year plan for assisting
small peasant farmers: "integrated rural development". He was
confident that, given more credit and more opportunity to adopt
modern techniques, small farmers could significantly expand their
production. The objective, as a later World Bank policy paper
explained, is "the modernization and monetization of rural society
and . . . its transition from traditional isolation to integration with
the national economy."[8] Integration is defined as "greater interac-
tion between the modern and traditional sectors, especially in the
form of increased trade in farm produce and technical inputs and
services." In other words, integrated rural development seeks to
transform subsistence peasant agriculture into commercial,
capitalist agriculture by locking the small producer into the agribusiness food system as a consumer of agricultural inputs (seed, fertilizers, chemicals, machinery, technology, etc.) and as a producer of
crops suitable for further processing and marketing both nationally
and internationally. In addition to providing credit and technical
assistance, such programs would extend basic employment, education and health services to the countryside, thus making it an "integrated" approach. The anticipated results were a general mitigation
of poverty, more jobs, a slowing of migration from the countryside
to urban slums, more food for domestic consumption, less need to
import foodstuffs, and finally, additional foreign exchange for
urban and industrial development.

After the Nairobi speech, the World Bank's funding for rural
development quadrupled. Between 1974 and 1978, the Bank made
over $5.3 billion worth of loans compared to only $100 million spent
annually on rural development in earlier years. (See Table 6-XIV.)
Quickly the new concept gained top billing (if not top budgeting) in
the programs of regional development banks and national aid agencies. Third World governments, even those perennially indifferent
to their rural poor, went out of their way to design programs and
funding submissions to fit the favoured category. In a few short
years, integrated rural development and basic needs approaches to
aid giving had become global development fads.

False Expectations

Aid-watchers in the industrialized countries held (some still hold)
high expectations that the lofty rhetoric of the new aid signified a
quantum advance in its quality. They hoped that the usual commercial and political motives for aid were being replaced by real concern
for the poorest people. After the rhetoric is boiled down however,

Table 6-XIV

World Bank Lending for Rural Development*

Fiscal Year	Number of Projects	Lending (millions US $)
Annual average 1969-73	10	109
1974	25	450
1975	41	1,012
1976	39	799
1977	56	1,322
1978	49	1,728
Total 1974-78	210	5,311

* Includes lending to projects directed towards benefitting the rural poor as well as multisectoral projects in which agriculture plays an important role.
Source: Leif E. Christofferson, "The World Bank and Rural Poverty", in **Finance and Development**, December, 1978.

there is little left of the new recipe.

In fact, little has changed. Three-quarters of the World Bank's loans still go to commercial developments — electric power, railroad, highway, mining and manufacturing projects — which make investments by transnational corporations in the Third World both possible and profitable. The Bank now disguises some of these traditional programs by classifying them as part of rural development projects; they are justified as necessary infrastructure for the development of the countryside.

Despite all the talk of aiding the small peasant farmer, 75% of the World Bank's agricultural credit — and the Bank is the single largest source of such funds — still goes to medium and large landowners. In Latin America that means that a high proportion of the Bank's disbursements supports the 7% of all landowners who possess 93% of the cropland. And substantial aid still flows to large-scale, export agriculture instead of small-scale, domestic food production. In 1978 alone, the World Bank extended $258.5 million in loans for non-food crops such as tea, tobacco, jute and rubber and an additional $221 million for food crops such as vegetables, sugar and cashews explicitly designated for export. In Latin America, a shocking 70% of the Bank's agricultural credit subsidizes livestock production to satisfy the tastes of local elites and serve rich-world dinner tables.[9]

Meanwhile, the funds remaining for small food producers will do nothing for the millions of landless peasants in the Third World. Although they are an estimated 35% of the active agricultural population, the landless are excluded from rural development schemes, written off as poor credit risks because they lack the means of producing food. Neither the landless nor those peasants with subsistence-size parcels of land will gain greater access to the means of food production through the rural development schemes of northern aid agencies. Peasants want substantial land reform, but the new aid offers only technique. As the World Bank explains, the new schemes "put primary emphasis not on the redistribution of income and wealth . . . but rather on increasing the productivity of the poor." Measures such as land reform are downplayed because "avoiding opposition from powerful and influential sections of the rural community [read: large landowners] is essential if the Bank's progress is not to be subverted from within."[10]

At CIDA there has been an equally unimpressive change of heart since the new aid was announced. In the first three years after releasing its *Strategy*, the Agency's disbursements of bilateral aid for rural development actually declined from 29.5% of total commitments to 23.6%. Other "basic needs" areas were also neglected: commitments for education and training dropped from 5% of all commitments in 1976 to 3.3% in 1978; commitments for health, welfare, housing and water supply fell from 12.1% to 6.2% over the same period. In contrast, CIDA allotments increased for traditional projects of power generation and distribution (from 7.5% in 1976 to 17.6% in 1978) and transport (from 15.6% to 31.6%).[11] A sleight-of-hand allows CIDA to disguise some non-basic-needs projects under a "priority sector" classification when they are deemed part of a broader rural development effort. Such is the case in the Lesotho Thaba Tseka project described earlier where three-quarters of CIDA's $6 million contribution was spent on construction — not rural development as promised.[12]

Canada in Colombia

Canada broke ground in the field on "new aid" by its involvement in a prototype basic needs project in the South American country of Colombia. In 1976 Colombia's president, Alfonso Lopez Michelson, unveiled a program of integrated rural development (DRI) jointly financed by the Inter-American Development Bank (contributing a $64 million loan), the World Bank (1 $52 million loan), and CIDA ($13.5 million in loans and a further $500,000 grant). CIDA's minority participation belies Canada's leadership role in the project. The International Development Research Centre conducted a pilot project at Caqueza, near the capital city of Bogota, which became the basis for the DRI concept, a concept explicitly designed to "have applications in other parts of the world, particularly in Latin America."[13] Canadian embassy officials in Bogota also boasted that CIDA's willingness to put up financing for DRI was instrumental in securing later loans from the World Bank and the IDB.

DRI planners faced a classic situation of underdevelopment in Colombia. Nutritional deficiencies ravage 60% of all children in that country. In the countryside, an infant is more likely to die before the age of five than a North American adult before the age of sixty. One million rural families own no land at all, and three-quarters of those owning small land parcels occupy only 7.2% of the cultivable terrain. Working their small plots, these peasants produce basic crops for consumption — a poor man's diet of potatoes, beans, cassava, corn and raw sugar.[14] Yet even as the country's poor go malnourished, a small, obscenely rich elite — 5% of the rural population — monopolizes two-thirds of the cropland to produce coffee, sugar, cotton, beef and even marijuana for export.

The age-old breach between landed and landless was widened by the modernization of Colombian agriculture after World War II. The government actively promoted and subsidized the development of modern estates producing agro-exports. International aid agencies proffered supposed answers to the rural problem but these only made things worse.[15] Food aid from the United States succeeded in opening up a commercial market for American wheat, and caused a decline in domestic wheat production as fertile valleys were turned over to the production of beef for export by wealthy landowners who, by 1973, were using two-thirds of the miracle strains of rice to feed livestock or produce beer.[16] Between 1961 and 1972, the World Bank, the IDB, and the US Agency for International Development had provided over $300 million in credits for mechanization, irrigation and other agricultural inputs almost exclusively for the large estates.

As these large estates converted into capitalist agribusinesses, small peasant farmers were pushed off the land. More than a million migrated from the countryside to the cities between 1951 and 1964. Over the next six years the number of landless peasants more than doubled.[17]

The Colombian government heralded DRI as an exemplary solution to these problems. Specifically, the government hoped that DRI would halt migration to the cities, replace imported foodstuffs with domestic crops, and restrain the rise in food prices for the urban work force. Lower food prices would in turn lead to a moderation in wage demands and trade union militancy, deterrents to foreign investment in industry. Government leaders also anticipated that DRI would help them consolidate their political power. In order to contain unrest in the countryside, DRI was applied specifically to regions with chronic political tensions, militant peasant organizations and sporadic guerrilla activity.

The World Bank views the five-year $355 million DRI as the project which most closely approximates its own concept of rural development in its "basic needs" phase. It also most clearly shows the inadequacies of the new aid panacea.

First of all, DRI excludes a large segment of Colombia's rural poor. One million landless peasant families and another one-quarter million small producers are judged unlikely generators of expanded food production. They get no DRI aid. The program circumvents, and is a poor substitute for, land reform. It replaces a token twelve-year land reform program which redistributed only 1.6% of the large estates. By the mid-1970s, continuing inequalities in land ownership had fomented the creation of strong peasant federations. The government and its allies dealt with this dissent by imprisoning 35,000 federation members and assassinating over 200 militants. While DRI's planners continue to avoid land reform, they somehow expect that three-quarters of the rural population will be satisfied if a few among them improve their productivity while all are still confined to only 7.2% of the cropland.

Canada's assigned role in the DRI program was to increase food production by small peasant farmers in the provinces of Sucre and Cordoba. Here, large estates cover three-quarters of the agricultural land. In the province of Sucre, fifty wealthy families own 62% of the land and use most of it for cattle grazing, each head of cattle feeding off twice as much land as the average peasant family tills for food.[18] But true to form, the CIDA program skirts the question of land ownership — despite the clamour for change in land tenure which had resulted in the assassination of three peasant leaders, the wounding of 20 others, and the imprisonment of 5,000 more in the province of Sucre since 1968. It bypasses the almost 25,000 peasant families who own less than one hectare of land and instead assists 7,489 families with between one and 20 hectares. It treats the supposed beneficiaries of the plan as a "target population" — never as participants, much less the protagonists, of their own development — selected because their labour can be shifted from subsistence to commercial agriculture, "modernized and monetized".

The final results of the DRI program cannot yet be assessed. But the harvest can be no better than the seeds that were planted. With a bias towards the already relatively better-off within the target group — those with between 10 and 20 hectares who have, in bankers' terms, the best payback capacity — DRI credits will strengthen this group as a "middle class" within the peasantry. Owners of small-to-medium size parcels of land tend to receive less credit and will be the ones most likely to default on their debt payments. Crushed by the credit system that was to have saved them, these bankrupt small farmers may be forced to sell their land to "middle class" farmers or to large landowners. In trying to meet debt payments, some recipients of DRI credits will be tempted to take their land out of food production and put it into more remunerative cash crops. Alternatively, they could try to expand their landholdings by pushing out the smallest producers. Either way, instead of becoming successful entrepreneurial farmers, DRI clients will experience an enormous increase in their indebtedness, and greater dependence on the capitalist marketplace, the services of government, bankers and agribusiness. In the long run, the Colombian countryside will be blighted by a continuing concentration of land ownership, more landless labourers, more rural unemployment, and a greater migration to the cities — all in blatant contradiction to the stated goals of DRI.

Peasant leader Juan de Dios Torres, a critic of DRI, says the plan integrates "the World Bank's interests with the interests of the *latifundistas*" (huge estate owners). He charges that DRI seeks to protect Colombia's large landowners and their export agriculture while coopting some peasant farmers and undermining their independent organizations.[19] Colombian economist Ernesto Parra adds that the rural development scheme is really trying to create a class of "little peasant capitalists" to act as a buffer between the impoverished many and the privileged few. Tied into the commercial agricultural system, the beneficiaries of DRI will share a common interest with large landowners in increased mechanization, the use of wage labour, and the concentration of land ownership. In the words of a 1978 Cornell University study, they are "likely to be assertive profit maximizers, politically active, determined in protecting their position."[20] The harvest of the plan is social control, not social progress. "Rural development really aids agrarian capitalists and landlords — politically, socially and economically," concluded Rosemary Galli of Redlands University in her study of DRI in Colombia.[21]

By 1980, before the five-year DRI program had run its full course, CIDA began preparations for its withdrawal from the scheme. Despite their rhetoric about helping the poor, Colombian authorities had proved unwilling to entertain even minimal reform of the structure of rural exploitation. A new central government elected in 1978 had also decided to stress energy and industrial progress instead of rural development. Its new president, Julio Cesar Turbay Alaya, opted for the politics of repression instead of the politics of reform, mounting a widespread anti-subversion campaign that caught peasant leaders, trade unionists and church activists in its net.

Canada Commerce

Canada's enthusiasm for DRI soured also because of CIDA's inability to use the program as a wedge to open new markets for Canadian goods in Latin America's fifth largest economy. Half of CIDA's $14 million commitment to DRI was tied to the procurement of Canadian fertilizers, pesticides, electric transmission lines, 60 jeep-type vehicles and 120 motorcycles. Such inputs in themselves seem inappropriate for helping peasant farmers. But Canadian aid officials in Bogota complained that they were having difficulty even in interesting Canadian suppliers in the small contracts offered by the program's tied aid provisions.

CIDA simply lacks the competence and resources to match its trendy commitment to rural development. The Agency's sectoral guidelines on the subject, developed in 1976, admit that Canada is "rather unprepared to tackle integrated rural development on a massive scale."

Canada has had little experience in rural development abroad. . . . Canada has no corps of tropical agronomists and we cannot assume responsibility for crop production programs for crops with which we have no familiarity.[22]

Nor can aid officials fall back on their own Canadian experiences in agriculture. After all, Canada's treatment of its own small farmers resembles the DRI-like schemes exported to the Third World. The small farmer is as endangered here as in Colombia. Between 1951 and 1971, the number of farms in Canada declined by a whopping 70% while the number of farmers was reduced from 21 to six percent of the total labour force.[23] That's hardly a strong selling point for Canada's rural development aid overseas.

CIDA is currently financing rural development schemes in Haiti, Peru, Lesotho, Indonesia, Rwanda, Mali and a handful of other countries, as well as in Colombia. Despite the procurement problems in Colombia, the private sector has noted the commercial potential of the new aid. Addressing a 1976 workshop on integrated rural development, George Hunt, president of Canagro Ltd., urged CIDA to give "more emphasis to building up the private sector, both farm and agribusiness" in its rural development projects overseas. Equating the growth of agribusiness with rural development, Mr. Hunt explained business's interests in aid to the Third World's rural poor:

Canada has a lot to offer in strengthening farm production and building an efficient agribusiness sector. . . . We have 1,500 farm machinery companies, of those, seven are full-line producers . . . we have thirty-nine firms registered as agricultural consultants. . . . Practically all of our banks have specialists in agricultural credit and agricultural production and we are becoming increasingly interested in international development.[24]

This interest indicated by agribusiness firms shows rural development's hidden agenda. Trends in development aid generally follow, not lead, the movements of private capital. Far from trailblazing, the aid emphasis on rural development is actually rushing to catch up with an unprecedented expansion of agribusiness activity in the Third World since the 1960s. Attracted by cheap land and labour, transnational food corporations have created much of the problem that integrated rural development now proposes to solve — although the cure is an integral part of the cause. In Latin America, for example, per capita production of subsistence crops — a sector largely controlled by giant corporations — increased by 27%

in the same period.[25]

The corporate transformation of land producing food for local consumption into land producing for the international market creates some grotesque situations. Transnational corporations, in league with local partners, monopolize half the cropland of the Caribbean and Central America, much of it producing for export while 70% of the children of the region suffer malnutrition. In the Dominican Republic, half the cultivable land is used by foreign corporations to produce sugar for export, while basic staples have to be imported at inflated prices.[26] A number of transnational agribusinesses are currently extricating themselves from the direct ownership of land to avoid the political and financial risks of being large landowners and the loss of assets should their land be nationalized. Their new investments in the Third World are directed at monopolizing the more profitable stages of food production such as the provision of inputs to cultivation at one end, marketing services at the other, and food processing in between. In many instances global food firms welcome the rural credit programs of international development agencies because they support cultivators who, on contract, supply their agribusiness subsidiaries with both traditional crops as well as dairy products, vegetable cash crops, animal feeds, agro-industrial products and tropical fruits.[27]

The "modernization and monetization" of agriculture promoted by the World Bank and national aid agencies like CIDA will accelerate this process of corporate penetration in the Third World countryside. Eager to benefit are bankers involved in rural credit services, agribusiness firms committed to the cultivation, processing and marketing of crops and livestock, and the manufacturers of agricultural machinery, fertilizers, pesticides, seed, feed and packaging. Social scientist Ernest Feder calculates that the World Bank's schemes alone will generate seven to ten billion dollars worth of sales for transnational corporations over the next few years.[28] Once again the recipients of aid become the instruments of market expansion for developed countries.

Aid-giving nations also hope that the rhetoric of basic needs will deflect Third World complaints about the injustices of the international economic system. By talking a basic needs line western spokespersons divert attention and debate from North-South issues of exploitation to the scandal of inequality *within* aid-receiving nations. In political terms, the basic needs approach has become a counter-offensive by the rich nations to the Third World's demands for a New International Economic Order.

CIDA prizes integrated rural development as an important innovation, Canada's best offer to the Third World. The Agency's 1979-80 annual report insists that the emphasis of Canada's aid program "will continue to be on the basic needs of people in the poorest countries, particularly in the rural areas."[29]

But when the rhetorical packaging surrounding basic needs aid is torn away, the new aid looks very much like the old. It is supposed to alleviate poverty, but skirts the causes of that poverty. The techniques prescribed by rural development promoters — the use of an integrated approach to rural reform, for example — are not in themselves always or necessarily negative. Nor is the emphasis on the centrality of the rural problem within the debate about underdevelopment misplaced. But no amount of technique or exhortation about the importance of the agricultural sector, even if it helps some small farmers produce more, will be of significant benefit to the world's rural poor without radical changes in land tenure systems. As Dr. D.L. Umali, the Asian representative of the Food and Agriculture Organization of the UN, explains:

the main constraints to a just development are not basically a matter of technology. The issue we face is not the technology of food production, but who controls the agricultural resources and the levers of power and who, therefore, benefits from them. Inequality in control over productive resources is the primary constraint on food production and on equitable distribution.[30]

Thus, basic needs are essentially a matter of political, social and economic power; they cannot be addressed without confronting the basic greed of national and international elites.

With an appearance of social progress masking a purpose of social control, the basic needs approach to rural development is the Trojan Horse of today's development aid.

The Global
7 Managers

M aybe what I did wrong was to challenge the power of the western economic system," former Prime Minister Michael Manley,
the leader Jamaicans once hailed as their "Joshua", reflected after
his defeat in the country's October 1980 national election. "For that I
will remain unrepentant and unreconstructed."[1]

The elections climaxed a year of escalating violence and economic chaos which ravaged the already desperately poor slums of
Kingston, the nation's capital. By the time the polls closed, about
700 Jamaicans had been killed in street fighting between partisans of
Manley's democratic-socialist People's National Party (PNP) and the
conservative Jamaican Labour Party (JLP), headed by Edward Seaga,
the victor in the election. Thousands more, appalled at the disorder,
packed their bags and boarded a plane for a more stable work envi-
ronment.

The crisis had been precipitated early in the year by the Manley
government's refusal to comply with demands imposed by the
International Monetary Fund (IMF) for a $150 million cut in the
national budget as a condition for continued Fund support. The
breakdown of negotiations with the Fund prompted a flurry of
ministerial visits and negotiations with private banks and aid agencies as the government scrambled to prevent total economic collapse. A bad mark from the IMF guarantees difficulties with a host of
other international institutions.

In April, representatives of Jamaica's private creditors, including the Royal Bank of Canada and the Bank of Nova Scotia, rejected an impassioned plea for emergency financial assistance. In late spring, Jamaicans awaited the arrival of a delegation representing the World Bank, the most powerful of all multilateral aid agencies and the IMF's closest partner in the field of international finance. The mission was dispatched to assess the economic situation and to discuss possibilities for future Bank projects.

At the same time, Manley began working out arrangements for a meeting of the Bank-sponsored Caribbean Group for Cooperation in Economic Development, which includes donor countries like Canada, the United States, West Germany, the Netherlands and Norway, as well as recipient nations and multilateral agencies. In the long run, Manley found that he could not placate both a restless, anxious electorate and a host of impatient creditors.

After his victory, Seaga quickly piloted Jamaica back to the spot richer powers had assigned it in the international order. Observers predicted that he would cut about 10,000 civil service jobs, an IMF-dictated austerity measure Manley had refused to implement. Before the end of the year, the new Prime Minister had visited Washington to restore peace with the Fund and with the US government.

He subsequently reported that he expected IMF approval for loans totalling $550 million. Banks started discussing the rescheduling of Jamaica's debt before Seaga formally concluded an agreement with the Fund, a concession denied to Manley.

In January, Reagan and Seaga discussed the possibility of organizing a private high-level group of Jamaicans and Americans, which would promote joint projects. Washington signed a $40 million loan agreement with the JLP government, boosting US aid to Jamaica during the 1981 fiscal year to more than $60 million. The White House statement on the deal noted Seaga's intention to "rebuild his country's economy, with particular emphasis on revitalizing the private sector."[2] On a jaunt to Jamaica during the same month, Canada's External Affairs Minister Mark MacGuigan announced that he hoped to double aid for the Caribbean region, and to boost significantly the allocation for Jamaica.*

* Canada had extended aid to Jamaica even during the most difficult periods of the Manley administration, partly because Trudeau is Manley's personal friend. But Ottawa policy makers doubtless realize that Seaga will better serve the long term interests of the rich donor nations. In December, 1980, it was announced that Manley had accepted a one-year fellowship at Canada's International Development Research Centre to write a book on the Third World and the New International Economic Order. Manley later decided against Research Centre support for his work to avoid embarrassing Trudeau.

Seaga has suggested that the Reagan administration back an anti-communist alliance in the Caribbean, funded through a new "Marshall Plan" for Jamaica and other countries in the region. The Plan would involve a cooperative effort by the US, its allies, the IMF and the World Bank to pump in over $2 billion.

Jamaica's protracted negotiations with its numerous international supervisors clearly indicate that it is not a sovereign state, free to develop economic and social policies tailored to its own needs. Since Manley signed an agreement with the IMF in 1977, the government has been forced to surrender much of its authority to a supranational government headed by the IMF and the World Bank, institutions controlled by the United States and other major capitalist powers.

The refusal of an impoverished Third World nation like Jamaica to implement IMF policies was a daring, but in the short term, doomed attempt to reassert national independence. "I find it very dreadful that any country which dares to challenge the hegemony of the great powers can have such vengeance wrought upon it in economic terms," Manley reflected after his defeat. This vengeance has been inflicted as a deterrent to other poor nations which may be tempted to cross the lines drawn for them by leaders of the supranational government.

A Cog in the Wheel: Canada's Role in Multilateral Agencies

The International Bank for Reconstruction and Development (IBRD), better known as the World Bank, and the IMF are senior partners in a network of institutions that includes the Inter-American Development Bank (IDB), the Caribbean Development Bank (CDB), the Asian Development Bank (ADB), the African Development Fund (AFDF), the United Nations Development Program (UNDP) and a number of other UN agencies, as well as national development agencies such as Canada's CIDA. (See Table 7-XV.)

Since the late sixties, national development agencies have been steadily boosting their contributions to the World Bank and the regional development banks, enabling them to control an ever higher proportion of the total world development budget. The IBRD, in which members' power is determined by the amount of their subscriptions, is now the largest single source of international development finance.[3] The regional banks, which work closely with the World Bank, are less affluent, but still potent forces in the sphere of foreign aid.

This network of institutions has developed the collective clout to dictate the economic and social policies of recipient nations, and to

Table 7-XV
Who Calls the Shots?
Weighted Voting in Multilateral Institutions
(in % votes)

WORLD BANK (30.6.80)		INTER-AMERICAN DEV. BK. (31.12.79)		ASIAN DEV. BANK (31.12.79)		CARIBBEAN DEV. BANK (31.12.79)		AFRICAN DEV. FUND (31.12.79)	
a) Major Developed Donors		**a) 24 Regional Developing Members:**	56.10%	**a) Regional Developing Members:**	43.88%	**a) Regional Developing Members:**	66.48%	**a) Regional Developing Members:** (African Dev. Bank)	50.00%
United States	21.11%	**b) Regional Developed Members:**		**b) Developed Members:**		**b) Non-Regional Members:**		**b) Non-Regional Members:**	
U.K.	7.82	United States	34.85%	Japan	14.44%	Canada	16.76%	Japan	10.05%
W. Germany	5.32	Canada	4.73	United States	9.98	U.K.	16.76	Canada	5.92
France	5.31	Sub-total	39.58	Australia	6.40	Sub-total	33.52	West Germany	5.44
Japan	5.30	**c) Non-Regional Developed Members:**	4.32%	Canada	5.83	100.00%		United States	3.95
Canada	3.39	100.00%		Others	19.47			Sweden	3.60
Italy	2.62			Sub-total	56.12			16 others	28.96
Netherlands	2.36			100.00%				Sub-total	50.00
Belgium	2.24							100.00%	
Australia	2.00								
Sub-total	56.48								
b) 125 other members	43.52								
100.00%									

Sources: World Bank, **Annual Report 1979**; Inter-American Development Bank, **Annual Report 1979**; Caribbean Development Bank, **Annual Report 1979**; Asian Development Bank, **Annual Report 1979**; African Development Fund, **Annual Report 1979**.

impose crippling sanctions on those who try to chart an independent course. All the evidence indicates that this power will become
even more comprehensive during the eighties.

Most Canadians are familiar with CIDA's activities, if only
because of its periodic mistakes and mishaps overseas. The World
Bank and the IMF are generally perceived as much more remote
institutions, with no apparent connection to Ottawa's development
assistance programs. But over 35% of the Agency's budget currently
disappears into the coffers of these and other multilateral agencies,
beyond the direct control of Ottawa and Canadian voters.

Canada is a member of the fraternity of rich, developed
countries, but it is still a dependent nation, designated to play a
subordinate role in the network of international development
institutions. Unlike the recipient nations, Ottawa has not yet been
forced to accept direct instructions about its internal development
programs. Its subjection to their authority, though less complete
than the control experienced by poor nations, is evident in both
government statements and practices.

The Trilateral Commission, an international think tank which
has profoundly influenced recent US foreign policy, has correctly
situated Canada within the international system. "There is a clear
difference between leadership and systemic concern. Smaller
countries [such as Switzerland and the Netherlands] frequently
adopt policies geared to systemic as well as purely national objectives — not because they are leaders, but because they rely so heavily on the functioning of the international order that their national
interest is to actively promote its success."[4]

Canada's relatively insignificant share of voting power within
the largest multilateral institutions — 3.39% in the World Bank and
4.73% in the Inter-American Development Bank — cannot easily be
manipulated to promote distinctive foreign policy goals. In the vast
majority of cases, Ottawa simply cooperates with the objectives formulated by the most powerful member states, without even considering the possibility of developing a separate Canadian agenda.

Ottawa has backed the recent drive to increase the power and
resources of multilateral agencies by allocating a steadily increasing
proportion of its development assistance resources to these institutions. In its 1975 *Strategy*, CIDA pledged to increase its multilateral
aid, up to a maximum of 35% of its total disbursements.[5] By
1979-80, the Agency had exceeded even this high target.

Canada has not balked at this reallocation of its aid resources,
although it can expect few immediate tangible returns on its contributions. These aid dollars are not tied to procurement in Canada,
and Canadian companies have generally performed poorly in securing contracts for projects funded through the World Bank and other
multilateral agencies. By June 1977, Ottawa had contributed $745

million in paid-up World Bank shares and subscriptions, but Canadian entrepreneurs had procured only $416 million of Bank-financed contracts. The gap between Canada's contributions and its procurements has been larger than the shortfall suffered by any other member country. "For every dollar contributed, Japan has received $3.16 in contracts, while the US has got $1.08. But Canada has received only 56 cents."[6]

Canada's track record within multilateral institutions suggests that it participates only because it has to pay its dues within the fraternity of developed capitalist powers. But Ottawa has transformed necessity into a virtue by devising a few schemes to use multilateral allocations for its own advantage.

First of all, Canada is the only nation in the world with a membership in every international development bank, and has enhanced its image as a generous donor simply through its conscientious clubsmanship. Its participation in these institutions helps to develop an awareness of Canada even in Third World countries where CIDA has mounted no bilateral projects.

Ottawa will never be more than a second string player within the World Bank, the IMF and the Inter-American Development Bank. But its contributions have been used to develop a distinctively Canadian presence in the smaller regional development banks. Canada and the United Kingdom, the two non-regional members of the Caribbean Development Bank, split a third of the total votes, and Canada is currently the Bank's largest donor member. Canada's role in the CDB builds its influence in a region where it has substantial trade, investment and banking interests, as well as bilateral aid commitments.

Ottawa exercises less influence in the Asian Development Bank, but the voting strength of Australia and Canada combined exceeds the weight assigned to the United States, the second most powerful developed member nation. According to CIDA, Canada was the "prime mover" in the establishment of the African Development Fund, the concessional arm of the African Development Bank, and it remains a major contributor.[7]

This catholic distribution of multilateral aid not only helps to build small spheres of Canadian influence overseas, it also facilitates tidy and economical housekeeping at home. In 1978-79, for instance, only 3% of CIDA's staff, a total of 33 employees, was needed to administer all of Canada's multilateral aid disbursements. Funds for multilateral institutions flow smoothly and quickly through the Agency, and never lead to embarrassments about Canadian bureaucratic bungling. Because they have spent their money quickly, and presumably wisely, CIDA administrators can then ask for even more money the following year.

CIDA and the government as a whole also appreciate the fact that contributions to multilateral development banks escape the year by year scrutiny to which bilateral programs are subjected. Once Canada has acquired bank shares, its commitments are reviewed only when periodic replenishments are required. Canadian appointees to these institutions, moreover, are accountable neither to Canadian legislators nor to the Canadian public. Their remoteness has been a convenience for the Ministry of External Affairs, and a focus of repeated complaints by critics of Canadian foreign policy.

CIDA has justified its contributions to multilateral agencies by praising them for their "acceptability: collective participation by recipient nations in the councils of international institutions gives these states an opportunity to influence on a regular basis the institutions' policies and programs." Ottawa also applauds their "cooperative nature: along with other international organizations, multilateral assistance institutions are potential building blocks for understanding, trust, and peace among nations."[8]

But Ottawa's foreign policy makers know through experience that the policies of these institutions are neither cooperatively developed, nor acceptable, to many recipient nations. They also understand and accept Canada's role as facilitator of strategies conceived by their more powerful allies. They comply with the laws of the supranational government because they know their obedience will generate rewards suited to their rank in the global pecking order. They also know the penalties for defiance, because they have often participated in the punishment of deviants.

Bretton Woods and Beyond: Building the Global Order

Canada was a founding member of the post-World War II global order, unlike Jamaica and many other Third World countries which were still controlled by the old colonial powers.* Western businessmen, political leaders, and intellectuals had started making blueprints for a new international system well before the end of hostilities. They tried to mould a structure which would protect the US and other advanced capitalist powers from the economic slumps and protectionist policies of the thirties, as well as from the violent conflicts of the forties.

The most highly publicized of these post-war institutions was the United Nations, which was billed as a forum where nations, big

* The nations of Latin America, which had achieved independence in the early nineteenth century were practically the only Third World participants in the deliberations which shaped the post-war global order. They were present — actually, if not formally — as observers.

and small, would gather to settle their disputes and promote global harmony. The *New York Post* rejoiced that the 1945 San Francisco conference, which drafted and approved the United Nations charter, was the "most important gathering since the Last Supper".[9]

A far more effective system of world government had in fact been developed about a year earlier at the less publicized Bretton Woods, New Hampshire conference, where delegates from 44 countries gathered to approve plans for the IMF and the IBRD. The United States and Britain dominated the proceedings, while poor countries and middle powers like Canada simply assented to their proposals. The USSR participated in the negotiations, but decided against membership in the Fund and the Bank.

Canadian economist A.F.W. Plumtree, who was present at the conference, makes an argument for the importance of Canada's role at Bretton Woods, but admits that the Canadian initiative "was a reflection not so much of independent originality in Ottawa as of a sensitivity to those elements that would, when put together, prove to be acceptable both in Washington and London."*[10]

The adoption of the Bretton Woods system was simply the first phase of Washington's continuing drive to ensure the survival and success of western capitalism. The US and its allies found it necessary to adapt these structures to changing realities in the early sixties, and again in the early seventies, but the adjustments were facelifts meant to rejuvenate the organism in the pursuit of its original goals. According to the Trilateral Commission, one of the chief architects of the third wave in post-war institutional development, "Each phase of institution building has had two political objectives: the ratification of the power structure underlying international relationships at the time, and the integration of newcomers into those relationships."[11]

The US emerged from the war as the strongest and richest nation in the world, and the Bretton Woods system was designed, first of all, to facilitate the free flow of American goods and investment capital around the world. The IMF was appointed international financial policeman, empowered to ensure currency convertibility and to facilitate the exchange of goods and services across national borders. Participating nations also equipped it with resources to help other members experiencing short term balance of payments difficulties. Membership in the World Bank was restricted to nations who had already joined the IMF.

* The third major pillar of the post-war order was soldered into place when General Agreement on Tariffs and Trade (GATT) was ratified in 1947. The GATT was designed to regulate international commerce, while the Bretton Woods system was set up to stabilize monetary systems and to finance the development of new market and investment opportunities around the world.

From the start, the IMF and the IBRD cooperated closely in their promotion of political and economic stability within western spheres of influence. They established neighbouring offices in Washington, organized joint annual meetings, and developed a routine of continual consultation about affairs of mutual interest. Through an informal agreement, the president of the World Bank has always been an American, and the IMF Managing Director, a European.

Power within the Bretton Woods system was determined by the amount of the member's capital subscription. Washington was the biggest contributor to both institutions. It subscribed nearly 40% of the Bank's capital and so controlled nearly 40% of the votes. Until 1956, its control of the Fund was so absolute "that decisions were made effectively by the US Secretary of the Treasury."[12]

The World Bank was created as a new type of international investment institution, with a mandate to extend or guarantee loans for post-war reconstruction and development. It started business with a subscribed capital of US $7,670 million. In 1947, the Bank offered its first loans, totalling about $500 million, to support the reconstruction effort in four European countries. After the US developed the Marshall Plan in 1948, IBRD officials focused their attention on projects in Third World countries.

IBRD directors, now the chief financial patrons of the world's poor countries, are first and foremost bankers, whose natural peers are the directors of Chase Manhattan and Barclay's. One of the Bank's primary aims, specified in its Articles of Agreement, is to promote foreign investment. Its loans are extended at rates lower than, but related to, market rates, and it has shown a profit every single year since 1948.

The priority Bank administrators have assigned to the interests of private capital is obvious in its choice of recipients. Only two of its top ten loan recipients in 1978-79, supposedly a period of concentration on the poorest of the world's poor countries, were nations classified as "low income" by the IBRD. The others were so-called "middle income" nations, which are generally more suitable hosts for foreign investors.[13] The Bank's commitment to foreign investment has been vital to companies based in the US and other developed countries, which after World War II rapidly established subsidiaries around the world and evolved into the now notorious "transnationals".

Eugene Rotberg, the Bank's current treasurer, stresses that: "We are not a social welfare agency committed to making transfer payments to solve the problems of misery and poverty," but also insists that "there is no conflict between our developmental efforts on the one hand, and the interests of either our shareholders or bondholders on the other."[14] The continuing tension between the IBRD's identities as Bank and development agency was in fact deliberately built into the original structure.

The conflict was highlighted in 1956, when the Bank established an affiliate, the International Finance Corporation (IFC). The IBRD had been authorized to extend loans to governments or to private enterprises, but loans to private companies had to be guaranteed by the government of the host country. Many companies preferred to avoid entanglements with overseas governments.

The IFC was empowered to fund private enterprise and its loans were proffered with no political strings. It was conceived as a smaller operation than the Bank, and by 1970, its subscribed capital totalled only $110 million.*

The mandate of the United Nations Development Program (UNDP), established around the same time as the Bretton Woods institutions, shows the true status of the United Nations within the new international order. The UNDP was born to play poor relative to the Bank and the IMF. Unlike its more affluent kin, the UNDP assigned each participating member one vote. The US and its most powerful allies decided that, for this reason, the Program couldn't be trusted to use money and power wisely. The UN agency was not allowed any continuing sources of revenue, and was forced to ask members for new contributions each year. It was assigned the task of providing preliminary technical assistance for projects undertaken by the Bank or other development agencies.

The supranational institutions established after the war functioned smoothly as long as Washington was the absolutely supreme power in the western world. But by 1960, some adjustments were necessary to gear their operations to changing global realities. During the late fifties, the US economy suffered a recession, and massive deficits showed up in its balance of payments: $3.5 billion in 1958, $3.7 billion in 1959, and $3.9 billion in 1960.

The European Economic Community (EEC), and Japan — the second and third members of the seventies' Trilateral trinity — were developing new economic and political clout as they completed the process of post-war reconstruction. Washington strategists decided that they must be accorded authority and obligations suited to their new status, and their power within the World Bank and the IMF was increased. At the same time, the resources available for multilateral

---

* Canada's overall procurement in the IBRD network has been low. But the Bank and the IFC have funded the overseas operations of some of Canada's major corporations. After the war, Brascan (then Brazilian Traction) was the first company to secure a World Bank loan. More recently, the IFC offered a $15 million loan for EXMIBAL, INCO's Guatemalan nickel mining and partial refining operation. The IFC also approved a loan for the massive Trobetas bauxite project in Brazil. The financing was extended to Mineracao Rio do Norte SA, in which Canada's Alcan Aluminium holds a 19% interest. [15]

loans were dramatically increased and, in 1959, the World Bank quotas doubled, while IMF quotas rose by more than 50%.

In the early sixties, the western capitalist powers also started developing methods to incorporate possible dropouts, as well as impatient newcomers into the system. World Bank loans were too expensive for many less developed countries, so in 1960, the Bank established a soft loan affiliate, the International Development Association (IDA), which charges no interest on loans and allows 50 years for repayment.

The regional development banks were established during the same period as a supplement to IBRD initiatives in the Third World. The biggest and most powerful of these, the Inter-American Development Bank, opened its doors in the fall of 1960, less than a year after Castro's march on Havana. The African Development Bank, which was closed to non-regional members, was established in 1964. The Asian Development Bank began business in 1966, and the Caribbean Development Bank was launched in 1970. (The African Development Fund started operations in 1972.) All these banks established both hard and soft loan windows, similar to the IBRD and the IDA.

Several severe shocks to the global order in the early seventies, which are still reverberating a decade later, have required further modifications to the Bretton Woods system. By the late sixties, the Vietnam War was sapping US power and prestige, and its economy was again slumping after the boom years of the mid-sixties. In 1971, the Nixon administration broke one of the most basic rules of the IMF system by making a unilateral decision to suspend the dollar's convertibility to gold, and to let it float in relationship to other currencies. A devaluation of the US dollar was subsequently negotiated with other Fund members. These initiatives, which meant that the dollar no longer served as a fixed standard for other currencies, shook the post-war monetary system to its foundations, and radically changed the Fund's primary post-war role. Two years after the global monetary crisis, the OPEC nations started a series of drastic oil price hikes, creating what the oil companies and their allies have called a long term "energy crisis".

The Trilateral powers attempted to cushion the shock by retreading the IMF, and expanding the resources available to the World Bank and other multilateral aid agencies. US voting power within these institutions slipped during the decade, but Washington and its chief allies have made sure that they are still the pre-eminently powerful members. The 21.11% the US retains in the World Bank still permits it to exercise virtual veto power over major bank decisions. The top ten developed countries within the Bank command a 56.48% majority over the combined voting strength of the other 125 developed and underdeveloped member nations. The EEC countries voting together, as well as the US, can veto specified types of significant decisions within the Fund.

Surgery on the IMF during the seventies transformed it from guarantor of stable exchange rates to official financial guardian of nations — both developed and underdeveloped — suffering severe economic difficulties. Its loans are often relatively small, and are not classified as official development assistance. But IMF support, or lack of it, can be crucial for needy nations because:

• the Fund will not extend certain kinds of loans unless recipients agree to economic policies dictated by Fund administrators. These policies generally include tight wage controls, frequent increases in the prices of basic commodities, slashes in public spending, and openness to foreign investment.

• The IMF stamp of approval is generally a prerequisite for bilateral and multilateral development assistance, as well as for private bank loans. This aid is often far more substantial than the loans extended by the IMF itself. Wearing its new seventies style uniform, the IMF, more than ever before, has acted the role of international policeman.

The World Bank and other multilateral development institutions also assumed new authority as world governors during the past decade. The appointment of Robert McNamara as IBRD President in 1968 inaugurated a new era in its development. As head of the world's chief development institution, McNamara was as energetic and inventive as he had been earlier as Secretary of Defense, and earlier as President of the Ford Motor Company. He enhanced its already considerable prestige, pushed for new styles and mechanisms of aid dispensation, and for a constantly expanding pool of Bank capital. Total loans and grants extended by all multilateral agencies more than tripled from $2.1 billion in 1970 to $7.5 billion in 1976, and the World Bank accounted for a high proportion of this total.[16]

By the time McNamara retired in 1980, World Bank lending to the Third World was 12 times greater than it had been when he assumed office. The capital increase planned before his resignation will allow the Bank to double its lending in the eighties, and achieve a 2,000% increase in the two decades since his appointment.[17]

The tremendous expansion in multilateral aid cannot, of course, be attributed solely to the dynamism of a single individual. A number of converging forces made the increase necessary. The large multilateral institutions, first of all, have the financial resources and technical skills to mount massive Third World infrastructure projects which generate exports and investment from the rich nations. They are also well situated to coordinate the efforts of several agencies toward a single goal.

There were also pressing political reasons for the shift to multilateral channels. In 1969, the Commission on International Development, chaired by Lester Pearson, recommended that the multilateral share of the total world aid budget be boosted from approximately 10% to at least 20%. The Commission's report noted that "international organizations do much to endow development assistance with the character of a truly international effort, reducing any overtones of charity or interventionism which have at times embittered the aid process in the past."[18]

A retreat from overt intervention was especially important for Washington, because its programs and its foreign policy as a whole were being subjected to harsh criticism at home and overseas. Members of the Trilateral Commission have noted that "American initiatives are often undesirable, because they trigger negative reactions by virtue of being American."[19]

International agencies, billed as cooperative enterprises, provided a convenient cover for continuing US initiatives. James Grant, President of the Overseas Development Council during the middle seventies, and a veteran of the US Agency for International Development's pacification program in Vietnam, explained his preference for multilateral agencies by pointing out that "they have greater potential for intervening effectively into the domestic affairs of a developing country."[20]

The use of these agencies for channeling assistance to some of Washington's closest allies became a necessity after 1975, when the US Congress applied human rights restrictions to key bilateral aid programs. The human rights rider, introduced into aid legislation by Democratic Representative Tom Harkin, cut US assistance to regimes which engage "in a consistent pattern of gross violations of internationally recognized human rights."

Jimmy Carter adopted the human rights slogan, but discouraged Congress from excesses of zeal. He, like Nixon before him, tried to circumvent US legislators and continue support for repressive regimes like the governments of Chile, South Korea and the Philippines by channeling funds through multilateral agencies not covered by the Harkin amendment. The spending by agencies not covered by human rights legislation more than doubled from $7.8 billion in fiscal year 1971 to $17.2 billion in fiscal year 1976. "In the past six years, the share of traditional aid outlets has dropped from 46% to 31%," the Centre for International Policy noted in 1977.[21] This increase in multilateral aid was only a short term solution for the executive branch because, during the late seventies, the stipulations of the Harkin amendment were extended to cover key international agencies.

A right-wing Republican President and Republican Senate piloting the aid program through the early eighties will have few qualms about the repressive policies of US allies. But the election of Ronald Reagan does not necessarily presage massive cutbacks in Washington's support for multilateral institutions.

Some American foreign policy makers favour a new emphasis on politically targeted bilateral aid, and the administration has cut back on the first installment of a three-year contribution to the IDA, the World Bank's soft loan window. US Treasury chief Don Regan has drawn up just short of accusations that the IBRD encourages socialism.

But cooler heads in government realize the strategic importance of the multilateral development banks. Deputy Assistant Secretary of State Ernest B. Johnston reminded a House of Representatives subcommittee in early 1981 that "the United States took the lead in creating and maintaining the MDB's [multilateral banks] over the last 35 years not only because they are a cost effective means of providing development capital, but also because they play a vital role in the maintenance and operation of the whole economic system."

Deputy Secretary of the Treasury, R.T. McNamar, testifying before the same subcommittee, pointed out that "a look at the largest World Bank borrowers in fiscal year 1980 — Brazil, Turkey, Indonesia, Korea, Thailand, Colombia, and the Philippines — provides a good indication of how this leveraged lending contributes to US security by way of its contributions to growth and material well-being, and thus to stability in vital regions of the world."

These top Bank clients are not only key American allies. They are nations strapped with heavy financial burdens, and their total debts in 1978, $165 million, accounted for 47% of total Third World indebtedness. They badly need continuing multilateral loans. (See Table 7-XVI.)

Despite its current flirtation with a bilateralist concept of foreign policy, the US in the long run also needs the multilateral institu-

Table 7-XVI

Top Ten World Bank Recipients — 1979

	Foreign Debt — 1978 US$ billions	Loans IBRD and IDA US$ millions
1. India	20.5	1,492
2. Indonesia	18.8	830
3. Brazil	33.3	674
4. Mexico	31.2	552
5. Korea, Republic of	18.2	397
6. Philippines	7.5	395.5
7. Morocco	7.4	349
8. Egypt	14.1	322.5
9. Turkey	9.7	312.5
10. Colombia	4.3	311.5

Source: Lappé, Collins, Kinley, **Aid As Obstacle** (San Francisco: Institute for Food and Development Policy, 1980); World Bank, **World Development Report 1980** (Washington, 1980).

tions. Washington, like the other advanced capitalist powers, is still attempting to adjust to the economic tremors first felt in the early seventies. The World Bank, the IMF, and the regional development banks will continue to be important stabilizing forces, protecting the international order from the shock of a major cataclysm.

Punishing Dissidents: Two Case Studies

No government can retain its power without an effective system of sanctions against those who violate its laws. Managers of the IMF and the World Bank realized from the start that intervention in the political affairs of participating members would be as important to their job as overall management of the global economic system. These organizations have been continually praised as cooperative, apolitical development agencies, and the World Bank's Articles of Agreement specify that : "Only a look at the largest economic considerations shall be relevant to the Bank's decisions; it must not be influenced by the political character of the member or members concerned. Nor must the Bank and its officers interfere in the political affairs of any member."[22] But even Bank managers admit that "economic policy may be linked to political policy and thus Bank decisions may be influenced or have an influence on the domestic affairs of a country."[23]

This acknowledgement is an understatement of the hard fact that the IMF, the World Bank, and other multilateral agencies can, in cooperation with their most powerful members, plan the rise and fall of governments.

Jamaica's 1980 debacle was only the climax of a long struggle with the Fund, the US government, and private corporations and banks. The conflict originated in 1974, when Manley, who was first elected in 1972, initiated a gradual nationalization of the nation's bauxite industry, and launched a national political program the PNP called "democratic socialism".

The US responded with a campaign of political and economic destabilization.* AID turned down a Jamaican request for a $2.5 million food grant in 1975, and the US Export-Import Bank dropped Jamaica's credit rating from top to bottom category in early 1976.[24]

During a Christmas visit to Jamaica in 1975, US Secretary of State Henry Kissinger let Manley know that the economic boycott would

---

* The term "destabilization" is generally associated with the machinations of the Central Intelligence Agency. In practice, US destabilization campaigns, launched to weaken governments perceived as threats to American interests, have included a wide range of disruptive tactics, including economic boycotts. The role of the CIA in Jamaica is still unclear. Its activities in Chile have been well documented.

be terminated if the Jamaican government accepted an IMF program. Manley initially refused the offer. But by 1977, the destabilization program had created such an acute economic crisis that the government capitulated. The Fund ordered harsh wage, price and budget controls that made a mockery of the PNP's plans for "democratic socialism". Manley's subsequent attempts to satisfy both international creditors and the Jamaican people left his government in fragments.

The destabilization of the Manley regime was a repeat in slow motion of a much more savage drive to smash the government of Chilean President Salvador Allende Gossens. Allende, who was more unequivocally a socialist than Manley, mobilized the Chilean Congress to vote unanimously for nationalization of the copper industry shortly after his election in 1970.

The American copper companies, which had long monopolized one of the country's chief resources, and the Nixon administration were enraged by this move and by the haggling over what the Americans considered fair compensation. Allende further violated the rules of the international capitalist system by refusing to negotiate an agreement with the IMF.

Washington, which had earlier interfered with the Chilean political process by trying to prevent Allende's election, decided that Chile had to be strangled economically, and during the next few years, it managed to cut drastically the flow of funds to the Allende regime. This economic boycott sapped the government's strength so that, by the fall of 1973, the Chilean military found it an easy target.

The Allende government submitted three applications, but the Inter-American Development Bank approved no new loans to Chile from 1970 to 1973. The World Bank also found that it had no funds for Chile during the early seventies. Privately, a World Bank officer offered a candid characterization of the credit squeeze. "Allende moved too fast. Didn't he realize that the worst thing you can do is kick an elephant?"[25] Chile's creditors, led by a vindictive United States, also made the process of rescheduling the nation's $2 billion foreign debt, much of which had been incurred by the previous government, a long and difficult process.

When the military seized power from Allende, international institutions suddenly and drastically changed their disposition toward Chile. In February, 1974, when the junta led by Augusto Pinochet asked the IBD for assistance in the field of agriculture, the Board rushed its approval for a $22 million loan. IBD loans during 1974 totalled $97.3 million, the largest amount of loans the Bank ever extended to Chile during a single year.[26]

The World Bank also changed its policy, and in fiscal year 1974 approved $13.5 million worth of loans to Chile. The totals for 1975 and 1976 were $20 million and $33 million. (See Table 7-XVII.) The 1976 loan, for rehabilitation of Chile's copper mining and refining facilities, generated unusual controversy among Bank directors.

Nine of the Board's twenty directors, controlling 41% of the Bank's total votes, expressed their disapproval of the gross human rights violations committed by the Pinochet regime by abstaining or voting no on the loan. It was the only loan, of over 200 considered in 1976, on which the Board's vote was not unanimous. (The dissenting members represented Britain, France, Germany, Belgium, Holland, Austria, Luxembourg, Cyprus, Denmark, Norway, Sweden, Finland, Iceland, Romania, Yugoslavia, Israel, and many Middle Eastern nations.)

Table 7-XVII

World Bank Loans to Selected Countries

	Political Regime	Period	Loans (millions of $)	Annual Average
Brazil	Democratic	1953-61	149	16
	Populist	1962-63	0	0
	Military	1964-77	2,961	211
Bolivia	Populist	1952-70	0	0
	Military	1970-77	195	24
Chile	Christian democracy	1965-70	98	16
	Socialist democracy	1971-73	0	0
	Military	1974-77	126	31

Source: Anne Penketh, "The Haves Benefit: Foreign Aid Eluding the Poor", **The Globe and Mail,** September 15, 1980, p. 7.

Between 1970 and 1975, when Washington started modifying its policies toward Chile and other regimes guilty of gross human rights violations, Canada cooperated completely in the enforcement of the US vendetta against Allende, as well as in its subsequent support for Pinochet.

When Canadian Church groups questioned Canada's role in multilateral organizations during the Allende years, External Affairs Minister Mitchell Sharp justified Canada's approval of IBD policy by explaining that the Bank's management "was not able to justify [Chile's] first application on economic grounds." When the other two applications were received "the economic situation in Chile was deteriorating rapidly, and, as a result, they still had not been considered for approval by the Board of Directors, on which Canada has a seat, at the time of the coup d'etat."[27]

Ottawa has never objected to multilateral aid for the junta, though it has extended no bilateral assistance since the coup, and did not associate itself with dissenting directors during consideration of the 1976 World Bank loan. At the IBD, Canada voted even for the $22 million loan rushed through the Bank with embarrassing haste just after the coup. Gerin-Lajoie countered criticism by explaining that "the loan was designated to respond to an emergency situation in the agricultural sector as the Chileans urgently needed funds to purchase agricultural equipment for the upcoming planting season."[28]

Because it has never added human rights stipulations to its bilateral or multilateral aid disbursements, Canada has, since the mid-seventies, sometimes been better able to represent US interests in international agencies than the US itself. If an American delegate to the BID, for instance, is forced to vote against a loan to Pinochet's junta, or another of Latin America's repressive regimes, he can count on Canada, playing its traditional role as US front man, to support assistance for the offending government.

Canadian policy makers have been unable to perceive any inconsistency in Ottawa's votes at the United Nations, condemning the junta, and its votes in multilateral aid agencies approving loans to the same regime. They have disingenuously maintained that economic support is an issue totally separate from political endorsement. Finance Minister John Turner, using and abusing the same principle stated in the World Bank's Articles of Agreement, responded to queries with the argument that "The government of Canada considers that approval of loans by international financial institutions should rest on technical and not political criteria. . . ."[29]

The experience of Manley and Allende shows that aid administrators posturing as apolitical technicians only thinly disguise their power to seriously undermine or to consolidate governments. The regimes of many other Third World leaders have been toppled in a similar fashion. The combined pressure applied by the US government, the World Bank, and the IMF helped to topple the populist government of Brazilian President Joao Goulart in 1964. (See Table 7-XV.) The military overthrew a democratic government in Ghana in the early seventies, after the imposition of austerity measures demanded by the Fund and the Bank.[30] Both institutions have propped up the repressive regime of Indonesian President Suharto, who seized power from the erratic anti-imperialist Achmed Sukarno in a bloody 1965 coup. By 1980, the World Bank had extended a cumulative total of $3,987.8 million in loans to Indonesia, making it the IBRD's fourth largest recipient.

The World Bank, the IMF and allied institutions will become even more potent political forces in the eighties, as heavily indebted, oil importing, underdeveloped countries are forced to turn to them for assistance. The poor countries' medium and long term debt totalled $US 439 billion at the end of 1980, and showed no signs of declining.[31] This staggering load will, in the short term, be insupportable without aid, and the inevitable accompanying advice, from wealthy nations and their agencies.

The World Bank in the Eighties

During its 35-year history, the World Bank-IMF team has demonstrated both the resilience necessary for survival and the initiative vital to the exercise of effective global leadership. Their administrators have accommodated themselves to the rigours of localized wars and global recession, placated the demands of emerging major powers on the international scene, restrained deviants, and prevented the poorest nations from dropping out of the system they have devised. They have ensured the continuing cooperation of middle powers like Canada by endowing them with influence proportional to their position within the international order. Through their flexibility, they have maintained the capacity to meet their original and primary commitments to the world's most advanced capitalist powers.

At the start of the eighties, the World Bank is lavishly endowed with a capital stock of approximately $40 billion, projected to rise to $80 billion. Its administrators have projected that its loans will total $24 billion per year by 1990.[32] Its strong arm companion, the IMF, remains ever ready to defend the Bank's honour. The two are better equipped than ever before to act as heads of a supranational government.

The Bank has developed the authority to define "development" in the world's poor countries, and will set the trends for the coming decade. When McNamara dictated a new focus on meeting the basic needs of the world's poorest people through rural development projects, national aid agencies around the world, including CIDA, did a hasty facelift on their projects so that they would at least resemble McNamara's model.

It is probable that the eighties will be styled as the era of energy development, though the Bank and other agencies have failed to meet the objectives they set for themselves during the previous decade. During the fiscal year 1980, the World Bank and the IDA continued to concentrate their resources on agriculture and rural development, and approved 85 such projects in 44 countries, for a total of $3,458.4 million allocated to that sector. But an almost equal amount of funding — $2,849.3 million was channeled to 39 energy development projects.

The World Bank's focus on energy will no doubt fuel a new drive to assimilate those troublesome mavericks, the OPEC nations, within the established world development network. By the mid-seventies, members of the Trilateral Commission were already worrying about the disposition of their big oil bankroll and hatching schemes to "avoid being gradually eclipsed by OPEC country institutions with aid programs that are not only geographically limited but often politically linked."[33]

Ottawa has already hitched Petro-Canada to the new bandwagon. Canada's 1980 National Energy Program includes a promise that the Crown Corporation will spin off a new firm, Petro-Canada International, which will undertake oil exploration in the less developed world. Petro-Canada International will "harness the skills of many private sector firms in Canada for the benefit of developing countries", and attempt to initiate joint ventures with other state-owned western oil companies, according to the government's statement. Ottawa has participated in preliminary discussions with the state oil companies of Mexico and Venezuela, exploring the possibilities for a major joint petroleum development project in Latin America and the Caribbean.[34] Venezuela's Foreign Minister, Jose Alberto Zambrano-Velasco, visited Ottawa in February 1981 to advance cooperative efforts. Alberta and Venezuela already exchange petroleum research information, and hope to launch large-scale joint research programs in the near future.

In the eighties, the Bank will expand its already well developed capacities to extract information and issue instructions to recipient governments. Indeed, a new IBRD program inaugurated in 1980 increases the Bank's resemblance to the IMF. The new Bank non-project structural adjustment loans are comparable to the stand-by credits offered by the Fund, and are meant specifically to help poor countries reduce their current account deficits. G.K. Helleiner, professor of political economy at the University of Toronto has observed that, because the activities of the two institutions are increasingly similar, it is becoming "harder and harder to tell what is development and what is stabilization."[35] Some representatives of the less developed world have expressed worry that the Bank might try to force these loans, and unwelcome IMF style adjustment policies, on reluctant recipients.[36]

The Bank, using its increased capital and clout, will launch new initiatives to coordinate the activities of public and private funding institutions. Private banks are glad to gather under the IBRD's expansive umbrella for two reasons: 1) Through co-financing operations with the World Bank they gain access to its voluminous technical and financial data. Private bankers know that the IBRD "has proven to be a tougher, harder lender than many commercial institutions. It asks questions and receives answers that are relevant to the making of loans but are rarely put by commercial institutions."[37] 2) World Bank information and backing has grown increasingly important to private banks since the mid-seventies. They overextended themselves in the Third World during the decade, expanding their lending from an average of $4 billion in the 1970-72 period, to an estimated $23 billion in 1979.[38]

Business Week reported in 1976 that US banks were alert to the opportunities presented by the new co-financing programs developed by the World Bank and some regional development banks.[39] The number of World Bank-private bank joint operations has continued to climb since then, and by September 1980, 33 co-financing loans had been arranged for 31 projects.

The commercial bank loan is extended at market rates and is often tied to the World Bank loan through an optional cross-default clause. The clause guarantees that if the borrower nation runs into difficulties paying off the commercial loan, its credit rating with the World Bank will suffer, a penalty Third World countries will try hard to avoid. No borrower has ever dared to default on a World Bank loan.

The World Bank's new President, Alden Winship Clausen, former chairman of the Bank of America, will be pushing for an even higher degree of private co-financing. Clausen, who took office last June, has noted that for every $1 the Bank puts into a project, it now attracts $3 to $4 from outside (banks and other private sources). "Can we make that $5 or $6?" Clausen speculates. "I think that clearly I want to explore that."

The Bank is also accelerating its efforts to mount joint projects with national development agencies. In fiscal 1980 alone, it co-financed seven projects with CIDA. In a five-year period, from 1969 to 1974, it joined forces with Sweden for 17 projects, with France for 24, and with the US for 14. It has also coordinated projects with the regional development banks.

The formation of IBRD-sponsored aid coordinating groups during the seventies is perhaps the clearest illustration of the Bank's growing power as informal governor of member Third World countries. The Caribbean Group for Cooperation in Economic Development, established in 1978, and convened by the Bank in association with the IMF, the BID, and the CDB, is only one of many similar groups uniting recipients, donors and multilateral agencies in a single forum. During 1980, aid coordinating groups for Bangladesh, Colombia, Egypt, Korea, Nepal, Pakistan, the Philippines, Sudan, Uganda, Zaire and the Caribbean staged formal bank-sponsored meetings.

The push for a comprehensive world development plan, conceived and implemented through the World Bank and its partners, is steadily diminishing the choices open to Third World governments. They are less and less able to preserve their, in many cases, newly-won independence. They have been taken on as clients by a team of managers who dictate to them both the meaning and the terms of development. They are in turn cajoled and punished if they are slow to accept direction.

But recent history shows that there are limits to their patience. During the seventies, many poor countries developed a cooperatively conceived plan for a New International Economic Order, a system designed to meet their own needs. The majority of underdeveloped nations is still new to the game of international alliances, but hard experience has been an effective coach.

New Challenges

The multilateral aid agencies organized since World War II have continually avowed that they are cooperative and apolitical institutions, mandated to devise techniques and fund projects that will correct the economic problems of underdevelopment. They have been praised by development assistance experts from Pearson to Brandt. (The report of the Brandt Commission offers suggestion for minor reforms in the World Bank.[40]) National aid agencies around the world have demonstrated their approval for the multilateral approach by steadily boosting their allocations for the major international agencies.

In reality, the World Bank and its partners have grown ever more powerful, not because they foster cooperation among nations, but because they have bound the world's poor nations to a system developed primarily by the US, and subsequently sustained by the cooperative efforts of the Trilateral powers. This world government has developed at least short term solutions for the periodic shocks that have hit the western economic system since World War II: the balance of payments and debt problems that have plagued countries both rich and poor, the demands of the newly rich developed countries, and the claims of the world's poorest.

They have absorbed an increasing proportion of the world development budget also because they have amassed reams of material analyzing Third World economies, and developed a technical competence needed by national aid agencies and private funding institutions. They have established themselves as the natural leaders of the development drive to advance western economic interests in the world's poor countries.

Canada is a small but necessary component in the post-war global system. It lacks the authority to control the levers, but it facilitates the smooth functioning of the massive machine. During the past decade, Ottawa boosted its support for multilateral institutions even beyond the levels promised in the mid-seventies. In the eighties, its contributions, as a proportion of CIDA's overall aid expenditures, may drop a few percentage points, but rapid growth will not be succeeded by a sudden decline.

The multilateral institutions are simply too important to the West. They will not be left malnourished even if domestic politics in the United States, Canada and other countries force cutbacks in government contributions to the multilateral development banks. New ways of amassing large amounts of capital for the use of these institutions are now being explored, as Finance Minister Allen MacEachen explained in a 1980 speech:

I expect that in the 1980s we will look to the international financial institutions to play an even greater leadership role. They are likely to grow at a much faster rate than the growth of government budgets earmarked for development assistance and the national economies of donor countries. Imaginative approaches are required to increase their borrowing on capital and other contributions subscribed by their members. This will be particularly important if there continues to be a reluctance or an inability on the part of some of their chief contributors to commit resources to them on the scale required.[41]

The institutions established at Bretton Woods have demonstrated their ability to adapt to rapidly changing global realities, but their success has not by any means been total. The wealth they have poured into the world's poor countries since World War II has not "developed" the vast majority of Third World nations, even on the terms formulated by the agencies themselves. According to World Bank statistics, the number of people living in a state of absolute poverty has actually increased during the past two decades.[42] The world development network has also experienced difficulties incorporating the OPEC nations, and in recycling the OPEC dollars flooding the world's money markets for their own uses.

During the last fifth of the twentieth century, the World Bank will be faced with these and perhaps, unexpected new challenges. The prolonged economic slump suffered by the countries of the developed world, and the indebtedness crippling the economies of many poor countries, portend a new crisis, the dimensions of which may exceed any experienced before by the global managers. It is conceivable that the system first developed at Bretton Woods could collapse completely, or require repairs that would leave it unrecognizable. If, in the future, new systems must be built on the wreckage of the old, they will function effectively and achieve authentic global development only if institutional power is radically redistributed among the world's rich and poor countries.

The alternative may be prolonged global chaos and conflict, provoked by the poor's struggle to liberate themselves from privation and political subjection. At a 1972 UN meeting in Santiago, Chile, Salvador Allende issued a warning which resonates a decade later: "The peoples of the world will not allow poverty and affluence to exist indefinitely side by side. They will not accept an international order which will perpetuate their backward state. They will seek and they will obtain their economic independence and will conquer underdevelopment. Nothing can prevent it — neither threats, nor corruption, nor force."

Part V: Conclusions

Canada and the
8   Third World

In July 1981, the leaders of the most powerful western nations assembled in Canada for the seventh western economic summit. Chaired by Prime Minister Trudeau, the meeting was highly touted in advance as an opportunity for the seven richest countries of the West, representing over half of world economic output and most of total international trade, to make substantial progress on North-South issues. In the months before the summit, Trudeau promoted the topic by travelling to meet with leaders of both industrialized and underdeveloped nations.

But when the prime ministers, presidents and chancellor of the seven summit nations — the United States, West Germany, Japan, Britain, France, Italy and Canada — cloistered themselves in the world's largest log cabin in Montebello, Quebec, their parochial concerns dominated the discussion and eclipsed Trudeau's North-South agenda. Undaunted and tuned to the hyperbole of the mass media event, External Affairs Minister Mark MacGuigan triumphantly announced a "major advance" in the North-South dialogue. His enthusiasm was lavished on a short reference in the summit's final communiqué to the effect that the seven countries were committed to talk about organizing future discussions on the subject of "global negotiations" — a term, inscribed pointedly in lower case not capital letters, referring to comprehensive negotiations among a wide range of northern and southern countries on

North-South issues. The final communiqué also tried to assuage anticipated Third World reaction of insult at the summit's inattention to the problems besetting most of humanity by including a promise to maintain or marginally increase the aid commitments of the big seven.

The Ottawa summit signalled clearly to the Third World that the seven wealthiest countries of the West, which together direct the course of the entire world's economy, remain unwilling to change the status quo. Preoccupied with their own economic problems and disagreements, they once more postponed consideration of significant North-South adjustments.[1]

The summit also threw into relief the basic tenets and contradictions of Canadian foreign policy towards the Third World. As a junior partner in the rich world's most exclusive club, Pierre Trudeau was unable to convince his fellow world leaders to focus their attention on the question of Third World underdevelopment. And, when the western nations refused to advance beyond narrowly-defined self-interest, Ottawa stayed with them. Ottawa policy makers believe that Canada's own self-interest requires that they ingratiate themselves with the senior members of the summit club. The federal government, therefore, would not break western solidarity by enunciating its own, distinct and more progressive policies towards the Third World. Rather, Ottawa opted for continuing its typical dualism in foreign policy on North-South issues — talking a good line but taking no major actions, except to once again trot out its commitment to foreign aid.

Canada's three-decade-old program finally has to be evaluated in the context of the North's collective inaction on more important non-aid issues. One way of approaching such an evaluation is by stacking aid up against Canada's own commercial relationships with the Third World that form part of the structures of underdevelopment for which aid is an inadequate remedy. This larger balance sheet shows that Canada is the real "aid" recipient in its overall dealings with the Third World.

Who Aids Whom?

Canada consistently comes out ahead in its trade relationships with non-oil producing Third World countries, partly because of the deteriorating terms of trade between North and South and because countries like Canada restrict imports from the Third World. Deteriorating terms of trade mean that the prices of commodities exported by non-oil underdeveloped countries have fallen by more than 40% over the last 20 years relative to the price of imports from industrialized countries. The United Nations Conference on Trade and Development (UNCTAD) has calculated that this caused a perverse transfer of income from underdeveloped to industrialized countries valued at some $17 billion. For a country like Tanzania, it means that while it required five metric tons of tea to buy a tractor in 1972, it took 13 tons to buy the same tractor in 1979.[2] Import restrictions against products from Third World nations further aggravate the trade imbalance. Tanzanian sales to Canada of jute-made baler twine, for example, have been declining in recent years because of federal import restrictions aimed at protecting small Canadian producers of synthetic twine, even though the biodegradable jute product is preferred by Canadian farmers.[3]

Because of these mechanisms, and simply because Canada sells more to the Third World than it buys, recipients of Canadian aid regularly experience a merchandise trade deficit with Canada. According to CIDA's 1976 Annual Review, our trade surplus with CIDA's aid partners rose from $272 million in 1973 to $655 million in 1975.[4] For the decade 1970-1979 as a whole, CIDA's bilateral aid to its top ten recipients amounted to $2.4 billion, while during the same period Canada exported $2.9 billion more in goods (excluding oil) than it imported from these same countries. (See Table 8-XVIII.) Tied aid accounts for a proportion of these exports, but even without CIDA-supported trade, Canada would chalk up a trade surplus with these aid recipients. Such statistics forced CIDA to admit to MP Douglas Roche in 1976 that "Canada, on balance, was the greater beneficiary in her economic relations with these aid partners."[5]

The Third World also confers economic advantages on Canada by hosting private direct investment. Canadian direct investments in the Third World were valued at $3.2 billion in 1977, a 70% increase over the previous five-year period. According to the OECD, by 1976 Canadian investors were placing more investment dollars in Third World countries than in traditional sites in industrialized nations, making Canada the seventh largest foreign investor in the Third World and the fifth most important source of direct investment capital after the United States, Britain, West Germany and Japan.[6]

Canadian investments overseas are generally more profitable than domestic investments, and investments in Third World countries generally more profitable than in other industrialized states. Part of these profits are remitted to Canada in the form of dividends and interest payments, while another portion, between a quarter and a half, is reinvested abroad to expand the stock of Canadian-owned foreign investments. In 1976, foreign earnings in the Third World by Canadian corporations were $422 million — about 47% of the amount Canada disbursed in aid for the same year. The amount remitted to Canada is about twice as great as the investment capital originally sent to underdeveloped countries. Between 1970 and 1976, for example, Canadian corporations brought home

Table 8-XVIII

Aid and Trade Balance Sheet

Canadian Aid and Trade with Main Recipients of Bilateral Aid
1970 to 1979
($ millions)

Aid Recipient	Bilateral Aid Disbursements	Canadian Merchandise Trade exports to	imports from	balance
India	791	1,626	554	+1,072
Pakistan	440	604	65	+ 538
Bangladesh	388	507	47	+ 460
Tanzania	171	133	58	+ 75
Indonesia	151	468	142	+ 326
Tunisia	118	155	1	+ 153
Sri Lanka	116	105	131	- 26
Ghana	115	171	61	+ 110
Nigeria	85	280	581	- 301
(excluding oil)			(60)	(+ 220)
Niger	79	— —	— —	— —
Total	2,454	4,049	1,640	+2,409
(excluding oil)			(1,119)	(+2,930)

— — no data available

Notes: Total bilateral aid statistics cover the period from fy 1969-70 to fy 1978-79 for the ten top recipients of Canadian aid during this period. Merchandise trade statistics are for the calendar years 1970 to 1979. A merchandise trade surplus in Canada's favour is represented by (+) and a Canadian trade deficit by (-). The trade figures cover merchandise trade only, whereas bilateral aid supports the export of Canadian services as well. Figures are rounded.

Sources: CIDA, **Annual Review** (various years); Statistics Canada, **Exports by countries** and **Imports by countries** (various years).

$1,304 million in remitted dividends and interest payments on their foreign investments compared to $666 million sent abroad in direct investment flows during the same period.[7]

Thus, when Canadian aid disbursements are tabulated together with Canada's net returns from trade and direct investment transactions with aid recipients, the balance of payments benefit is overwhelmingly in Canada's favour. This advantage is compounded by additional factors.

One of these factors is commercial lending, about which there is little information because of the privacy Ottawa has conceded to Canadian private banks. The Bank of International Settlements calculates that of the $178 billion debt owed by Third World nations to all private banks in 1976, Canadian banks were owed about $13.3 billion or 7.5% of the total.[8] Although much of this debt is owed to the international affiliates of Canadian banks operating in Eurodollar markets, profits nonetheless accrue to Canadian banks and return to Canada. The yardstick provided by the Bank for International Settlements suggests that Canadian banks probably take in well over a billion dollars a year in interest payments alone on their loans to Third World countries, which in turn boosts their already significant international earnings. Canadian banks are thus the beneficiaries of the Third World's current indebtedness and its constant need to borrow more to pay off past debts. For underdeveloped countries, this debt treadmill means that current debt service (interest and amortization) payments are now over one-and-a-half times greater than the amount received in official development assistance from the industrialized countries.[9]

Finally, Canada is a big winner in its relations with the Third World because of the "brain drain". A study by UNCTAD identifies Canada as one of the primary recipients of human capital from the Third World — especially skilled workers and educated professionals whom Ottawa attracts to meet domestic manpower requirements. Between 1963 and 1972, Canada admitted 56,000 skilled immigrants from underdeveloped countries whose talents had an imputed capital value of $11.5 billion. Canada's total aid flow to the Third World in the same period was $2.3 billion. Thus, weighed against aid, the "brain drain" provided a crude net benefit of $9.2 billion to Canada.[10]

On balance, then, commercial and human transfers from the Third World to Canada far exceed the most optimistic appraisals of the benefit of Canadian aid. The nations of the Third World are bolstering some parts of the Canadian economy and some individual private corporations much more than CIDA is supporting them. Flaws in foreign aid programs are clearly secondary in importance to the economic relationships which limit Third World development. Canada could do more to correct inequities between North and South by changing its trade, investment, financing, and technology transfer patterns than by increasing or improving development assistance schemes. The greatest help, in other words, would be simply to get off the backs of the world's poor.

But Canada's response to the Third World's call for a New International Economic Order, which many representatives of the South see as a scheme for shucking their burdens, has been alternately cautious, apathetic and hostile. Whatever the attitudes and platitudes espoused by Ottawa today, in action it has frustrated NIEO demands. The federal government continues to set trade, monetary, foreign investment and other policies with virtually no regard for their effect on underdeveloped countries. The current Liberal government has made few attempts to harmonize aid and non-aid policies as it promised in its 1975 *Strategy for International Development Cooperation*. In international trade negotiations, Canadian officials who meet their counterparts from underdeveloped countries across the negotiating table have reputations for being very hard-nosed and difficult on issues involving access of Third World prod-

ucts to Canadian markets. Reforms to the international order which
Canadian officials have supported are ones with minimal impact or
which coincide with immediate Canadian interests or the interests
of the North in general.* Overall, Canada's position in international
discussions of non-aid issues has been to support the intransigence
generally practised by other western nations.[11] The Ottawa summit
was only the most recent demonstration of Ottawa's loyalty to its
more powerful allies.

The NIEO — No Panacea

But while non-aid relationships are much more central causes of
underdevelopment than aid policies, the reform of international
economic structures is not the long-sought panacea for Third World
poverty. The NIEO, conceived as a total overhaul by many supporters and critics, does not really involve radical dismantling of the
current global economic system. It calls for more and fairer trade,
investment and external financing for underdeveloped countries,
together with greater clout for the Third World in existing interna-

* External Affairs Minister Mark MacGuigan cites the General System of
Preferences (GSP), the creation of new facilities in the International Monetary Fund (IMF), the establishment of a Common Fund, and the Law of the
Sea as examples of accomplishments towards a NIEO which Canada has
supported.[12] In fact, Ottawa's implementation of the GSP, a system of
preferential tariffs for Third World imports, has been slow and imperfect
and the system itself deals with only a fraction of the Third World's trade
concerns. As Canada's "key non-aid" development instrument, the GSP has
long been cancelled out by the escalation of restrictions in western nations
against Third World manufactures and by the formulation of a new General
Agreement on Tariffs and Trade which is so contrary to southern interests
that only a handful of Third World states have signed it. Canada's support
for new financing programs by institutions like the IMF — including the
ill-fated idea of an energy affiliate of the World Bank — is motivated less by
concern for the development consequences of Third World indebtedness
than by northern worry that financial default by underdeveloped states
would disrupt international financial markets and bankrupt over-extended
private banks. Negotiations towards the establishment of a Common Fund
have led to repeated concessions by the Third World that have reduced the
proposed program for stabilizing commodity prices to a shadow of its original self. And Canada's support for a new Law of the Sea concord — now in
danger of being completely scuttled by the Reagan Administration after
seven years of discussions — is a case of Canadian concern that seabed
mining will jeopardize Canadian land-based mining interests allying themselves with Third World concerns that all nations, but especially underdeveloped ones, benefit from humankind's common heritage. Whether it is
ever adopted or not, the current consensus document from the Law of the
Sea Conference allows transnational corporations to dominate exploitation
of the seabed's wealth and grants Canada one of the biggest land grabs in
history.[13]

tional institutions like the IMF and the World Bank. Although it proposes to lessen the degree of Third World dependency on northern capital and technology, it would not eliminate it and some aspects of the platform would bind the Third World even more closely to industrialized economies.

One of the major problems with this reform package is that its supposed benefits would likely be concentrated in a few, and often the least needy, hands. Its provisions would probably transfer resources to the larger, so-called "middle income" Third World nations while the poorest countries would receive little. It can also work as much, if not more, to the benefit of transnational corporations as to the welfare of the Third World. For example, the transnational corporations already control between one-quarter and one-third of total world production and an estimated one-third of all international commerce.[14] Thus, better terms of trade negotiated through the NIEO could benefit transnational corporations through their Third World subsidiaries and do so by exploiting Third World labour and dislocating northern jobs.*

A fairer international economic system simply does not automatically mean a more equal and just relationship between social classes within Third World nations and an improvement of the conditions of life for the world's poorest. When governments of the South are committed to authentic development for the majority of their population, some of the reforms proposed by the NIEO may greatly assist the process of liberating development. But many proponents of the NIEO are in fact some of the most elitist, repressive and dictatorial regimes in the world. Under these regimes, the benefits of measures like improved and stabilized commodity prices would be

---

* An example of the limits to reform in trade and industrialization patterns between North and South can be found in the well-intentioned appeals in Canada for lowering trade barriers against textile imports from the Third World. Lower Canadian textile tariffs would certainly profit transnational corporations; 15 giant TNC traders control 85-90% of world cotton trade, 12 large firms produce 60% of the world's chemical fibres, and another 35 to 40 large corporations control a broad range of global textile activity. A substantial portion of an unrestricted Canadian textile market would be captured not by underdeveloped countries but by other industrialized producers which already are as much a source of import competition as Third World exporters. Because Third World production of textiles is based on the availability of extremely low wage-labour, and is also a transient industry, in the long run greater market access for Third World textiles in Canada would further lock underdeveloped producers into exploitative labour conditions and export dependency causing further underdevelopment. Although Canada's current tariff restrictions on textiles are no substitute for a long-range, more self-reliant textile industry policy, lowering these barriers in the present situation could cause immediate dislocations for Canadian workers without stimulating Third World development.[15]

monopolized by the rich. For example, during recent peaks in prices for sugar, coffee and soybeans, huge profits were pocketed by transnational marketing firms while in countries like Brazil large landowners and agribusiness companies increased land rents to peasants, forced peasants off their small plots and reduced the amount of land growing food.[16]

Thus, change in international economic structures cannot in themselves promote authentic development. This can begin only with the transformation of political structures *within* underdeveloped countries. Nonetheless, reforms of international institutions and structures are necessary because when Third World countries like Chile and Jamaica establish governments that embark on programs to benefit their poor majority, these structures and institutions isolate, punish, subvert and sometimes destroy the development experiment. Thus, the liberation of the Third World may not be complete without the transformation of international structures, but such transformation should be viewed as secondary and complementary to national political transformation. In the long run, radical changes in international structures may be effected only as a consequence of the struggle for liberation within Third World countries.

Canada's Aid Scoreboard

The above caveats should not be used as excuses either to ditch entirely or to perpetuate CIDA's current aid program. But they cannot redeem the federal government's abysmal record on non-aid issues and should not be used to evade changes in non-aid areas of Canadian foreign policy.

As for Canadian aid itself, it may be useful to review the success or failure of the Agency in meeting its own objectives, before outlining the contours of possible reforms.

Donor nations have used development assistance for more than three decades to advance general foreign policy objectives of the western alliance — and not without some success. Employed as both a carrot and a stick, western foreign aid programs have indeed succeeded in helping protect northern, capitalist interests by promulgating western values and consumption cultures, establishing new friendships, lubricating international commerce, and securing access for the West to Third World raw materials, markets, and investment opportunities. But today, Third World governments are increasingly inclined to pursue their own political agendas even under the threat of aid cut offs. For example, despite Canada's long-standing aid programs and vocal disapproval, India went ahead and exploded a nuclear device using Canadian technology.

Other donor nations, such as the United States, are now learning that massive injections of aid to client states may forestall political upheaval temporarily, but, as in the case of Iran, cannot prevent, and may even provoke, eventual revolution. The reason is that even while achieving western commercial and political foreign policy goals, development assistance has not increased development, but rather economic dependency and political subservience which are aspects of underdevelopment and neo-colonialism.

Canada has scored no better in its three-pronged use of aid to achieve political, commercial and developmental foreign policy objectives.

CIDA's scoreboard marks for achieving distinctively Canadian political objectives are somewhat mixed. Aid has allowed Ottawa to block Quebec's attempts to establish international support for its unique aspirations, but this use of aid is clearly at odds with its supposed development purpose. Instead of dealing with the causes of conflict within the Canadian federation, it transfers some Canada-Quebec confrontations to a Third World arena. It can also be admitted that aid has served as Ottawa's ante into the North-South poker game. It establishes Canada's right to a say in NIEO debates and meets the expectations that other donor nations have of Canada as a member of the rich world's club. But aid as a political ante perversely also serves as an excuse *not* to make concessions on non-aid issues. And because of the Third World's emphasis on the latter, action on non-aid issues would probably prove Canadian willingness to shoulder responsibilities in North-South negotiations much more than even a generous foreign aid increase.

Besides these mixed political achievements, there is no evidence that Canada has won important, specifically-Canadian political successes through aid giving. In multilateral institutions, Canada turns over its political ambitions and foreign policy sovereignty to the larger voting blocks, led by Washington, that dominate the politics of these institutions. Ottawa's bilateral programs are dwarfed by the contributions of other donors who rank ahead of Canada as aid sources in most of the countries that are CIDA priorities. In the Caribbean, where Canada is often the first or second most important source of aid, the political impact of Canadian assistance may be greater, but so too is the suspicion of Canada as an imperialist power. Finally, nowhere is Canadian aid a significant source of recipient government revenue. (See Table 8-XVIII.) As a donor, CIDA wields a twig, not a big stick.

On the commercial scoreboard, there is no evidence that aid has developed significant, permanent export markets in the Third World for Canadian goods and services. Aid simply can't do the job. Although they support immediate exports and provide taxpayer-financed subsidies for a small clique of Canadian-based enterprises,

Table 8-XIX

Comparative Tables Relating to Canadian Bilateral Aid
to Major Recipients
1977
Canadian Bilateral Aid

Selected Aid Recipients	Disbursements (US $ millions)	As % of net bilateral aid from all DAC**	Rank among other DAC donors	As % of recipient government expenditure	As % of Canadian exports
India	36.8	8%	5th	0.2%	27%
Pakistan	67.5	21%	2nd	2.7%	90%
Bangladesh	42.1	11%	4th	— —	71%
Tanzania	9.7	4%	8th	1.3%	151%
Indonesia	11.8	3%	8th	0.2%	18%
Tunisia	9.5	6%	5th	— —	83%
Sri Lanka	16.2	13%	3rd	2.8%	99%
Ghana	13.5	26%	2nd	1.0%	54%
Nigeria*	14.7	32%	1st	0.1%	46%
Niger*	13.7	17%	5th	— —	— —
Cameroon	8.7	7%	5th	1.5%	621%
Malawi	14.8	27%	2nd	9.4%	462%
Zambia	11.5	12%	4th	1.2%	86%
Ivory Coast	6.5	9%	2nd	— —	47%
Jamaica	3.9	17%	3rd	0.3%	10%
Barbados	1.7	55%	1st	0.3%	10%
Belize	1.5	26%	2nd	— —	94%
Haiti	4.7	12%	2nd	2.4%	29%
Trinidad & Tobago*	0.9	39%	2nd	— —	2%

* data for 1976 employed for historical representivity of Canadian aid flows and for consistency with available data for other columns

** Development Assistance Committee of the OECD.

Notes: Aid disbursement statistics are taken from the Organization for Economic Cooperation and Development (OECD) and are for the calendar year, in US dollars. Canadian export statistics employed to construct the final column are in Canadian dollars and also only represent merchandise exports while bilateral aid also supports the exports of services; therefore, the percentages in this column only generally reflect the degree to which total Canadian exports (goods and services) to aid recipients are reliant on aid. The countries selected for this table include the top fifteen recipients of bilateral aid during 1970-80 and four Caribbean countries selected because Canada is a major source of their aid receipts.

Sources: OECD, **Geographic Distribution of Financial Flows to Developing Countries, 1971-59 1977,** (OECD, Paris, 1978); Statistics Canada, **Exports by Country,** (fourth quarter 1979)

many of them foreign-owned, CIDA programs are both inadequate and inappropriate means of advancing an export-led growth strategy that itself should be challenged. Ottawa policy makers are deluding themselves if they really believe that aid can promote long-lasting markets by providing goods and services that recipient countries wouldn't buy if they had the choice.

CIDA's current levels of assistance come with so many project restrictions, tying provisions, inappropriate technology and misguided development concepts that the overall developmental benefits of Canadian aid are either negligible or negative. Although it concludes that aid giving should be continued, the 1978 study by the Economic Council of Canada on our relations with the Third World admits that aid has made no measurable contribution to economic growth in underdeveloped countries, that it is inefficiently allocated and that there is little evidence that it has reduced income disparities whether within or between nations.[17] Development that may have occurred in some Third World countries as a result of CIDA effort is overshadowed by the underdevelopment generated elsewhere.

Reforming Canadian Aid

CIDA's failure to achieve its own objectives suggests that more than just the aid delivery system is in need of an overhaul. Changes in Canadian aid giving must be comprehensive. They must be directed not only at the type of aid offered — the aid package is commonly the subject of aid critiques — but more importantly at redrafting aid purposes and the criteria for selecting aid partners.

The only justifiable purpose for aid giving is assisting Third World countries in their struggles towards integral development. As a minimum this means CIDA must drop its charade of trying to meet development and commercial objectives simultaneously. It means ending the hypocrisy of calling export promotion, surplus food disposal, and public subsidization of private corporations "aid". It means rejecting the use of aid to transfer — in traditional or new, Brandtian forms — the economic problems of Canada to the South. Concretely this translates into cancelling CIDA programs and policies for export and investment promotion. The programs of CIDA's Industrial Cooperation Division for subsidizing private companies investing in the Third World should be taken out of the aid program if not abandoned altogether as unnecessary corporate welfare. Food aid should be severely cut back and reserved for well-planned, disinterested emergency efforts. Canada's bilateral aid should be unilaterally untied and the first priority of untied aid should be the support of high local-cost projects that few other donors are willing to consider because of their own tying restrictions.

Unlike commercial purposes, political content cannot be eliminated from aid giving because authentic development is always a political process as much as an economic and social one. But to the degree CIDA continues to subordinate development needs to ideological preferences, western campaigns against enemy "isms", and outright patronage, Canada will be seen as a purveyor of underdevelopment and neo-colonialism. Instead, the political content of Canadian aid needs to be radically redefined. The politics that guide the Agency should be those of solidarity with oppressed peoples and their struggles for political and economic liberation.

If these were the political goals of Canadian aid giving, CIDA would have to develop a more precise and selective criterion for identifying aid partners. Aid would be reserved for popularly-supported governments that seriously want to eradicate poverty at its roots in a self-reliant way. Development assistance should not be given to any underdeveloped country that maintains gross social inequalities or denies fundamental human rights. If Third World regimes are not interested in promoting the welfare of their majority poor, externally-financed aid is unlikely to be able to do much for the people. Even the best aid when given to elitist and repressive regimes will bypass the poor and almost inevitably reinforce the structures of domination. On the other hand, governments that are committed to authentic development may have some chance, difficult as it may be, of employing even imperfect types of aid for the benefit of their people.

Human rights must be a central criterion for selecting aid partners and determining aid effectiveness because they are an integral part of the development process. Wherever human rights are systematically violated — not just political and civil rights but also economic, social, religious and cultural rights — underdevelopment occurs. The abuse of civil and political rights is not only a direct violation of the integrity of the person but an additional impediment to integral development, because the political participation of individuals and groups in society is restricted. In the same way, the abuse of economic, social and cultural rights makes the full realization of political and civil rights impossible because the economic and social participation of different social classes is grossly unequal. In other words, the new goal for aid giving — and another criterion for selecting aid partners — should be the advancement not merely of "basic needs", but the more encompassing fulfillment of "basic rights".

Shifting the political purpose of Canadian aid towards basic rights and solidarity with oppressed peoples firstly implies disengaging our aid program from the imperial strategies and structures of the largest western powers. In the current political context, CIDA must reject the plans of the Reagan administration to use western aid in a new Cold War campaign to rebuild fortress America. In international financial institutions, which in the long run may require complete replacement, Canada should in the short run adopt an independent position that favours respect for human rights and resists attempts by larger powers to use these structures to discipline and limit Third World development experiments.

Secondly, CIDA should reduce the number of countries to which it provides aid — perhaps along the lines of the more selective program of the Swedish aid agency — in order to give priority support to those nations earnestly engaged in eradicating poverty. In the short run this may mean decreasing the amount of aid allocations and the abandoning of aid targetry. So be it. Dispensing a tainted aid elixir in gallon jugs instead of quart bottles does not speed a remedy. Supplying smaller amounts of better quality aid to countries where it will benefit the majority and correct injustices will do more good than continuing to support indifferent and elitist governments with larger amounts of aid with the illusory hope that some crumbs will trickle down to the poor. A litmus test of the quality of Canadian aid might be whether it helps mobilize people through cooptation and the reinforcement of exploitative structures. In repressive and elitist countries, CIDA could increase its support for Canadian non-governmental organizations, in such a way as not to compromise their independence, so that these NGOs can aid counterpart groups in the Third World in combating the causes of poverty.* In addition, more could be done for the poor in such countries by more direct political instruments of foreign policy such as international pressure to end human rights violations, and by demonstrations of increased respect for legitimate aspirations of popular movements.

---

*Although NGOs are generally praised for being effective, disinterested, grass-roots-oriented mechanisms of aid giving, not all NGOs are agents for authentic development. In fact, some Canadian and international NGOs are as paternalistic supporters of the political status quo as the worst forms of government aid giving. For the many Canadians who support NGOs through private contributions, a small checklist of questions might be used to determine if a given NGO is a progressive or regressive agent:

- Is the NGO committed to combatting the root causes of poverty and underdevelopment as they exist in both Canada and the Third World, and in international structures?
- Does the NGO put the decision-making control over projects in the hands of local Third World organizations without fostering economic dependency?
- Are the projects and organizations funded by the NGO clearly assessing their own positions, work and objectives within the larger framework of society and seeking to change the basic relationships of injustice?
- Does the NGO's public face in Canada — especially its fund raising

Unfortunately, the outlook for the implementation of such reform proposals is not optimistic. Canadian aid policy, after all, is a creature of Canadian foreign policy and Ottawa sets foreign policy on the basis of its analysis of the "national interests". But the "national interests" is a slippery term. In practice, Ottawa's definition is highly circumscribed by considerations of the welfare of the corporate elite and by Canada's dependent, junior partner status within the US economic and political orbit. A far-reaching overhaul of foreign policy and aid programming depends on the political transformation of our own political economy and the subsequent redefinition of the national interests — a political task similar in many ways to struggles required in Third World countries.

The question of political power is thus at the crux of the aid and development debate in both Canada and the Third World. Exhortations for reform directed at those with power usually fall on deaf ears because, as the former anti-slavery leader Frederick Douglas noted, "power never concedes anything without a struggle; it never has and it never will." But when the aid debate leads to a recognition of the questions of power, it can help empower organized groups in both Canada and the Third World — trade unions, peasants, non-governmental organizations, political movements, churches — in their struggle to gain power to make essential choices.

As the last two decades of this century unfold, Canadians will likely have increased opportunities — if only because of the continuing economic crisis and its consequences in unemployment and inflation — to understand that they share with the people of the Third World some common problems of underdevelopment and dependency and some common obstacles in the international concentrations of economic and political power. In turn, this growing awareness may form the basis for increasing expressions of support and solidarity between North and South. In the long run, such solidarity is in the real national interests of Canada.

---

appeals — distort or correctly portray the causes of underdevelopment?
• Is the NGO itself democratic in the way it relates to its Canadian constituency? (NGOs that are not accountable to their donors are less likely to mature in their concepts of development.)

In Canada there is also a network of NGOs which addresses Third World issues not by providing aid but by educating Canadians and building solidarity. Church, trade union, and community groups working on human rights and solidarity issues can do as much for authentic development by freeing political prisoners from their cells and by supporting popular movements of workers and peasants as large aid institutions can do with all their money.

Endnotes

Introduction

[1] *North-South: A Program for Survival. The Report of the Independent Commission on International Development Issues under the Chairmanship of Willy Brandt* (Cambridge, Mass.: The MIT Press, 1980).

[2] *Ibid.*, p. 238.

[3] *Ibid.*, p. 267.

[4] Among the Brandt Proposals for a "massive transfer of resources from North to South" are: increased official development assistance rising to 1% of GNP by the year 2000, increased share capital and borrowing power by the multilateral development banks, the allocation of special drawing rights, the funding of a World Development Fund from progressive international taxation, and concessional financing for mineral exploration.

[5] World Bank, *World Development Report, 1980* (Washington: World Bank, 1980), p. 9.

[6] *The Globe and Mail*, January 19, 1981.

[7] *World Business Weekly*, January 1, 1981.

[8] *The Globe and Mail*, October 1, 1980.

[9] *The Globe and Mail*, August 25, 1980.

[10] For more on the Shulman episode see *Toronto Sun*, January 20, 1977; *The Globe and Mail*, January 20 and 24, 1977; the *Toronto Star*, January 20 and 21, 1977. Another Shulman criticism was directed at a $1.2 million CIDA grant for a physiotherapist training school in South Vietnam. CIDA's director of communications, Paul Doucet, easily deflected the criticism with the comment: "Maybe Mr. Shulman doesn't know that there was a war there and it's a good thing to help rehabilitate thousands of maimed people."

[11] *Maclean's*, February 16, 1981; December 29, 1980.

[12] Peter Worthington, "How Aid Helps Dictators", *Toronto Sun*, June 26, 1980.

[13] Canada, Department of Industry, Trade and Commerce, *Strengthening Canada Abroad: Final Report of the Export Promotion Review Committee* (Ottawa: IT&C, November 30, 1979), p. 35.

[14] See, for example, the two substantial reports of all-party parliamentary committees: Canada, House of Commons, *International Development: Report to Parliament of the Standing Committee on External Affairs and National Defence* (Ottawa: House of Commons, April 14, 1976); Canada, House of Commons, *Parliamentary Task Force on North-South Relations* (Ottawa: Supply & Services, 1980).

[15] *North-South: A Program for Survival*, p. 243.

Chapter 1. At First Glance: Public Perceptions of Canadian Aid

[1] *Toronto Sun*, January 21, 1977.
[2] *Toronto Sun*, January 28, 1977.
[3] *Montreal Star*, January 20, 1977.
[4] *Toronto Star*, January 17, 1975.
[5] *Ibid.*
[6] *Ottawa Citizen*, January 2, 1975.
[7] *Montreal Star*, January 24, 1975.
[8] *The Globe and Mail*, January 14, 1977.
[9] *Toronto Star*, November 1, 1975.
[10] CIDA, *Canada and Development Cooperation, Annual Review, 1975-76*, p. 50.
[11] CIDA, "1977 Annual Aid Review: Memorandum of Canada to the Development Assistance Committee of the Organization for Economic Cooperation and Development", April, 1979.
[12] *Toronto Star*, July 22, 1979.
[13] CIDA, *Annual Review 1975-76*, p. 46.
[14] *Ibid.*
[15] CIDA, *Cooperation Canada*, no. 26, 1977, p. 12.
[16] Richard Nixon, "Asia After Vietnam", *Foreign Affairs*, October, 1967.
[17] Jamie Swift and the Development Education Centre, *The Big Nickel: INCO at Home and Abroad*, (Kitchener: Between the Lines, 1977), p. 107.
[18] *Amnesty International Report*, 1980, p. 199.
[19] "Pacific", *Foreign Policy for Canadians*, published by authority of the Honourable Mitchell Sharp, Secretary of State for External Affairs, (Ottawa: Information Canada, 1970), p. 20.
[20] *Ottawa Citizen*, December 21, 1974.
[21] *Montreal Star*, January 24, 1975.
[22] CIDA, *Annual Review 1975-76*, p. 34.
[23] *Development Directions*, November/December 1978, p. 29.
[24] *Montreal Star*, January 24, 1975.
[25] *Ibid.*
[26] *Toronto Star*, January 29, 1975.
[27] *Toronto Star*, January 11, 1975, and *Ottawa Citizen*, December 19, 1974.
[28] *Ottawa Citizen*, December 19, 1974.
[29] *Financial Times of Canada*, February 14, 1977.
[30] "Notes for an Appearance by Michel Dupuy to the Standing Committee of the House of Commons on External Affairs and National Defence", April 19, 1977.
[31] *The Globe and Mail*, July 9, 1977.
[32] CIDA, *Contact*, no. 38, March, 1975.
[33] David Van Praagh, "Canada and Southeast Asia", in *Canada and the Third World*, Peyton V. Lyon and Tareq Y. Ismael, eds., (Toronto: Macmillan Company of Canada, 1976), p. 321.
[34] *Far Eastern Economic Review*, December 26, 1975.
[35] Cheryl Payer, *The Debt Trap: The International Monetary Fund and the Third World*, (Monthly Review Press, 1974), pp. 86-89.
[36] Tanmih Ghn, September 30, 1976.
[37] *Toronto Star*, February 3, 1975.
[38] *Dev/Ed News*, early Spring 1981, p. 13.

Chapter 2. The Aid Program: Uneven Growth and Mixed Objectives

[1] *The Colombo Plan: Vision into Reality* (Colombo: Information Department of the Colombo Plan Bureau, 1976), p. 3.

[2] Keith Spicer, "Clubmanship Upstaged: Canada's Twenty Years in the Colombo Plan", *International Journal*, Vol. XXV, no. 1, Winter 1969-1970, p. 29.

[3] Keith Spicer, *A Samaritan State? External Aid in Canada's Foreign Policy* (Toronto: University of Toronto Press, 1966), p. 107.

[4] CIDA, *Annual Review*, 1967-68, p. 2.

[5] CIDA, *Annual Report*, 1967, p. 24.

[6] CIDA, *Annual Review*, 1969, p. 5.

[7] Memo from Paul Gerin-Lajoie to all CIDA officers, January 30, 1973.

[8] *Canada: Strategy for International Development Cooperation 1975-1980* (Information Division, Communications Branch, Canadian International Development Agency, 1975), p. 24.

[9] CIDA, *Annual Review*, 1977-78, p. 11.

[10] *North-South: A Program for Survival* (Cambridge: The MIT Press, 1980), p. 17.

[11] CIDA, *Annual Report*, 1975-76, p. 77.

[12] *Strategy*, p. 23.

[13] Mitchell Sharp, "Canada's Stake in International Programs", *Dialogue*, 1961, p. 47.

[14] *Foreign Policy for Canadians*: "International Development", (Ottawa: Information Canada, 1970), p. 12.

[15] Quoted in Spicer, *A Samaritan State*, p. 11.

[16] S.C. Triantis, "Canada's Interest in Foreign Aid", *World Politics*, Vol. 24, no. 1, p. 14.

[17] Canada, *House of Commons Debates*, Feb. 22, 1950, p. 131.

[18] *Toronto Star*, August 30, 1976.

[19] Barrie M. Morrison, "Canada and South Asia", *Canada and the Third World*, Peyton V. Lyon and Tareq Y. Ismael, eds., (Toronto: Macmillan of Canada, 1976), p. 25.

[20] Quoted in Clyde Sanger, *Half A Loaf: Canada's Semi-Role Among Developing Countries*, (Toronto: Ryerson Press, 1969), p. 203.

[21] *Foreign Policy for Canadians*: "International Development", pp. 9-10.

[22] Michel Dupuy, "Notes for an address by Michel Dupuy to the Empire Club of Toronto, November 3, 1977", p. 5.

[23] "See You in Bongo Bongo: Trade Versus Aid", *Last Post*, September 1973, p. 50.

Chapter 3. CIDA's Regional Programs: Global Reach

[1] Cited in Keith Spicer, "Clubmanship Upstaged: Canada's Twenty Years in the Colombo Plan", *International Journal*, Vol. XXV, no. 1, Winter 1969-70, p. 25.

[2] Cited in Linda Freeman, "The Nature of Canadian Interests in Black Southern Africa", unpublished doctoral dissertation (University of Toronto, 1978), p. 39.

[3] Keith Spicer, *A Samaritan State? External Aid in Canada's Foreign Policy* (Toronto: University of Toronto Press, 1966), p. 47.

[4] Peter C. Briant, *Canada's External Aid Program* (Private Planning Association of Canada, 1965), p. 30; also see Thomas C. Bruneau *et al, CIDA: The Organization of Canadian Overseas Assistance* (Centre for Developing Area Studies, McGill University, 1978), p. 12.

[5] Bepin Behair, *Facets of Foreign Aid* (Bombay: Vora & Co., 1968), pp. 98-99.

[6] Barrie M. Morrison, "Canada and South Asia", in Peyton V. Lyon and Tareq Y. Ismael, eds., *Canada and the Third World* (Toronto: Macmillan of Canada, 1976), pp. 17-18.

[7] Keith Spicer, *A Samaritan State?*, p. 127.

[8] Barrie M. Morrison, "Canada and South Asia", p. 31.

[9] Claire Culhane, *Why is Canada in Vietnam? The Truth About Our Foreign Aid* (Toronto: NC Press, 1972), p. 95.

[10] Statistics Canada, *Statistics Canada Daily*, August 8, 1980, p. 3.

[11] Canada, *Senate Report* of the Standing Committee on Foreign Affairs of the Senate of Canada on Canada-Caribbean Relations (Ottawa: Queen's Printer, 1970), p. 31.

[12] CIDA, "A Review of Canadian Development Assistance Policy in the Western Hemisphere", mimeo, circa 1974.

[13] Robert Chodos, *The Caribbean Connection: The Double-Edged Canadian Presence in the West Indies* (Toronto: James Lorimer & Co., 1977), pp. 198-206.

[14] External Affairs and National Defence Standing Committee of the House of Commons, May 27, 1976, p. 42.

[15] Jack Cahil, "MacGuigan Aims to Make Idealism Practical", *Toronto Star*, January 31, 1981.

[16] Robert O. Matthews, "Canada and Anglophone Africa", in Peyton V. Lyon and Tareq Y. Ismael, eds., *Canada and the Third World* (Toronto: Macmillan of Canada, 1976), p. 61.

[17] *House of Commons Debates*, 1957-1958, Vol. IV, p. 4016.

[18] Department of External Affairs, *Annual Report 1967*, p. 42; also see Linda Freeman, "The Nature of Canadian Interests in Black Southern Africa", p. 125.

[19] *Ibid.*, p. 125.

[20] Department of External Affairs, *Annual Report 1972*.

[21] Department of External Affairs, *Annual Report* (various years); Robert Matthews, "Canada and Anglophone Africa", p. 111.

[22] Linda Freeman, "Canada and Africa in the 1970s", in *International Journal*, Vol. XXXV, no. 4, Autumn 1980, p. 804; CIDA, *News Release*, no. 81-5, January 29, 1981.

[23] Quoted in Keith Spicer, "Clubmanship Upstaged", p. 26.

[24] Gregory Armstrong, "Aid Policies as a Reflection of Canadian Domestic Concerns", in *International Perspectives*, March-April 1975, p. 46.

[25] Linda Freeman, "Canada and Africa in the 1970s", p. 802.

26 Clyde Sanger, "Canada and Development in the Third World", in Peyton Lyon and Tareq Y. Ismael, eds., *Canada and the Third World*, p. 283.

27 Jeffrey Simpson, "Senegal to Get Aid from Petro-Canada", *The Globe and Mail*, January 13, 1981.

28 Department of External Affairs, *Annual Report 1979*.

29 Linda Freeman, "Canadian Interests in Black Southern Africa", p. 975.

30 CIDA, *Annual Report 1979-80*, p. 14.

31 Department of External Affairs, *Foreign Policy for Canadians: United Nations* (Ottawa: Information Canada, 1970), pp. 20, 19.

32 Quoted in Keith Spicer, *A Samaritan State?*, p. 62.

33 CIDA, "Canada's Development Assistance to Latin America", Briefing Paper no. 5, circa 1973.

34 CIDA, *Annual Review 1967-68*, provides details on export credits, food aid to the Dominican Republic and the IDB loans to Latin America during this period. Concerning Chile, the former US ambassador to Chile, Edward Korry, has recently gone on record to state that more than $20 million in illegal US funds were channelled into the country by the CIA prior to the 1964 election. See: *Latin America Weekly Report*, February 20, 1981.

35 Quoted in Peter C. Dobell, *Canada's Search for New Roles* (London: Royal Institute of International Affairs, 1972), p. 115.

36 CIDA, "Latin American Task Force: Development Assistance", mimeo, August, 1969.

37 CIDA, *Annual Review 1973-74*, p. 47.

38 CIDA, "A Review of Canadian Development Assistance Policy in the Western Hemisphere", mimeo, 1974.

39 CIDA, "Canada's Development Assistance to Latin America", p. 2.

40 *Ibid.*

41 CIDA, "A Review of Canadian Development Assistance Policy in the Western Hemisphere", pp. 40-43 and 43-47.

42 *Ibid.*

43 Associated Press Wire Service copy, dateline Bridgetown, Barbados, January 13, 1981.

44 "Foreign Aid to Junta is Curbed", *The Globe and Mail*, November 29, 1981; CIDA, "Canada Provides Food Aid to Nicaragua", *News Release*, no. 81-21, June 8, 1981.

Chapter 4. Underdevelopment Assistance

1 Sources for the following account of the CIDA-sponsored bakery project in Tanzania are the following: Andrew C. Coulson, "The Automated Bread Factory", mimeo, University of Dar es Salaam Department of Economics, April, 1975; "Is Canadian Bread Best for Tanzania", *The New Scientist*, January 23, 1975; David MacDonald, "Magazine Criticizes Tanzania Bakery Project", *Montreal Star*, January 24, 1975; Canada, House of Commons, *Minutes of the Standing Committee on External Affairs and National Defence*, May 29, 1975 (see answers provided by CIDA to questions asked by MP D. Roche); Canadian Baker Perkins Limited, *Annual Financial Statements* (various years); Telephone interview with Canadian Baker Perkins Ltd., April 24, 1981; Statistics Canada, *Inter-Corporate Ownership 1975* (Ottawa: Supply & Services, 1978); CIDA, "Canada to Assist in Growing Wheat", *News Release*, June 8, 1977.

2 Pierre P. Sicard, "Notes for an Address Before the Canadian Export Association", (Ottawa: CIDA, October 31, 1977).

3 W.W. Rostow, *The Stages of Economic Growth: A Non-Communist Manifesto* (Cambridge University Press, 1960).

4 Rostow's theory, although severely criticized, continued to permeate some of CIDA's development thinking throughout the 1970s. A 1974 brief to Cabinet by the Agency proposed expanding Canada's economic relationships "particularly in countries that are close to economic 'take-off' ". In addressing a parliamentary committee in early 1981, the External Affairs Minister discussed the rationale for giving some aid to so-called middle income countries: "If we can assist some countries to cross the barrier between the developing and developed category, we are surely achieving something worthwhile...." See Minutes of the *Standing Committee on External Affairs and National Defence*, Issue no. 40, April 12, 1980, p. 12.

5 A mid-1960s study on Canadian aid sponsored by Canadian business associations explained the savings theory in most simplistic terms: "The position of many of the developing countries is analogous to that of a business that uses all of its current output to sustain production. Nothing is left over for new investment toward future growth.... There are thus two solutions to the problem of international economic development: forced savings... or external assistance, public or private, from industrial nations.... Foreign capital and technical assistance are needed to fill the gap between the resources needed for the desired rate of development and the resources released through taxation and private saving." See Peter C. Briant, *Canada's External Aid Program* (The Canadian Trade Committee and the Private Planning Association of Canada, April 1965). Also on the savings theory see: Paul Rosenstein Rodan, "International Aid for Underdeveloped Countries", *Review of Economics and Statistics*, May, 1961; Hollis Chenery and A. Stout, "Foreign Assistance and Economic Development", *American Economic Review*, September, 1966.

6 Garrett Hardin, "Living on a Lifeboat", *BioScience*, October, 1974.

7 CIDA, *Annual Review* (various years).

8 John Crispo, "All Foreign Aid Should Be for Birth Control", *The Globe and Mail*, November 28, 1974. Hardin's neo-Malthusian ideas are retreaded in a recent, right-wing attack on Canadian aid by Paul Fromm and James Hull, *Down the Drain? A Critical Re-examination of Canadian Foreign Aid* (Toronto: Griffin House, 1981).

9 *Fortune*, November, 1976, p. 115.

¹⁰ World Bank, *World Development Report 1980*, pp. 56-58; Wasim Zaman, "The World Population Situation", *Third World Quarterly*, Vol. II, no. 3, July, 1980.
¹¹ Quoted in Barry Zwicker, "One of the Last Chances to Defuse the Population Bomb", *Toronto Star*, April 1, 1974.
¹² Quoted in *The New Internationalist*, June, 1977, p. 3.
¹³ The attraction of the population-based theory of underdevelopment is in its political function rather than its validity. The observation of the *Encyclopaedia Britannica* in 1911 still holds true for the neo-Malthusians of today: "It can scarcely be doubted that the favour which was at once accorded to the views of Malthus in certain circles was due in part to an impression, very welcome to the higher ranks of society, that they tended to relieve the rich and powerful of responsibility for the condition of the working classes, by showing that the latter had chiefly themselves to blame, and not either the negligence of their superiors or the institutions of the country. The application of his doctrines, too, made by some of his successors had the effect of discouraging all active effort for social improvement." Cited in Denis Goulet and Michael Hudson, *The Myth of Aid: The Hidden Agenda of the Development Reports* (New York: IDOC, 1971), p. 127.
¹⁴ Michael Harrington, *The Vast Majority: A Journey to the World's Poor* (New York: Simon & Schuster, 1977), p. 27.
¹⁵ Agency for International Development (AID), "U.S. Overseas Loans and Grants", (Washington D.C., 1967 and 1974.)
¹⁶ South Korea's post-war industrialization is full of ironies and contradictions. Economic growth was first boosted by a far-reaching land reform program — fully half the cultivable land changed hands between 1948 and 1957 — backed by the occupying US army. Washington's use of land redistribution as a means to combat communism has been repeated since South Korea in South Vietnam and El Salvador, both "Cold War" situations in Washington's view. But the US has opposed such reform almost everywhere else as a threat to US interests and the status quo.

During the 1960s and 1970s, South Korea's rapid economic growth was achieved by attracting foreign capital through tax incentives and low wages, channelling investments into export industries, and neglecting the domestic market — particularly agriculture. This strategy led to the contracting of over $26 billion in external debt and at the same time left the country extremely vulnerable to international economic fluctuations. Surplus US food and food aid had to be imported to keep food prices artificially low — at the expense of agriculture — to maintain international wage competitiveness.

The country's heralded success in export-oriented manufacturing has rested not only on exploited labour but also on US assistance. Between 1953 and 1978, South Korea's textile industry, for example, relied on over $390 million in US aid credits to purchase raw cotton imports at prices substantially below the world average. The channelling of foreign capital into the export sector has resulted in a dual economy with the foreign sector almost completely severed from the domestic structure; domestic industries do not supply raw materials, machinery or semi-finished goods to the export sector and the export industries supply very little to the domestic market. Today, this export-based house of cards is threatened by the very transnational corporations that constructed it. TNCs are now beginning to relocate Korean subsidiaries in other Asian countries where labour is even more exploited. See: *Canada Asia Currents*, periodically published by the

Canada-Asia Working Group; *Multinational Monitor*, June, 1981; *The New Internationalist*, no. 81, November, 1979; *Development Finance*, March-April, 1978.
[17] Dag Ehrenpreis, *On Development and Underdevelopment: Part I — What is Development?* (reprinted by CIDA Policy Analysis Division, March, 1976), p. 20.
[18] See: J.C. Duarte, *Aspectos da Distribuicao no Brasil em 1970* (Piracicaba: ESALQ-USP, 1971); Arruda, de Souza and Alfonso, *Multinationals and Brazil* (Toronto: Latin America Research Unit, 1975), p. 34; Sao Paulo Justice and Peace Commission, *Sao Paulo: Growth and Poverty* (London: CIIR and Bowerdean Press, 1978), p. 46.
[19] CIDA, "A Review of Canadian Development Assistance Policy in the Western Hemisphere", (Ottawa, 1974).
[20] *Ibid*.
[21] For a brief analysis of economic dualism see: Keith Griffin, "Underdevelopment in Theory," *The Political Economy of Development and Underdevelopment*, C. Wilber, ed., (New York: Random House, 1973).
[22] Adelman and Morris, "An Anatomy of Income Distribution Patterns in Developing Nations", *Development Digest* (published by AID), October, 1971.
[23] Hollis Chenery, "Trade, Aid and Economic Development", *International Development 1965*, Solomon and Robock, eds., (New York: Oceana Pub., 1966). For a general critique of the savings theory see: K. Griffin, "Foreign Capital, Domestic Savings and Economic Development", *Bulletin*, Oxford University Institute of Economics and Statistics, May, 1971.
[24] P.F. Wickenden, Chief, Transport Economics, Department of Industry, Trade and Commerce, *Personal Communication*, March, 1976, cited in S.E. Bird *et al*, *Are Our Aid Programs Exporting Our Bad Habits*, mimeo, Carleton University, Ottawa. A study by the British-North American Committee comes to the same conclusion: "The net benefit of tourism to the balance of payments is often much less than it might be, particularly in the smaller islands, because so much of the food the tourists eat and the things they buy in the shops are imported from abroad." See: David Powell, *Problems of Economic Development in the Caribbean* (London: British-North American Committee, 1973), p. 42.
[25] CIDA, *Strategy for International Development Cooperation 1975-1980*, pp. 6-7.
[26] World Bank, *Prospects for Developing Countries, 1975-1985* (Washington: World Bank, 1977).
[27] Lester B. Pearson *et al*, *Partners in Development: Report of the Commission on International Development* (New York: Praeger, 1969), p. 172.
[28] On Canada's tied aid record see the following sources: CIDA, "Aid Tying and Untying", mimeo, 1970; Nihal Kappagoda, *The Cost of Foreign Aid to Developing Countries* (Ottawa: IRDC, 1978); the North-South Institute, *North South Encounter* (Ottawa: 1977).
[29] L.B. Pearson, *Partners in Development*, p. 172.
[30] Strong originally set this figure in 1970 and repeated it for the CBC television program *The Fifth Estate*, April 4, 1978. See also: G.K. Helleiner, "Canadian Commercial Relations with the Third World", *Unequal Partners — Development in the Seventies. Where Does Canada Stand?*, Linda Freeman, ed., (Toronto: OXFAM of Canada, 1970), p. 4.
[31] Author's interview with Mr. Earl Hindley, Cali, Columbia, January, 1976.
[32] Douglas Roche, *What Development Is All About* (Toronto: NC Press, 1979), p. 131.

33 This quote and the following information concerning the Botswana power plant is found in Linda Freeman, *The Nature of Canadian Interests in Black Southern Africa*, unpublished doctoral thesis, University of Toronto, 1978.
34 *Ibid.*, p. 852.
35 Cited in Richard Gott, "Close Your Frontiers", a speech to the ICD Conference at the University of Kent at Canterbury, January, 1975.
36 Clyde Sanger, "Canada and Development in the Third World", *Canada and the Third World*, Peyton V. Lyon and Tareq Y. Ismael, eds., (Toronto: Macmillan, 1976), p. 290.
37 G.K. Helleiner, "The Development Business — Next Steps", *International Journal*, Vol. XXV, no. 1, Winter, 1969-70, pp. 166-7.
38 *African Development*, June 1976, p. 561.
39 Thomas C. Bruneau *et al*, "CIDA: The Organization of Canadian Overseas Assistance", Centre for Developing Area Studies, McGill University, October, 1978, p. 28. Some observers suggest that the figures used in this study, based on interviews with CIDA officials, nonetheless may overstate the percentage of "non-victim" initiation of aid projects.
40 Linda Freeman, *Canadian Interests in Black Southern Africa*, p. 958.
41 For more on the problem of tying restricting CIDA's participation in rural development and basic needs projects see: Douglas Roche, *What Development Is All About*, p. 89; and North-South Institute, *North South Encounter*, p. 127.
42 *Toronto Star*, June 30, 1981, p. A10.
43 Canada, House of Commons, *Minutes of the Standing Committee on External Affairs and National Defense*, April 21, 1981, pp. 12, 30. [Hereafter referred to as "Standing Committee".]
44 Parliamentary Task Force on North-South Relations, *Report to the House of Commons on the Relations Between Developed and Developing Countries* (Ottawa: Supply & Services, 1980), p. 74.
45 CIDA, "Message From the President of the Agency — Directions for the Agency", internal document, President's office, December, 1977, p. 1.
46 *Standing Committee*, April 6, 1978, p. 22.
47 An earlier CIDA formulation of the "mutual interests" theme was expressed in the Agency's *1969 Annual Review*: "While our assistance is designed primarily to help them, it brings important benefits to us — expanded markets, valuable experience for our people, and, hopefully, in the long run, a better, more secure world for our children." Following Dupuy's formulation of the concept, Marcel Masse had adopted the same argument for aid. Masse told the Toronto Canadian Club in early 1981 that the aid program "creates wealth in our country as well as in others." See: Marcel Masse, "The Third World: A Canadian Challenge", notes for a speech to the Canadian Club, Toronto, April 6, 1981, p. 10.
48 Paul Gerin-Lajoie, "The Economic Impact of Canada's Foreign Aid Program on the Canadian Economy", notes for a speech to the Montreal Board of Trade, Montreal, March 12, 1973, pp. 9-11.
49 Michel Dupuy, "Notes for an Address to the Empire Club of Toronto", November 3, 1977, p. 5.
50 North-South Institute, *North South Encounter*, p. 122.
51 The North-South Institute calculates that the current value of the loans forgiven, discounted by their original grant element, was only $35 million. See North-South Institute, *Third World Deficits and the Debt Crisis* (Ottawa: 1978), p. 27.

[52] Lester B. Pearson *et al, Partners in Development,* pp. 140-1.
[53] CIDA, *Annual Aid Review 1978 — Memorandum of Canada to the Development Assistance Committee of the* OECD, Ottawa, 1980.
[54] Lester B. Pearson *et al, Partners in Development,* p. 141.
[55] Jane Chudy, "Why Canadian Business Is Not Getting More World Bank Contracts", *Development Directions,* August/September 1978, pp. 22-25.
[56] Keith Hay, "The Implications for the Canadian Economy of CIDA's Bilateral Tied Aid Programs", paper prepared for the Economic Council of Canada, March 30, 1978, p. 50, Table 8.
[57] CIDA, "Active Contracts — Region and Country", mimeo, February 28, 1981.
[58] Hay's data is cited in the Economic Council of Canada, *For A Common Future — A Study of Canada's Relations with Developing Countries* (Ottawa: Supply & Services, 1979), p. 107.
[59] Michel Dupuy, "Notes For an Address to the Empire Club of Toronto", November 3, 1977, pp. 5-6.
[60] R. Oram's article in *The Globe and Mail — Report on Business,* January 22, 1977, makes an exaggerated claim that one dollar in consultancy fees can generate up to $10 worth of equipment orders.
[61] *Canada Commerce,* June 1979, p. 19.
[62] Douglas Roche, *What Development Is All About,* p. 89.
[63] Economic Council of Canada, *For A Common Future,* p. 106. The Council says that if aid were untied Canadian aid dollars would nonetheless work their way back to Canada when spent on goods in other donor nations and then by these donors on Canadian goods.
[64] CBC television, *The Fifth Estate,* April 4, 1978.
[65] For the CEA's denial that tied aid is a subsidy and for an example of their defence of tying see: Canada, House of Commons, *Minutes of the Special Standing Committee on North-South Relations* [hereafter *Special Committee*], Issue no. 23, November 3, 1980.
[66] For this argument by business see: Export Promotion Review Committee, *Strengthening Canada Abroad* (Ottawa: Dept. of IT&C, November 30, 1979), p. 36; and The Canadian Manufacturers' Association, "Submission to the Parliamentary Task Force on North-South Relations", mimeo, August, 1980, p. 4.
[67] For a business discussion of *credit mixte* see the following items: Canadian Export Association, *Review and Digest Bulletin,* December, 1977 and August, 1978; Canadian Export Association, *Export News Bulletin,* February, 1979; and Canadian Export Association, "Brief to Special Committee on North-South Relations", in *Special Committee,* Issue no. 23, November 3, 1980.
[68] *Special Committee,* Issue no. 23, November 3, 1980, p. 22.
[69] Sheldon Gordon, "Canadian Aid Policy: What's In It For Us?", *International Perspectives,* May/June 1976, p. 22.
[70] Canada, Treasury Board, "L'étude sur les effets de délier à la source et sans restrictions le programme canadien d'aide bilatérale, 1975".
[71] *The Fifth Estate,* April 4, 1978.
[72] Export Development Corporation, *Annual Report 1975.*
[73] James H. Adams, "Transnational Investment in the Third World: Issues for Canadians", in North-South Institute, *In the Canadian Interest,* p. 142. The CBIIAC describes its purposes as "harmonizing Canadian business approaches to international matters and providing effective liaison with the government and an effective communications system overall."
[74] Canadian Export Association, *Review and Digest Bulletin,* December, 1977.

[75] Cited in *Dev/Ed News*, early Spring, 1981, p. 13.
[76] Cited in David Lewis, *Louder Voices: The Corporate Welfare Bums* (Toronto: James, Lewis and Samuel, 1972), p. iv.
[77] The statistical material for the following section on Canada's balance of payments problems, unless otherwise noted, is extracted or computed from two basic Statistics Canada publications: *The Quarterly Estimates of Canada's Balance of International Payments*, Fourth Quarter 1980; and *Canada's International Investment Position 1977*. Also employed is R. Carty, "The Bottom Line: In the Red on the Canadian Balance Sheet", *This Magazine*, December, 1977.
[78] Thomas Claridge, "Science Council Finds Manufacturing Decline", *The Globe and Mail*, February 2, 1979.
[79] The current account deficit, over $5 billion in each of 1978 and 1979, declined to $1.5 billion during 1980 due to increases in merchandise exports. But there was little cause for celebration. The merchandise trade increase was almost totally due to increases in the value, not the volume, of raw material exports. Because the manufacturing trade deficit continued to expand, and because the prices Canada receives for exported raw materials are dependent on volatile commodity markets and exchange rates, the structural problems in the current account remain serious.
[80] The EDC also seems to allocate a large portion of its financial facilities to foreign-owned corporations. In a 1973 parliamentary review of the EDC it was calculated that almost 45% of EDC loans benefitted the Canadian subsidiaries of US-based transnational corporations. See a discussion of the role of the EDC in the trade strategy in "A Partner for Cerro Colorado: The Export Development Corporation", *LAWG Letter*, Vol. VI, no. 4 and 5, January-April 1980.
[81] Robert Stephens, "Be More Aggressive on Export Front Trade Minister Tells Manufacturers", *Toronto Star*, September 13, 1979.
[82] Stephen Duncan, "Subsidiaries May Lose Export Financing", *The Financial Post*, November 13, 1976. According to the *Economist* (14/1/78), over one-half of foreign subsidiaries in Canada have some restrictions on their exports applied by their parent firms.
[83] Directives by parent firms to their subsidiaries not to export from Canada may account for Canada's poor procurement record in international financial institutions. Although Canadian companies do well in winning 50% of the contracts they compete on, they enter the competition in fewer than 100 out of 7,000 opportunities provided by multilateral development banks. See: *Special Committee*, Issue no. 23, November 3, 1980, p. 23. The problem was also admitted by Industry, Trade and Commerce Minister Herb Gray in his testimony to the North-South Task Force: "the structure of much of Canadian industry in the branch-plant form without a mandate from the foreign parent who seeks export opportunities freely, inhibits trade with developing countries as much as it does with world markets generally." See: *Special Committee*, Issue no. 24, November 4, 1980, p. 57.
[84] Statistics Canada, *Exports by Country* (various years).
[85] Computed with Treasury Board data and Statistics Canada, *Exports by Country*, January-December, 1975.
[86] Economic Council of Canada, *For A Common Future*, p. 70.
[87] Lester B. Pearson, *Partners in Development*, p. 173.
[88] Marcel Masse, "The Third World: A Canadian Challenge", p. 11.
[89] Export Promotion Review Committee, *Strengthening Canada Abroad* (The Hatch Report); Canadian Manufacturers' Association, "Submission to the Parliamentary Task Force on North-South Relations"; Canadian Export

Association, "Brief to Special Committee on North/South Relations". These three documents coincide in their recommendations concerning the future of aid policy. Unless otherwise noted, quotes which appear in the following paragraph are from the Hatch Report.

[90] Mark MacGuigan, "Notes for Remarks to the Canadian Business Association, the Canadian Club of Hong Kong, and the Canadian University Assocation", Hong Kong, July 2, 1980, p. 5.

[91] Mark MacGuigan, "Bilateral Approach to Foreign Policy", speech to the Empire Club of Canada, Toronto, January 22, 1981. The move toward a bilateralist foreign policy began under the short-lived Conservative government of Prime Minister Joe Clark with musings by then External Affairs Minister Flora Macdonald that Canada would link aid giving more directly to Canadian self-interest and seek to deepen relationships with NICs. See two major speeches by Flora Macdonald — to the Canadian Club of Canada, Montreal, September 17, 1979; and to the Empire Club, Toronto, October 4, 1979.

[92] North-South Institute, *In the Canadian Interest,* p. 57.

[93] Mark MacGuigan, "Bilateral Approach to Foreign Policy", p. 1.

[94] *Financial Post,* May 16, 1981.

[95] *Financial Post,* April 11, 1981.

[96] *Financial Post,* May 16, 1981.

[97] Jack Cahill, "Canadians Who Help the Third World", *Toronto Star,* June 30, 1981.

[98] *Special Committee,* Issue no. 24, November 24, 1980, p. 46.

[99] *The Globe and Mail,* April 7, 1981.

[100] "Senegal to Get Aid from Petro-Canada", *The Globe and Mail,* January 13, 1981; "Timely Third World Plan", *Toronto Star,* November 23, 1980.

[101] On the nature of the state see: Leo Panitch, ed., *The Canadian State – Political Economy and Political Power* (Toronto: University of Toronto Press, 1977); Nicos Poulantza, *Classes in Contemporary Capitalism* (London: 1975); Ralph Miliband, *The State in Capitalist Society* (London: 1969); James O'Connor, *The Fiscal Crisis of the State* (New York: 1973).

[102] Douglas Roche, *What Development Is All About,* p. 152.

Chapter 5. Food Aid: Blessed Are the Givers

[1] See the classic study by Josue de Castro, *The Geopolitics of Hunger* (New York: Monthly Review Press, 1977).

[2] Walter Cohen, "Herbert Hoover Feeds the World", in *The Trojan Horse: A Radical Look at Foreign Aid*, Steve Weissman *et al*, ed., (Palo Alto: Ramparts Press, 1975).

[3] Frances Moore Lappé and Joseph Collins, *Food First: Beyond the Myth of Scarcity* (Boston: Houghton Mifflin Co., 1977), pp. 327-43.

[4] North American Congress on Latin America, "Agricultural Trade Development and Assistance Act of 1954 — PL 480", in NACLA's *Latin America and Empire Report*, May-June, 1971, p. 3; and Michael Hudson, *The Myth of Aid* (New York: IDOC, 1971). Former US Secretary of Agriculture Earl Butz is candid in his explanation of the creation of PL 480: "I think the Food for Peace was started primarily as a means of disposing of our surplus stocks. We called it Food for Peace because that was a convenient way to sell it politically in this country." (Quoted in *Ceres*, March-April 1974.) The multiple intentions of the program were clearly described in the Act's sub-title: "An act to increase the consumption of United States agricultural commodities in foreign countries, to improve foreign relations of the United States and for other purposes."

[5] Frances Moore Lappé and Joseph Collins, *Food First*, p. 343.

[6] Steve Talbot, "Food as A Political Weapon", in *The Trojan Horse*, p. 165.

[7] Political motives and a nudge from Washington probably explain Canada's grant of $298,000 in food aid to the Dominican Republic in 1966. It was the only such allocation during the 1960s when Canada had no bilateral aid dealings with Latin America. The grant came shortly after the US military invasion of the Dominican Republic and the installation of a pro-American head of state who was eager to employ food aid to placate a very restless populace. See *Canadian Aid: Whose Priorities?* (Toronto: Latin American Working Group, 1973).

[8] CIDA, *Canada and Development Cooperation: Annual Review 1975-1976*, p. 88.

[9] Keith Spicer, *A Samaritan State? External Aid in Canada's Foreign Policy* (Toronto: University of Toronto Press, 1966), p. 181.

[10] *Ibid.*, p. 182.

[11] Theodore Cohn, "Food Surpluses and Canadian Food Aid", a paper presented to the Canadian Political Science Association Annual Meeting, Quebec City, June 2, 1976; Theodore Cohn, "Canadian Food Policy and the Third World", *Current History*, November, 1980. Cohn's excellent studies are relied upon for information concerning Canadian surplus stocks and food aid allocations. In the late 1970s, CIDA committed itself to providing a minimum of 600,000 tonnes of grain annually under its food aid program. But since commitments above this level are based on value, not volume, Canada will continue to ship fluctuating amounts of grains in accordance with the price of wheat.

[12] Semolina is the gritty, coarse particles of wheat left after the finer flour has passed through the belting machine. CIDA began including semolina in its food aid package in 1971-72 for shipment to countries affected by the Sahelian drought. Also included in food aid packages for the Third World on a regular basis are the lower quality classifications of wheat which garner a lower price and are more difficult for Canada to sell on a commercial basis. These classifications contain slightly less protein than first class wheat.

[13] The events leading up to the invention of "Beef Loaf" show how food aid cannot be discussed apart from an analysis of national agricultural and trade policies. During the 1960s, as beef production began to outstrip consumption in both the United States and Canada, a trade conflict developed concerning the entry of beef imports into each nation from the other. Both federal governments tried to protect domestic producers by keeping out imports, while simultaneously fighting to remain in the market of the other country. Finding a surplus of beef in the early 1970s, Agriculture Minister Eugene Whelan attempted to protect the Canadian market by imposing a non-tariff barrier which excluded US cattle containing the growth hormone DES. Washington countered with import restrictions on Canadian beef products. The surplus beef dilemma of 1974 led to the imaginative, if not well-considered, inclusion of "Beef Loaf" in food aid shipments.

[14] "Can't give milk away — Whelan", *Toronto Star*, March 3, 1976, p. A21; "Help Needed", *The Globe and Mail*, February 19, 1976, p. 6, ed.

[15] See: Maxwell M. Mintrobe *et al*, *Harrison's Principles of Internal Medicine*, Seventh Edition (New York: McGraw Hill, 1975), pp. 209, 1471; A.M. Harvey *et al*, *The Principles and Practice of Medicine, Eighteenth Edition* (New York: Appleton-Century-Crofts, 1972), pp. 759-60; Paul B. Beeson and Walsh McDermott, ed., *Textbook of Medicine, Fourteenth Edition* (Toronto: W.B. Saunders Co., 1975), pp. 1232-3. Individuals who are deficient in lactase enzymes cannot digest lactose, the principal carbohydrate of milk. The commonest cause of lactase deficiency seems to be a genetically-determined decrease in lactase activity after infancy or early childhood, although acquired lactase deficiency is often seen in association with gastrointestinal diseases such as tropical sprue and bacterial infections of the intestinal tract, often evident among large segments of the populations of Third World countries.

[16] As early as 1955, a senior aid administrator told Parliament that "it is most unfortunate that many of these people should not have enough to eat, but they will always be in that condition unless we use our funds to put them in a better condition. . . . They will never become self-supporting if we send them food." See: House of Commons, *Standing Committee on External Affairs*, 1955, p. 704.

[17] Kai Bird and Susan Goldmark, "The Food Aid Conspiracy", in *The New Internationalist*, no. 49, March, 1977; see also Bob Anderson and Kathy Mezei, "Welcome to the Party: Aid for Bangladesh", *The Canadian Forum*, June, 1975.

[18] CIDA, "Report to the Secretary of State for External Affairs by Mr. Paul Gerin-Lajoie, President, CIDA, On the Mission to Bangladesh", April 10, 1975.

[19] The North-South Institute, *World Food and the Canadian Breadbasket* (Ottawa: North-South Institute, 1978), pp. 51-2. The government's admission that CIDA has little control over the use of counterpart funds opens the possibility that Canadian food aid, like its American parallel, can be used by recipient governments to finance police and military budgets. The North-South Institute strongly urged, without success, the declassification of the confidential study by CIDA and the Treasury Board entitled "Evaluation of the Canadian Food Aid Programme, May 1977".

[20] Tomasson Junnuzi and James Peach, *Report on the Hierarchy of Interests in Land in Bangladesh* (Washington: AID, September, 1977), p. 88. For a brief discussion of food-for-work programs see Lappé, Collins and Kinley, *Aid As Obstacle* (San Francisco: Institute for Food and Development Policy,

1980).
21 Jane Craig, *Land, People and Power: The Question of Third World Land Reform* (Toronto: OXFAM-Canada, 1977), p. 8.
22 Economic Council of Canada, *For a Common Future: A Study of Canada's Relations with Developing Countries* (Ottawa: Supply and Services, 1978), p. 94. The main recipients of Canadian food aid are India, Bangladesh, Pakistan, Sri Lanka, Indonesia, Egypt, the Sahel region of Africa, Tanzania and Ghana.
23 Canada, House of Commons, *Minutes of the Special Committee on North-South Relations*, Issue no. 24, November 4, 1980, p. 23.
24 GATT-Fly, "Canada's Food Trade — By Bread Alone?", mimeo, August, 1978.

Chapter 6. Harvest of Discontent: "Basic Needs" Aid to the Rural Poor

[1] Ross Henderson, "Canada's Aid Programme Seeks Political Change", *The Globe and Mail*, March 5, 1975, p. 4.

[2] CIDA, *Strategy for International Development Cooperation 1975-1980* (Ottawa: Information Canada, 1975), p. 23.

[3] CIDA, "Facts: Agricultural Development", July, 1977.

[4] Leif E. Christofferson, "The Bank and Rural Poverty", *Finance and Development*, December, 1979, p. 19.

[5] Robert McNamara, "Address to the Board of Governors of the World Bank, Nairobi, Kenya, September 24, 1973" (Washington: World Bank). The statistics for Latin America are from Erik Eckholm, "Smaller Farms: One Way to Get Greater Global Food Production", *Toronto Star*, July 8, 1979, p. A8. Comparable statistics are offered by the Food and Agriculture Organization (FAO) of the United Nations which notes that in Latin America 67.2% of all land holdings occupy only 3.6% of the agricultural land while in Africa, the region where land ownership is least skewed, 66% of the landowners still only control 22.4% of the agricultural land; see *Development Forum*, May, 1979, p. 6.

[6] Leif Christofferson, "The Bank and Rural Poverty".

[7] Robert McNamara, "Address to the Board of Governors of the World Bank, Nairobi, Kenya, September 24, 1973".

[8] World Bank, *Rural Development Sector Policy Paper*, (Washington: World Bank, 1975), p. 3.

[9] The Institute for Food and Development Policy, "The Aid Debate: Assessing the Impact of US Foreign Assistance and the World Bank", (San Francisco: 1979), p. 25. Also see World Bank, *Assault on World Poverty* (Baltimore: John Hopkins University Press, 1975) pp. 106, 118, 125; and World Bank, *Annual Report 1978*, pp. 72-79.

[10] Robert McNamara, "Address to the Board of Governors of the World Bank", and World Bank, *Rural Development Sector Policy Paper*.

[11] CIDA, *Annual Aid Review 1978*: Memorandum of Canada to the Development Assistance Committee of the Organization for Economic Cooperation and Development (Ottawa: CIDA, 1980), p. 27. The 1977 *Annual Aid Review* prepared by CIDA for DAC contains a discussion of CIDA's basic needs strategy. Government spending restraint in 1977 and 1978 froze CIDA spending and the Agency seems to have made the necessary adjustments by cutting spending plans precisely in areas deemed a "priority".

[12] Jackie Smith, "CIDA in Africa: Goodbye $6 million", *Toronto Star*, July 22, 1979.

[13] B. Nestel and H. Zandstra, "Caqueza: An Evaluation of the First Two Years", (Ottawa: IDRC, undated).

[14] Accion Campesina Colombiana, "Bases de apoyo para la estrategia y la politica del movimiento campesino Colombiano", report of the Third Congress of the ACC, Cartago Valle, December 5-8, 1974, annex p. 5.

[15] Leonard Dudley and Roger Sandilards, "The Side Effects of Foreign Aid: The Case of PL 480 Wheat in Colombia", *Economic Development and Cultural Change*, January, 1975, p. 321.

[16] Frances Moore Lappé and Joseph Collins, *Food First: Beyond the Myth of Scarcity* (Boston: Houghton Mifflin Co., 1977), see pp. 127, 129, 136, 137, 264-6.

[17] Alejandro Reyes Posada, "Aparceria y capitalismo agrario", *Controversia* (Bogota), no. 38, 1975, pp. 43, 52, 53.

[18] Asociacion Nacional de Usuarios Campesinos, "Conclusiones del Tercer Congreso", (Bogota, August-September 1974), mimeo, p. 5.

[19] Quoted in the bulletin of the NGO parallel conference to the World Conference on Agrarian Reform and Rural Development, Rome, 1979.

[20] See Ernesto Parra, "El Plan de Desarollo Lopez — I: plan de desarollo rural integrado, DRI", *Controversia*, no. 39, 1975; also, ———, "Landlessness and Nearlandlessness in Developing Countries", (Ithaca: Center for International Studies, Cornell University, 1978).

[21] Rosemary Galli, "Rural Development as Social Control: International Agencies and Class Struggle in the Colombian Countryside", *Latin American Perspectives*, Issue 19, Fall 1978, p. 71.

[22] CIDA, "Rural Development and Renewable Resources — Sectoral Guidelines No. 1", (Ottawa: CIDA, 1976), pp. A9, B9, A12.

[23] John W. Warnock, "The Political Economy of the Food Industry in Canada: Oligopoly and American Domination", *Our Generation*, Vol. II, no. 4, Winter 1976.

[24] George Hunt, "Canadian Agriculture's Potential to Assist Internationally", in Proceedings: International Rural Development Workshop (Ottawa: Agricultural Economics Research Council of Canada, 1976).

[25] US Department of Agriculture, *Agriculture in the Americas: Statistical Data* (Washington: 1975).

[26] Frances Moore Lappé and Joseph Collins, *Food First*.

[27] For a discussion of contract agriculture see Lewis D. Solomon, *Multinational Corporations and the Emerging World Order* (New York: Kennikat Press, 1978). For additional material on the expansion of agribusiness in the Third World consult: William K. Chung, "Sales by Majority-Owned Foreign Affiliates of US Companies in 1975", *Survey of Current Business*, February 1977; and R. David Belli, "Capital expenditures by majority-owned foreign affiliates of US companies, 1976 and 1977", *Survey of Current Business*, March, 1977.

[28] Ernest Feder, "Penetration of the Agricultures of the Underdeveloped Countries by the Industrial Nations and the Multinational Concerns", (Denn Haag: Institute of Social Studies, undated), mimeo. Also see, Ernest Feder, "McNamara's Little Green Revolution: The World Bank Scheme for the Liquidation of the Third World Peasantry", *Commercio Exterior* (English edition), August, 1976.

[29] CIDA, *Annual Report 1979-1980*, p. 9.

[30] Cited in Brian MacCall, "The Transition Toward Self-Reliance: Some Thoughts on the Role of People's Organizations", *IFDA Dossier*, 1980.

Chapter 7. The Global Managers

[1] *Latin America Weekly Report,* November 7, 1980.

[2] *The Globe and Mail,* January 20, 1981.

[3] Robert S. McNamara, "Address to the Board of Governors", (Washington: International Bank for Reconstruction and Development, 1978), p. 25.

[4] *The Reform of International Institutions: A Report of The Trilateral Task Force on International Institutions to the Trilateral Commission,* 1976, p. 12.

[5] *Canada: Strategy for International Development Cooperation,* (Ottawa: Information Division, CIDA, 1975), p. 22.

[6] Jane Chudy, "Why Canadian Business Is Not Getting More World Bank Contracts", *Development Directions,* August/September 1978, p. 23.

[7] CIDA, *Annual Review,* 1971-72, p. 55.

[8] CIDA, *Canada and Development Cooperation, Annual Review,* 1975-76, p. 63.

[9] Quoted by Shirley Hazzard in "The United Nations: Elderly Orphan", *The Nation,* October 22, 1973, p. 391.

[10] A.F.W. Plumtree, *Three Decades of Decision: Canada and the World Monetary System 1944-75,* (Toronto: McClelland and Stewart, 1977), p. 40.

[11] *The Reform of International Institutions,* p. 40.

[12] Cheryl Payer, *The Debt Trap: The International Monetary Fund and the Third World,* (New York: Monthly Review Press, 1974), p. 217.

[13] Frances Moore Lappé, Joseph Collins, and David Kinley, *Aid as Obstacle: Twenty Questions About Our Foreign Aid and the Hungry,* (Institute for Food and Development Policy, 1980), p. 33.

[14] Eugene H. Rotberg, *The World Bank: A Financial Appraisal,* (Washington: International Bank for Reconstruction and Development, 1978), p. 5.

[15] *Engineering and Mining Journal,* November, 1975, p. 155.

[16] Organization for Economic Cooperation and Development, *Development Cooperation, 1978 Review: Efforts and Policies of the Members of the Development Assistance Committee,* (Paris, 1978), p. 228.

[17] Ann Hughey, "Is the World Bank Biting Off More Than It Can Chew?", *Forbes,* May 26, 1980, p. 122.

[18] *Partners in Development: Report of the Commission on International Development,* (New York: Praeger Publishers, 1969), p. 214.

[19] *The Reform of International Institutions,* p. 26.

[20] Quoted by Steve Weissmen in "Foreign Aid: Who Needs It?", *The Trojan Horse: A Radical Look at Foreign Aid,* (Palo Alto: Ramparts Press, 1975), p. 17.

[21] *International Policy Report,* Vol. III, no. 1, January, 1977, (Washington: Center for International Policy), p. 3.

[22] *Policies and Operations: The World Bank Group,* 1974, p. 6.

[23] *The World Bank: Questions and Answers,* 1976, p. 7.

[24] "Caribbean Conflict: Jamaica and the US", NACLA *Report on the Americas,* Vol. XII, no. 3, May-June 1978, p. 30.

[25] Quoted in "The Role of the United States in the Overthrow of Allende", Latin American Working Group, 1973, p. 10.

[26] "Time of Reckoning: The US and Chile", NACLA's *Latin America and Empire Report,* Vol. X, no. 10, December, 1976, p. 28.

[27] Mitchell Sharp, telegram to Canadian Churches, 1974.

[28] Paul Gerin-Lajoie, correspondence with Canadian Churches, June 17, 1974. (For a full account of Canada's record on Chile in multilateral institutions, see "Worlds Apart: Economic Relations and Human Rights", LAWG *Letter,* Vol. V, no. 4/5, pp. 29-33.)

²⁹ John Turner, correspondence with Canadian Churches, July 2, 1974.

³⁰ *Forbes*, May 26, 1980, p. 127.

³¹ World Bank, *World Development Report 1979*, (Washington: The International Bank for Reconstruction and Development, 1979), p. 29.

³² World Bank, *World Development Report 1980*, (Washington: International Bank for Reconstruction and Development, 1980), p. 9.

³³ OPEC, *The Trilateral World, and the Developing Countries: New Arrangements for Cooperation, 1976-1980. A Report of the Trilateral Task Force on Relations with Developing Countries to the Executive Committee of The Trilateral Commission*, 1975, p. 15.

³⁴ *The National Energy Program 1980*, p. 53.

³⁵ G.K. Helleiner, Testimony at the Special Committee on North-South Relations, September 18, 1980, Issue no. 8, p. 6.

³⁶ *The Globe and Mail*, May 27, 1980.

³⁷ Rotberg, *The World Bank*, p. 7.

³⁸ World Bank, *Annual Report*, 1980, p. 69.

³⁹ *Business Week*, September 27, 1976.

⁴⁰ *North-South: A Program for Survival. The Report of the Independent Commission on International Development Issues under the Chairmanship of Willy Brandt*, (Cambridge: The MIT Press, 1980), p. 249.

⁴¹ Allen MacEachen, "North-South Dialogue and International Development", an address to the Society for International Development, Ottawa, November 16, 1980, p. 6. The way for multilateral institutions to expand their resources without new capital input by donors is by changing the regulations governing their "gearing ratios". At the World Bank, for example, this would mean changing the very conservative 1-to-1 ratio of bank borrowing relative to its capital. Some private banks have ratios of up to 28-to-1. See: *World Business Weekly*, March 23, 1981, pp. 6-7.

⁴² World Bank, *World Development Report 1980*, p. 35.

Chapter 8. Canada and the Third World

[1] James Rusk, "PM's North-South Initiatives Lose Ground", *The Globe and Mail*, July 21, 1981; and "Summit Blueprint Easy to Agree On but Hard to Follow," *The Globe and Mail*, July 22, 1981.

[2] See the testimony of Commonwealth General Secretary Shridath Ramphal to the Sub-Committee on International Development in House of Commons, *Minutes of the Standing Committee on External Affairs and National Defence*, Issue 2, March 31, 1977, p. 10. For the Tanzanian example see: "Tanzania's Economic Crisis Grows", *The Globe and Mail*, August 8, 1981.

[3] David Humphreys, "Tanzanian Twine Dilemma: A Test of Third World Relations", *The Globe and Mail*, June 18, 1979. Bangladesh's jute minister says that his country would rather see Canadian tariff restrictions against jute lifted than have $4 million worth of aid. See the testimony of CUSO's executive director, Ian Smillie, to the House of Commons *Special Committee on North-South Relations*, Issue no. 4, July 17, 1980, p. 20.

[4] CIDA, *Annual Review 1975*, pp. 150-151.

[5] CIDA, "Questions Submitted to CIDA by Mr. D. Roche MP, May 18, 1976".

[6] Organization for Economic Cooperation and Development, *Investing in Developing Countries*, 4th revised edition (Paris: OECD, 1978).

[7] Stephen W. Langdon, *Canadian Private Direct Investment and Technology Marketing in Developing Countries* (Ottawa: Supply & Services, 1980).

[8] Canada, House of Commons, *Minutes of the Standing Committee on External Affairs and National Defence*, May 17, 1977, p. 39.

[9] Calculated on the basis of 1977 from the World Bank's *World Development Report 1979* (Washington: World Bank, 1979).

[10] UNCTAD Secretariat, "The Reverse Transfer of Technology: Its Dimensions, Economic Effects and Policy Implications", (D/B/C.6/7) October 13, 1975. The Economic Council of Canada notes that the UNCTAD figures are calculated on the basis of the concept of the value of the discounted earnings over the lifetime of individual immigrants with particular skills. Another way to calculate the value of the "brain drain" to Canada would be the replacement cost — the amount Canada would have to spend to bring Canadians or immigrants to the level of skills embodied in current immigration. By this means of calculation, the ECC still puts the value of the brain drain to Canada at $2.9 billion over the 1963-1972 period, an amount still large enough to nullify the value of Canadian development assistance. See: Economic Council of Canada, *For a Common Future — Canada's Relations with Developing Countries* (Ottawa: Supply & Services, 1978), p. 117.

[11] For a discussion of Canada's official attitude toward some non-aid issues see: The North-South Institute, *In The Canadian Interest? Third World Development in the 1980s* (Ottawa: North-South Institute, 1980).

[12] Mark MacGuigan, "New Dimensions in North-South Relations: A Canadian Perspective", *Statements and Speeches* (External Affairs, Ottawa), no. 80/15.

[13] See: North-South Institute, *A Balance Sheet of Third World-Canada Relations* (Ottawa: 1979). This series of discussion papers addresses a wide range of Canada Third World relations including trade, food, investment, technology transfer, debt, immigration and aid.

[14] *North-South: A Program for Survival. The Report of the Independent Commis-*

sion on International Development Issues under the Chairmanship of Willy Brandt (Cambridge: The MIT Press, 1980).

[15] Chakravarthi Raghavan, "Industrialization of Third World for Benefit of TNCs or People?", *IFDA Dossier*, April/May, 1981; GATT-Fly, *The Textile and Clothing Industries in Canada: A Profile* (Toronto: 1980).

[16] For an excellent probing of the limits to platforms like the NIEO see: John Dillon, "The Limitations of the Trade Issue", published by GATT-Fly, (Toronto: July, 1973).

[17] Economic Council of Canada, *For A Common Future*, pp. 83-87.

Glossary

ADB — Asian Development Bank

AFDB — African Development Bank

AFDF — African Development Fund

AID — Agency for International Development

CALA — Canadian Association-Latin America and the Caribbean

CARICOM — Caribbean Common Market

CDB — Caribbean Development Bank

CEA — Canadian Export Association

CIDA — Canadian International Development Agency

CMA — Canadian Manufacturers Association

CUSO — Canadian University Service Overseas

DAC — Development Assistance Committee

DRI — A Program of integrated rural development in Colombia

EAO — External Aid Office

EDC — Export Development Corporation

GATT — General Agreement on Tariffs and Trade

GNP — Gross National Product

IBRD — International Bank for Reconstruction and Development

ICDA — Interdepartmental Committee on Development Assistance

ICERDC — Interdepartmental Committee on Economic Relations with Developing Countries

IDA — International Development Association

IDB — Inter-American Development Bank

IDRC — International Development Research Centre

IFC — International Finance Corporation

IMF — International Monetary Fund

ITC — (Department of) Industry, Trade and Commerce

MAF — Mission Administered Funds

NGO — Non-governmental Organization

NIC — Newly Industrializing Country

NIEO — New International Economic Order

OAS — Organization of American States

ODA — Official Development Assistance

OECD — Organization for Economic Cooperation and Development

OPEC — Organization of Petroleum Exporting Countries

UN — United Nations

UNDP — United Nations Development Program

LAWG

The Latin American Working Group (LAWG) is a
Toronto-based, independent, non-profit research and
education institute. Since 1966, LAWG has investigated
the political, economic and social relationships
between Canada and Latin America and has worked
to create a broader understanding among Canadians
of Latin American struggles for justice and
development. The group's publications include
occasional research studies and books, a quarterly
newsletter (the **LAWG Letter**) on Latin American affairs
and Canada-Latin America relations, the monthly
Latin America and Caribbean Labour Report, and
Central America Update. For further information
about LAWG's activities, its resource centre and its
publications, write:

Latin American Working Group
Box 2207, Station P
Toronto, Ontario
M5S 2T2

Index

Finance, Department of (Canada) 28,
31
Finland 157
food aid (*see* aid)
food crisis 118, 131
food-for-work 124, 125
Ford Motor Co. 152
foreign aid (*see* aid, CIDA *and* official
development assistance)
Foreign Policy for Canadians 51, 63, 65
France 8n, 45n, 60, 100, 114, 118, 144,
157, 161, 165
la Francophonie 55, 60
Freeman, Linda 90, 93
Frei, Eduardo 3, 64

G

GTE Lenkurt 103
Gabon 57, 59, 61
Gambia 61
General Agreement on Tariffs and
Trade (GATT) 5, 11, 148
General Manufacturing Co. 103
General Motors 42
General Steelwares 17
General System of Preferences (GSP)
170n
Gerin-Lajoie, Paul 20, 21, 33, 59, 95,
120, 158
Ghana 16, 17, 22, 23, 35, 46, 56-59,
168, 174, 193
global negotiations 4, 165
Gordon Sheldon 102
Goulart, Joao 158
Galli, Rosemary 137
Grain Millers Association 126
Grant, James 153
Gray, Herb 110, 189n
Greece 114
green revolution 131
Grenada 51, 53-55
Group of 77: 4
Guatemala 69, 86, 122, 125
Guinea 61
Guinea-Bissau 61
Guyana 50, 53, 54, 57

H

Haiti 6, 66, 67, 69, 138, 174
Hardin, Garrett 77
Harkin, Tom 153
Hatch Report 109
Hawker-Siddeley Canada Ltd. 19, 103
Hay, Keith 98, 99
Head, Ivan 126
Heath, Edward 3
Helleiner, G.K. 160
Holland 157
Honduras 66, 67, 69
Hoover, Herbert 114
House of Commons (*see* Parliament)
human rights 86, 153, 157, 158, 176,
177
Humphrey, Hubert 115
Hunt, George 138

I

Iceland 157
INCO Ltd. 24, 48, 150
Indcentre 72, 73
India 8n, 14, 17, 20, 28, 29, 35, 40,
46-49, 101, 113, 114, 116, 117, 154,
168, 172, 174, 193n
Indonesia 18, 19, 22, 24, 25, 48, 49,
86, 110, 138, 154, 158, 168, 174
Industry, Trade and Commerce,
Department of (Canada) 28, 30, 31,
43, 44, 83, 109, 110, 121, 122, 126
Inter-American Development Bank
(IDB) 36, 40, 64, 65, 67, 82, 134,
135, 143-146, 151, 156-158, 161,
183n
Interdepartmental Committee on
Development Assistance 31
Interdepartmental Committee on
Economic Relations with
Developing Countries 31
International Bank for Reconstruction
and Development (IBRD) (*see*
World Bank)
International Council for Adult
Education 37
International Development
Association (IDA) (*see* World Bank)
International Development Research
Centre (IDRC) 31, 32, 38, 97, 134,
142n

Perspectives on Underdevelopment

Perspectives on Underdevelopment, a new series from Between The Lines, will explore the multiple causes and various consequences of underdevelopment and inappropriate development. These books will discuss not only various aspects of the current global situation but also the struggles of those most closely affected by development issues to control their own present and future.

The intention of this series is to increase popular awareness of the distortion of economic and political life resulting from underdevelopment and from development imposed by those who do not have to live with its results.

Ties That Bind

Canada and the Third World: A Handbook

by The Development Education Centre

Fall 1981, 196 pp., paperback $8.95, cloth $15.95

Ties That Bind is a primer in the politics and economics of unequal development — a central aspect of present North-South relations. It lays bare the sinews of a global system that produces inequality by design rather than by accident.

As a collection of essays compiled and edited by the Development Education Centre, *Ties That Bind* situates Canada in the global economic order while exploring the patterns of aid, trade and investment which operate both externally in the world economy, and, more subtly, in Canada.

One essay takes an extensive look at the world trade system; another examines Canada's aid program and questions whether it is designed to help the Third World or to prop up Canadian business. A third analyzes the role of transnational corporations; and a fourth tackles the thorny problem of how North Americans perceive the Third World, challenging the "tyrant and victim" image of underdevelopment.

Through comparisons to Canadian situations, *Ties That Bind* not only provides a good introduction to the dynamics of underdevelopment, but also offers an immediate sense of the forces which create it.

A new title in the *Perspectives on Underdevelopment* series.

Bitter Grounds

Roots of Revolt in El Salvador

by Liisa North

Available early 1982.

Since the late seventies, El Salvador has been a much discussed country — in the media, public demonstrations and international forums. Missing from most of these discussions has been an attempt to link the current crisis with El Salvador's history.

El Salvador has had the longest uninterrupted rule by the military in all of Latin America. The oligarchy in this coffee-exporting country has squelched all attempts by the peasantry to form unions and has suspended free elections since 1931. Ninety-four per cent of Salvadoreans are landless and make less than $200 per year.

In *Bitter Grounds* author Liisa North traces the history from the mid-19th century to the present-day civil war. She analyses the political and economic structures that have prevented Salvadoreans from gaining effective control over their own destinies and economies for over one hundred years.

Bitter Grounds includes a chapter on current Canadian foreign policy towards El Salvador and appendices on the political and military forces dominating El Salvador.

Liisa North is an associate professor of political science at York University in Toronto and has worked closely with the Toronto Committee of Solidarity with the People of El Salvador.

between the lines

Other Titles Available from Between The Lines.

Imperialism, Nationalism and Canada
Essays from the Marxist Institute of Toronto
Edited by John Saul and Craig Heron

The Big Nickel
Inco at Home and Abroad
By Jamie Swift and the Development Education Centre

Reading, Writing, and Riches
Education and the Socio-Economic Order in North America
Edited by Randle W. Nelson and David Nock

Getting Doctored
Critical Reflections on Becoming a Physician
By Martin Shapiro, M.D.

Perceptions of Apartheid
The Church and Political Change in South Africa
By Ernie Regehr

The Phone Book
Working at the Bell
By Joan Newman Kuyek

Acid Rain: The Silent Crisis
By Phil Weller and the Waterloo Public Interest Research Group

The Land of Milk and Money
The National Report of the People's Food Commission

Power To Choose
Canda's Energy Options
By GATT-Fly